DEATHMATCH™

VOLUME ONE
KILLING IN THE NAME

ROSS RICHIE CEO & Founder • **MATT GAGNON** Editor-in-Chief • **FILIP SABLIK** VP-Publishing & Marketing • **LANCE KREITER** VP-Licensing & Merchandising • **PHIL BARBARO** Director of Finance • **BRYCE CARLSON** Managing Editor
DAFNA PLEBAN Editor • **SHANNON WATTERS** Editor • **ERIC HARBURN** Editor • **CHRIS ROSA** Assistant Editor • **ALEX GALER** Assistant Editor • **WHITNEY LEOPARD** Assistant Editor • **JASMINE AMIRI** Assistant Editor • **STEPHANIE GONZAGA** Graphic Designer
KASSANDRA HELLER Production Designer • **MIKE LOPEZ** Production Designer • **DEVIN FUNCHES** E-Commerce & Inventory Coordinator • **VINCE FREDERICK** Event Coordinator • **BRIANNA HART** Executive Assistant

BOOM! Studios, 5670 Wilshire Boulevard, Suite 450, Los Angeles, CA 90036-5679. Printed in USA. First Printing. ISBN: 978-1-60886-312-9

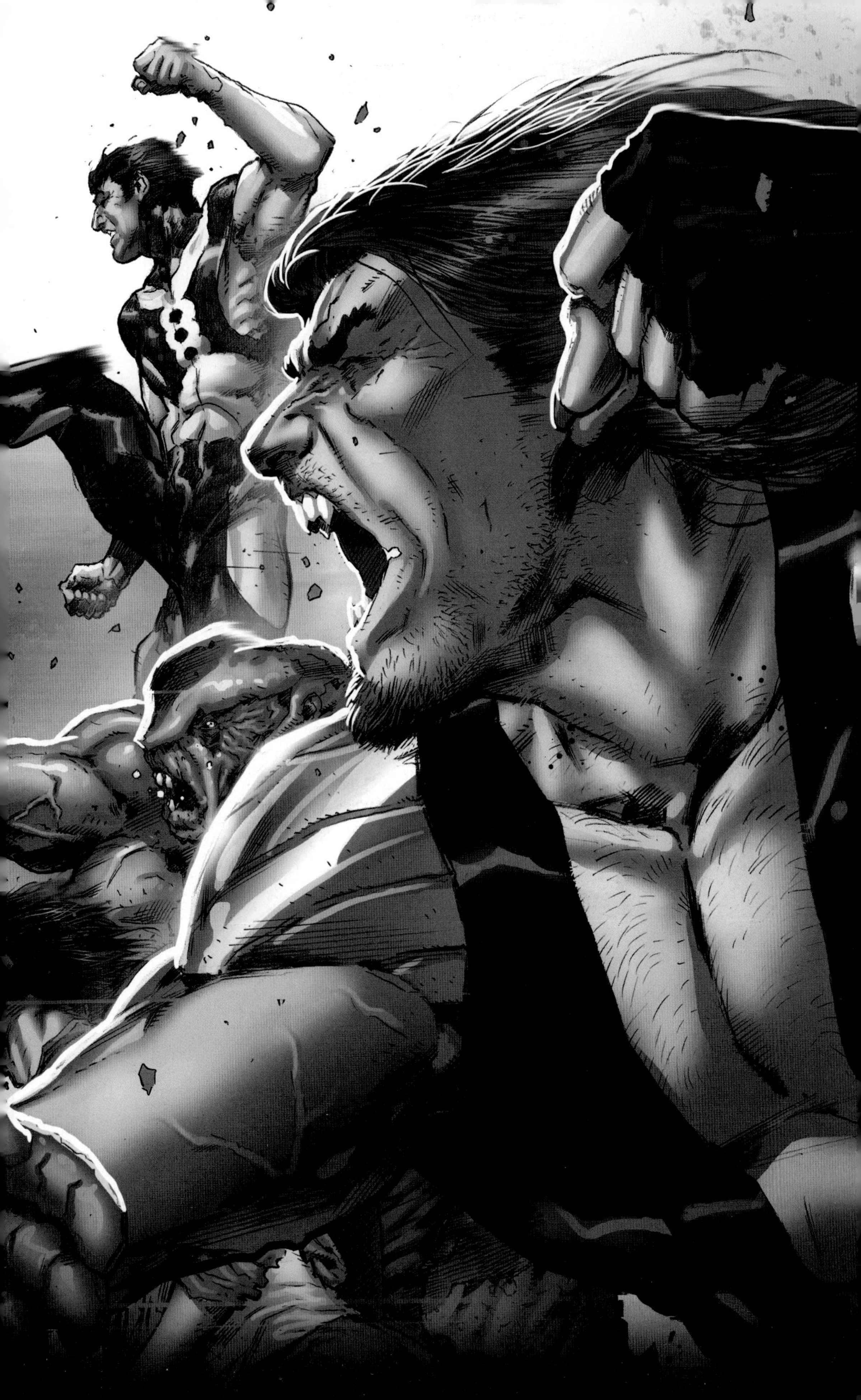

WRITTEN BY
PAUL JENKINS
ART BY
CARLOS MAGNO

COLORS BY
MICHAEL GARLAND

LETTERS BY
ED DUKESHIRE

COVER BY
CARLOS MAGNO
WITH COLORS BY ARCHIE VAN BUREN

EDITED BY
ERIC HARBURN

DESIGN BY
MIKE LOPEZ

LOGO DESIGN BY
PHIL SMITH

BASED ON A CONCEPT CREATED BY BRYCE CARLSON

CHAPTER ONE

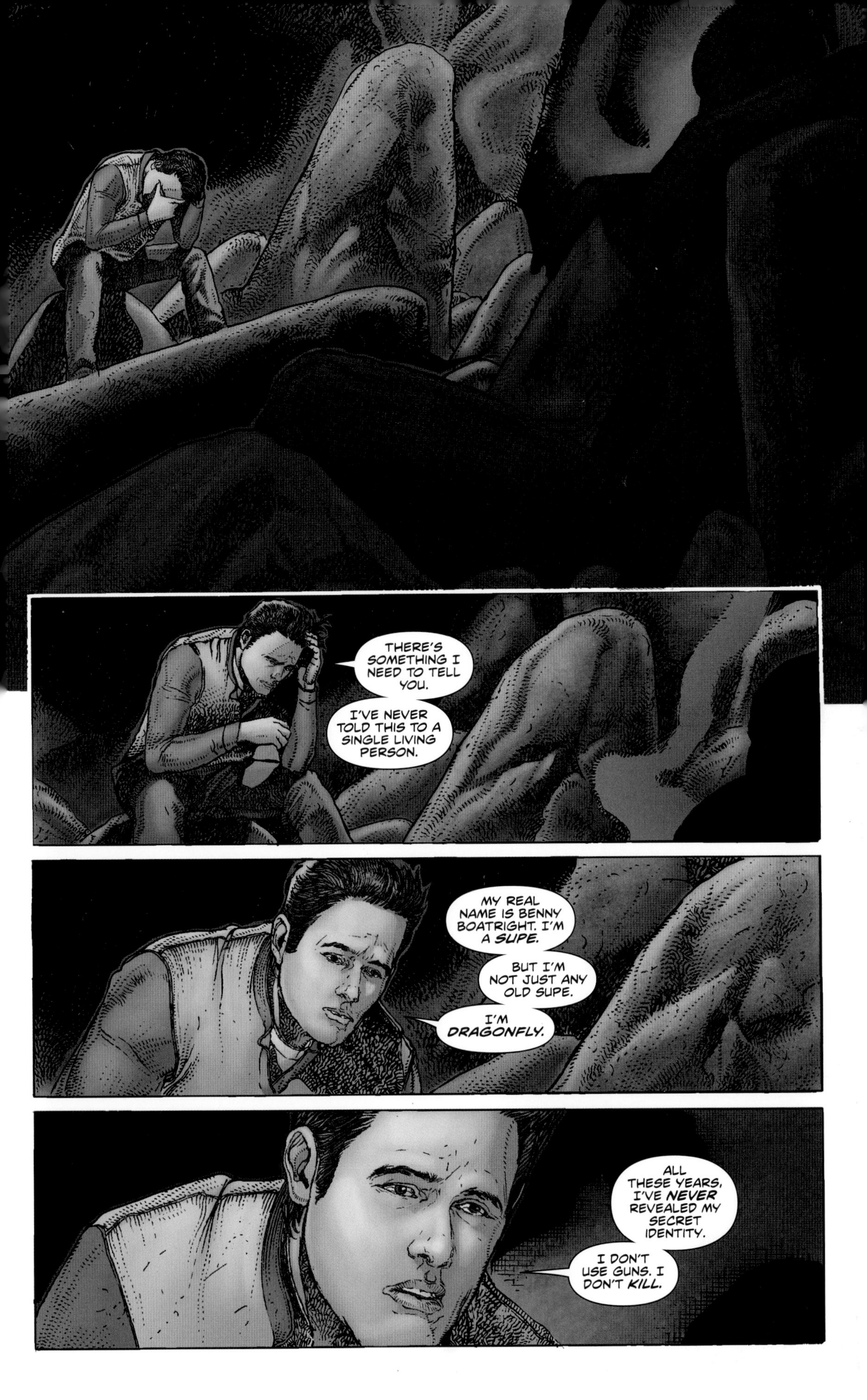
THERE'S SOMETHING I NEED TO TELL YOU.
I'VE NEVER TOLD THIS TO A SINGLE LIVING PERSON.
MY REAL NAME IS BENNY BOATRIGHT. I'M A *SUPE*.
BUT I'M NOT JUST ANY OLD SUPE.
I'M *DRAGONFLY*.
ALL THESE YEARS, I'VE *NEVER* REVEALED MY SECRET IDENTITY.
I DON'T USE GUNS. I DON'T *KILL*.

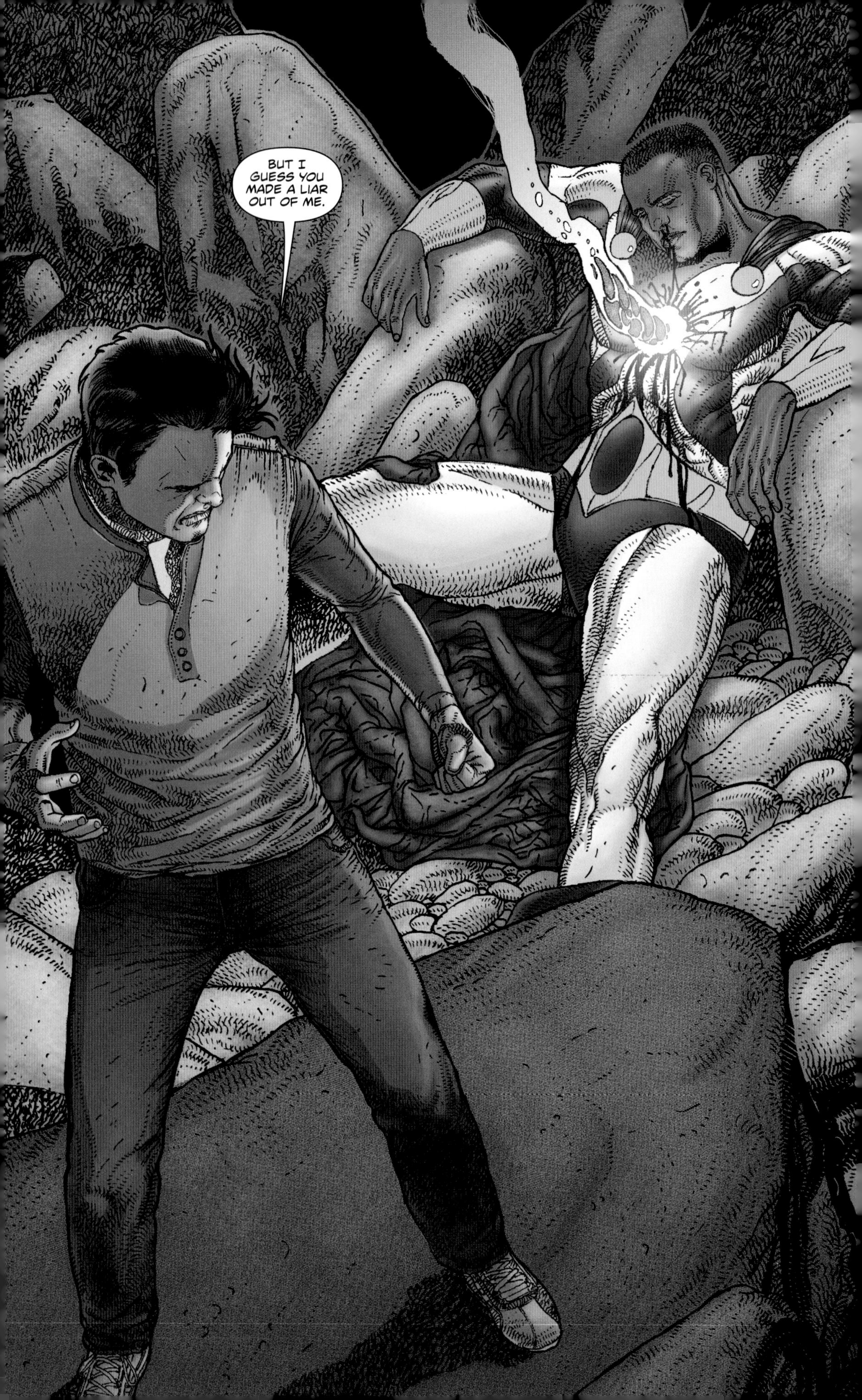
BUT I GUESS YOU MADE A LIAR OUT OF ME.

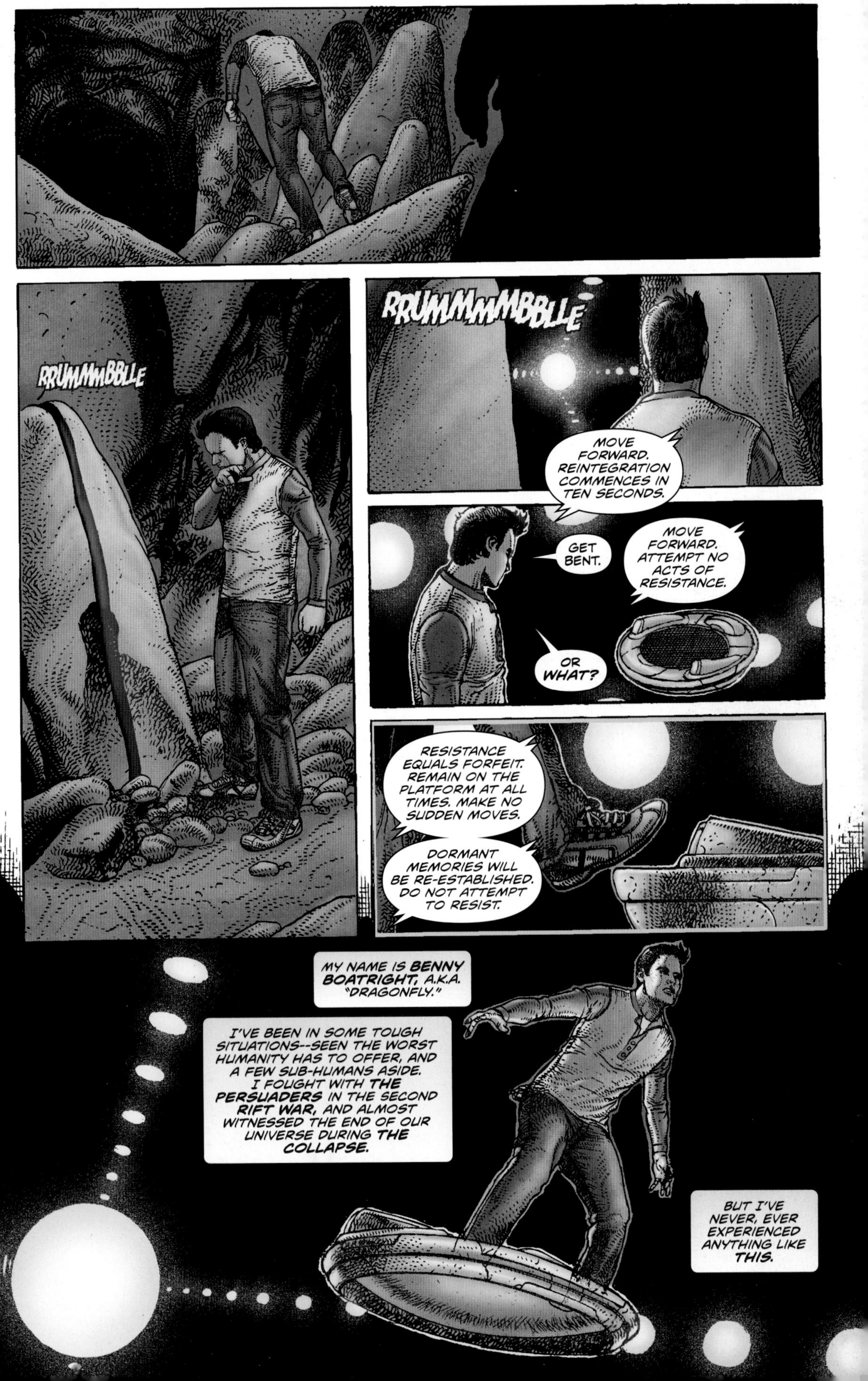
RRUMMMMBBLLE
RRUMMMMMBBLLE
MOVE FORWARD. REINTEGRATION COMMENCES IN TEN SECONDS.
GET BENT.
MOVE FORWARD. ATTEMPT NO ACTS OF RESISTANCE.
OR WHAT?
RESISTANCE EQUALS FORFEIT. REMAIN ON THE PLATFORM AT ALL TIMES. MAKE NO SUDDEN MOVES.
DORMANT MEMORIES WILL BE RE-ESTABLISHED. DO NOT ATTEMPT TO RESIST.
MY NAME IS BENNY BOATRIGHT, A.K.A. "DRAGONFLY."
I'VE BEEN IN SOME TOUGH SITUATIONS--SEEN THE WORST HUMANITY HAS TO OFFER, AND A FEW SUB-HUMANS ASIDE. I FOUGHT WITH THE PERSUADERS IN THE SECOND RIFT WAR, AND ALMOST WITNESSED THE END OF OUR UNIVERSE DURING THE COLLAPSE.
BUT I'VE NEVER, EVER EXPERIENCED ANYTHING LIKE THIS.

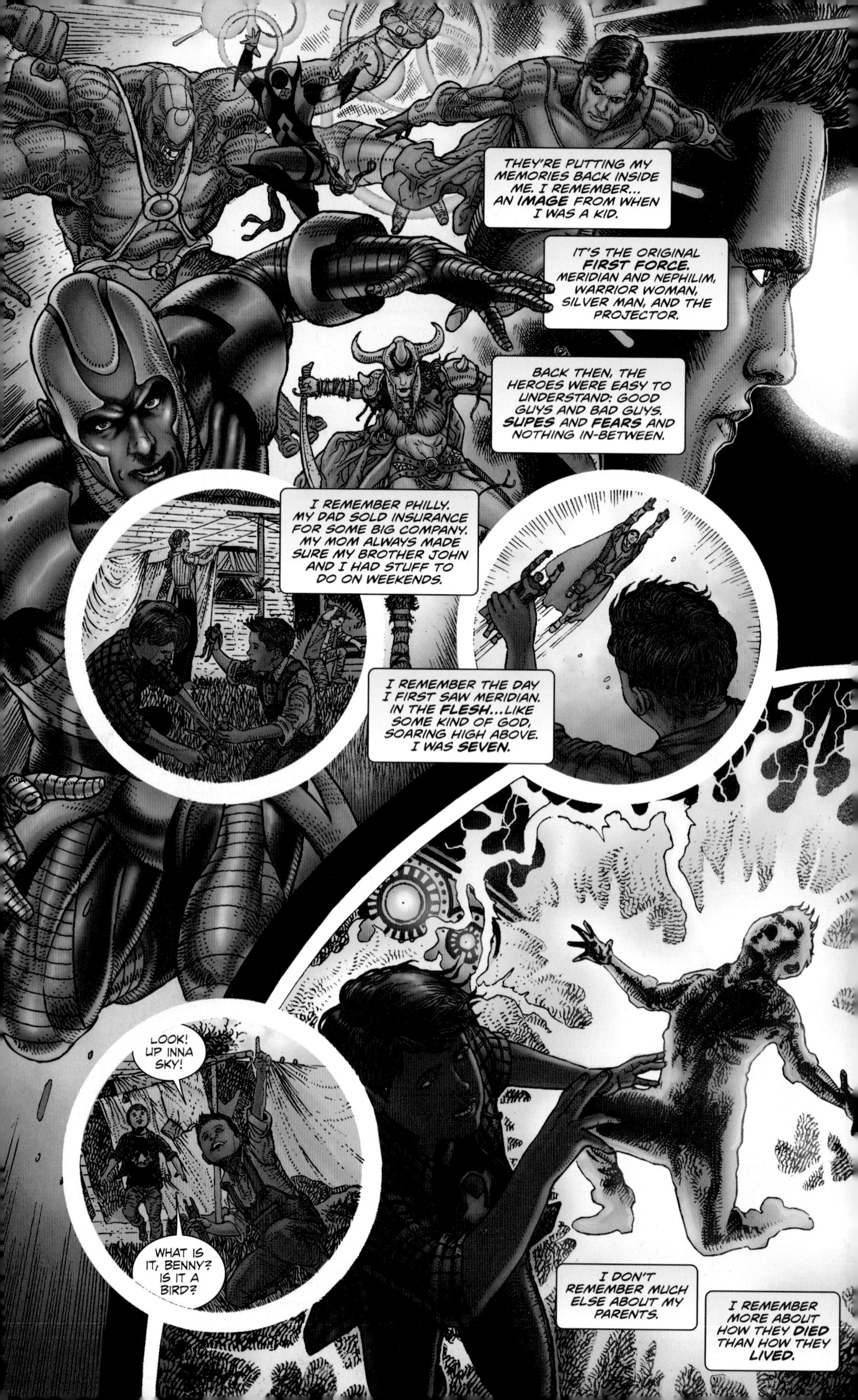

THEY'RE PUTTING MY MEMORIES BACK INSIDE ME. I REMEMBER... AN IMAGE FROM WHEN I WAS A KID.
IT'S THE ORIGINAL FIRST FORCE. MERIDIAN AND NEPHILIM, WARRIOR WOMAN, SILVER MAN, AND THE PROJECTOR.
BACK THEN, THE HEROES WERE EASY TO UNDERSTAND: GOOD GUYS AND BAD GUYS. SUPES AND FEARS AND NOTHING IN-BETWEEN.
I REMEMBER PHILLY. MY DAD SOLD INSURANCE FOR SOME BIG COMPANY. MY MOM ALWAYS MADE SURE MY BROTHER JOHN AND I HAD STUFF TO DO ON WEEKENDS.
I REMEMBER THE DAY I FIRST SAW MERIDIAN. IN THE FLESH...LIKE SOME KIND OF GOD, SOARING HIGH ABOVE. I WAS SEVEN.
LOOK! UP INNA SKY!
WHAT IS IT, BENNY? IS IT A BIRD?
I DON'T REMEMBER MUCH ELSE ABOUT MY PARENTS.
I REMEMBER MORE ABOUT HOW THEY DIED THAN HOW THEY LIVED.

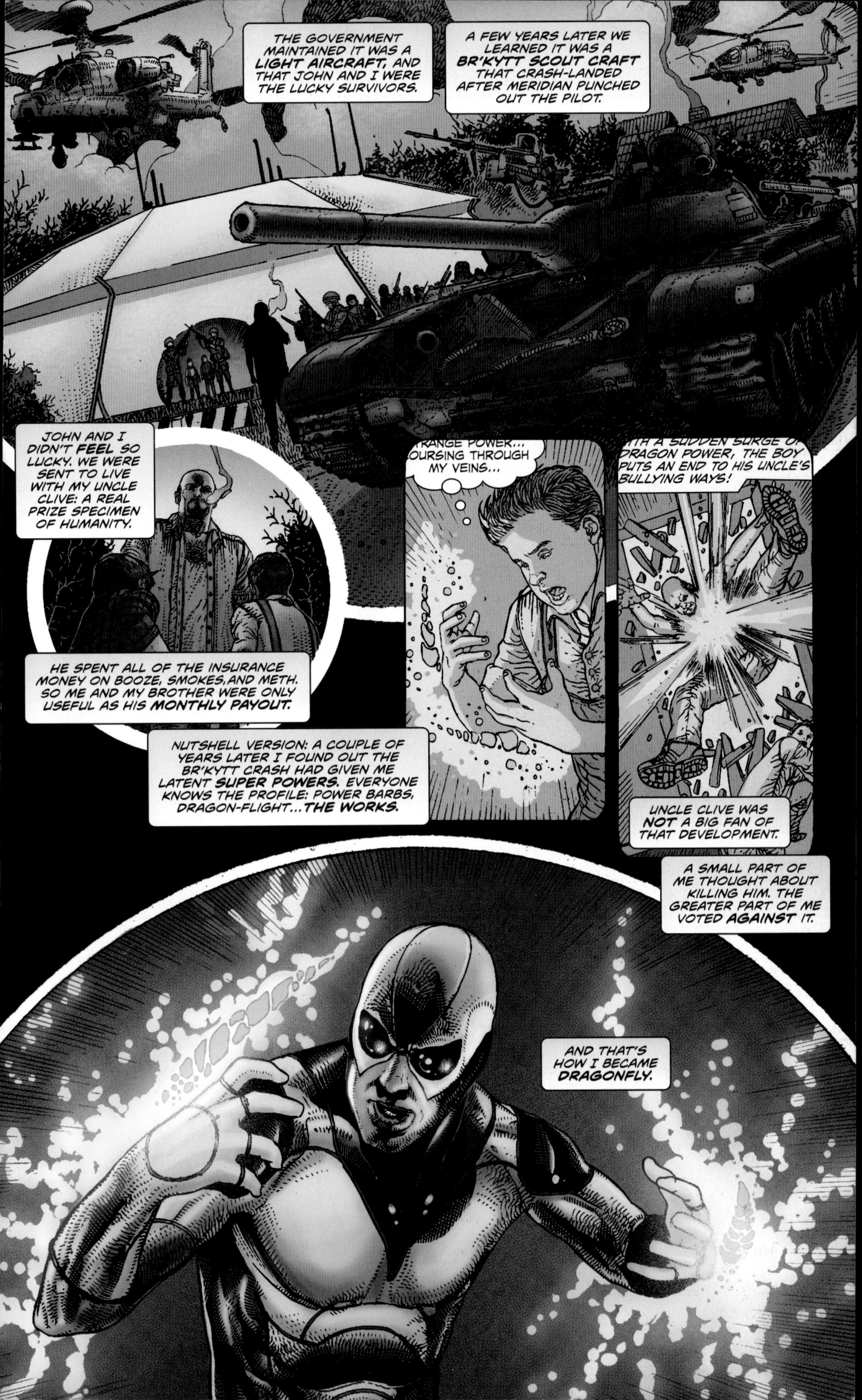

THE GOVERNMENT MAINTAINED IT WAS A LIGHT AIRCRAFT, AND THAT JOHN AND I WERE THE LUCKY SURVIVORS.
A FEW YEARS LATER WE LEARNED IT WAS A BR'KYTT SCOUT CRAFT THAT CRASH-LANDED AFTER MERIDIAN PUNCHED OUT THE PILOT.
JOHN AND I DIDN'T FEEL SO LUCKY. WE WERE SENT TO LIVE WITH MY UNCLE CLIVE: A REAL PRIZE SPECIMEN OF HUMANITY.
HE SPENT ALL OF THE INSURANCE MONEY ON BOOZE, SMOKES, AND METH. SO ME AND MY BROTHER WERE ONLY USEFUL AS HIS MONTHLY PAYOUT.
NUTSHELL VERSION: A COUPLE OF YEARS LATER I FOUND OUT THE BR'KYTT CRASH HAD GIVEN ME LATENT SUPER POWERS. EVERYONE KNOWS THE PROFILE: POWER BARBS, DRAGON-FLIGHT... THE WORKS.
RANGE POWER... OURSING THROUGH MY VEINS...
RAGON POWER, THE BOY UTS AN END TO HIS UNCLE'S BULLYING WAYS!
UNCLE CLIVE WAS NOT A BIG FAN OF THAT DEVELOPMENT.
A SMALL PART OF ME THOUGHT ABOUT KILLING HIM. THE GREATER PART OF ME VOTED AGAINST IT.
AND THAT'S HOW I BECAME DRAGONFLY.

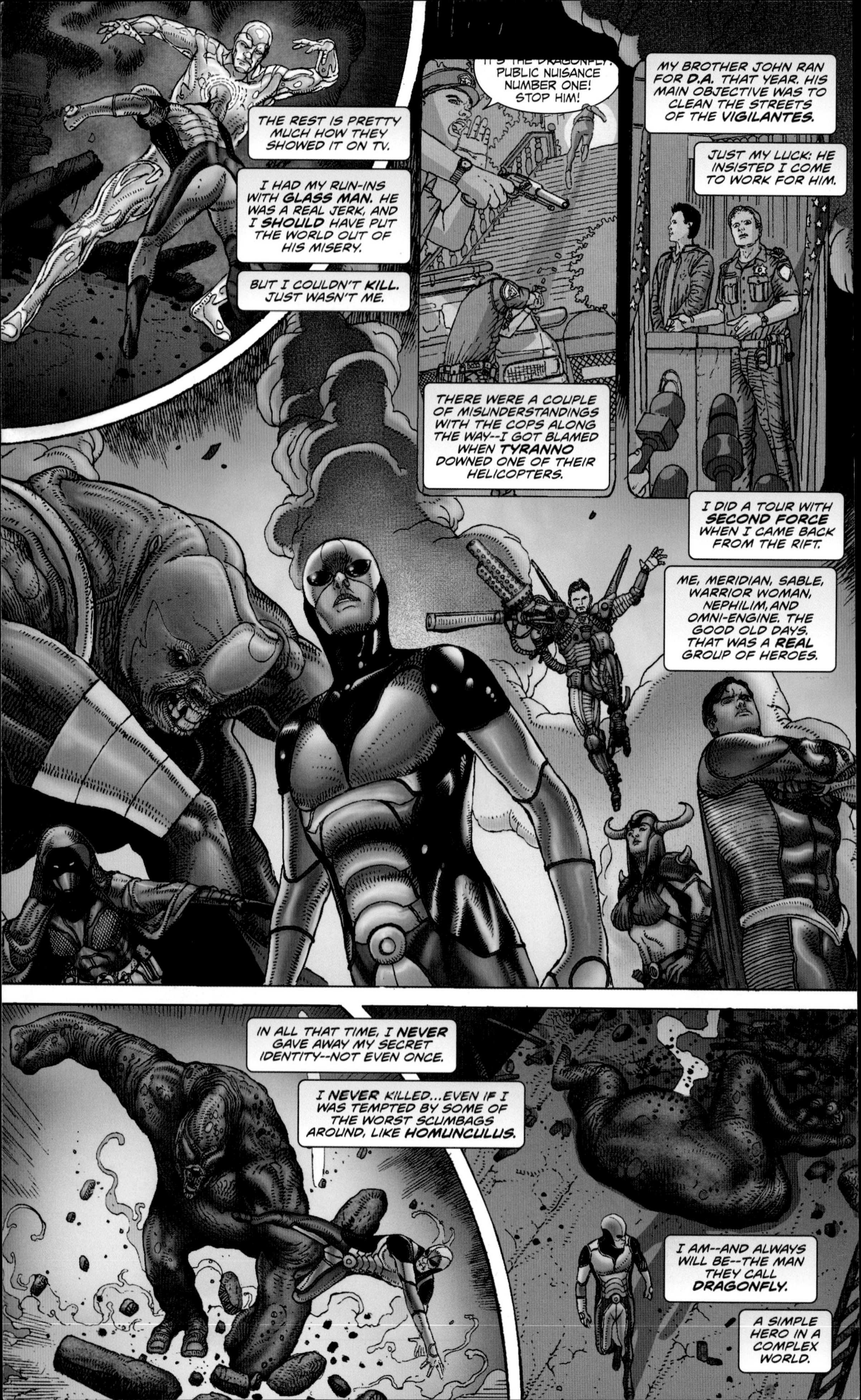
THE REST IS PRETTY MUCH HOW THEY SHOWED IT ON TV.
I HAD MY RUN-INS WITH **GLASS MAN.** HE WAS A REAL JERK, AND I **SHOULD** HAVE PUT THE WORLD OUT OF HIS MISERY.
BUT I COULDN'T **KILL.** JUST WASN'T ME.
PUBLIC NUISANCE NUMBER ONE! STOP HIM!
THERE WERE A COUPLE OF MISUNDERSTANDINGS WITH THE COPS ALONG THE WAY--I GOT BLAMED WHEN **TYRANNO** DOWNED ONE OF THEIR HELICOPTERS.
MY BROTHER JOHN RAN FOR **D.A.** THAT YEAR. HIS MAIN OBJECTIVE WAS TO CLEAN THE STREETS OF THE **VIGILANTES.**
JUST MY LUCK: HE INSISTED I COME TO WORK FOR HIM.
I DID A TOUR WITH **SECOND FORCE** WHEN I CAME BACK FROM THE RIFT.
ME, MERIDIAN, SABLE, WARRIOR WOMAN, NEPHILIM, AND OMNI-ENGINE. THE GOOD OLD DAYS. THAT WAS A **REAL** GROUP OF HEROES.
IN ALL THAT TIME, I **NEVER** GAVE AWAY MY SECRET IDENTITY--NOT EVEN ONCE.
I **NEVER** KILLED...EVEN IF I WAS TEMPTED BY SOME OF THE WORST SCUMBAGS AROUND, LIKE **HOMUNCULUS.**
I AM--AND ALWAYS WILL BE--THE MAN THEY CALL **DRAGONFLY.**
A SIMPLE HERO IN A COMPLEX WORLD.

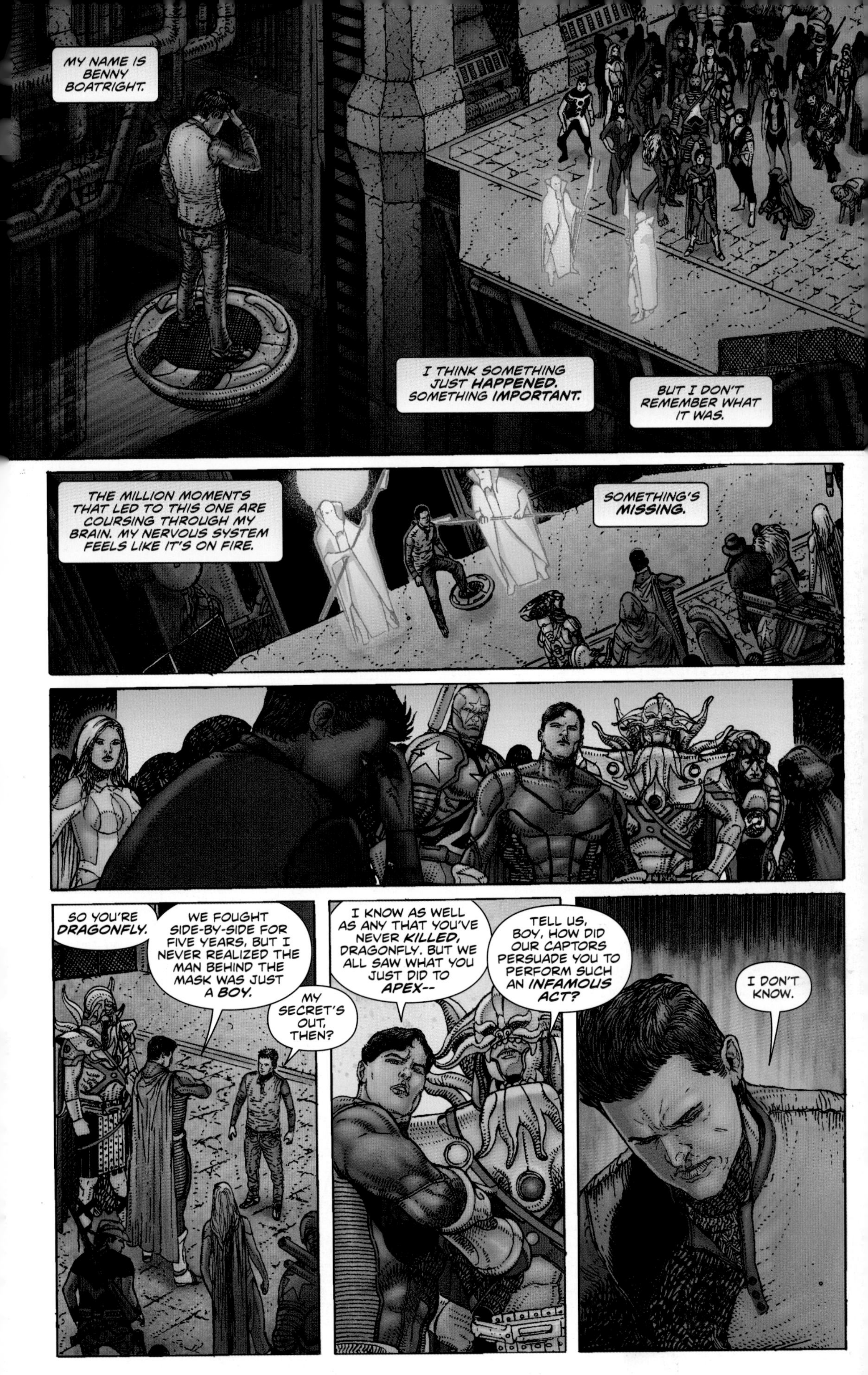
MY NAME IS BENNY BOATRIGHT.
I THINK SOMETHING JUST HAPPENED. SOMETHING IMPORTANT.
BUT I DON'T REMEMBER WHAT IT WAS.
THE MILLION MOMENTS THAT LED TO THIS ONE ARE COURSING THROUGH MY BRAIN. MY NERVOUS SYSTEM FEELS LIKE IT'S ON FIRE.
SOMETHING'S MISSING.
SO YOU'RE DRAGONFLY.
WE FOUGHT SIDE-BY-SIDE FOR FIVE YEARS, BUT I NEVER REALIZED THE MAN BEHIND THE MASK WAS JUST A BOY.
MY SECRET'S OUT, THEN?
I KNOW AS WELL AS ANY THAT YOU'VE NEVER KILLED, DRAGONFLY. BUT WE ALL SAW WHAT YOU JUST DID TO APEX--
TELL US, BOY, HOW DID OUR CAPTORS PERSUADE YOU TO PERFORM SUCH AN INFAMOUS ACT?
I DON'T KNOW.

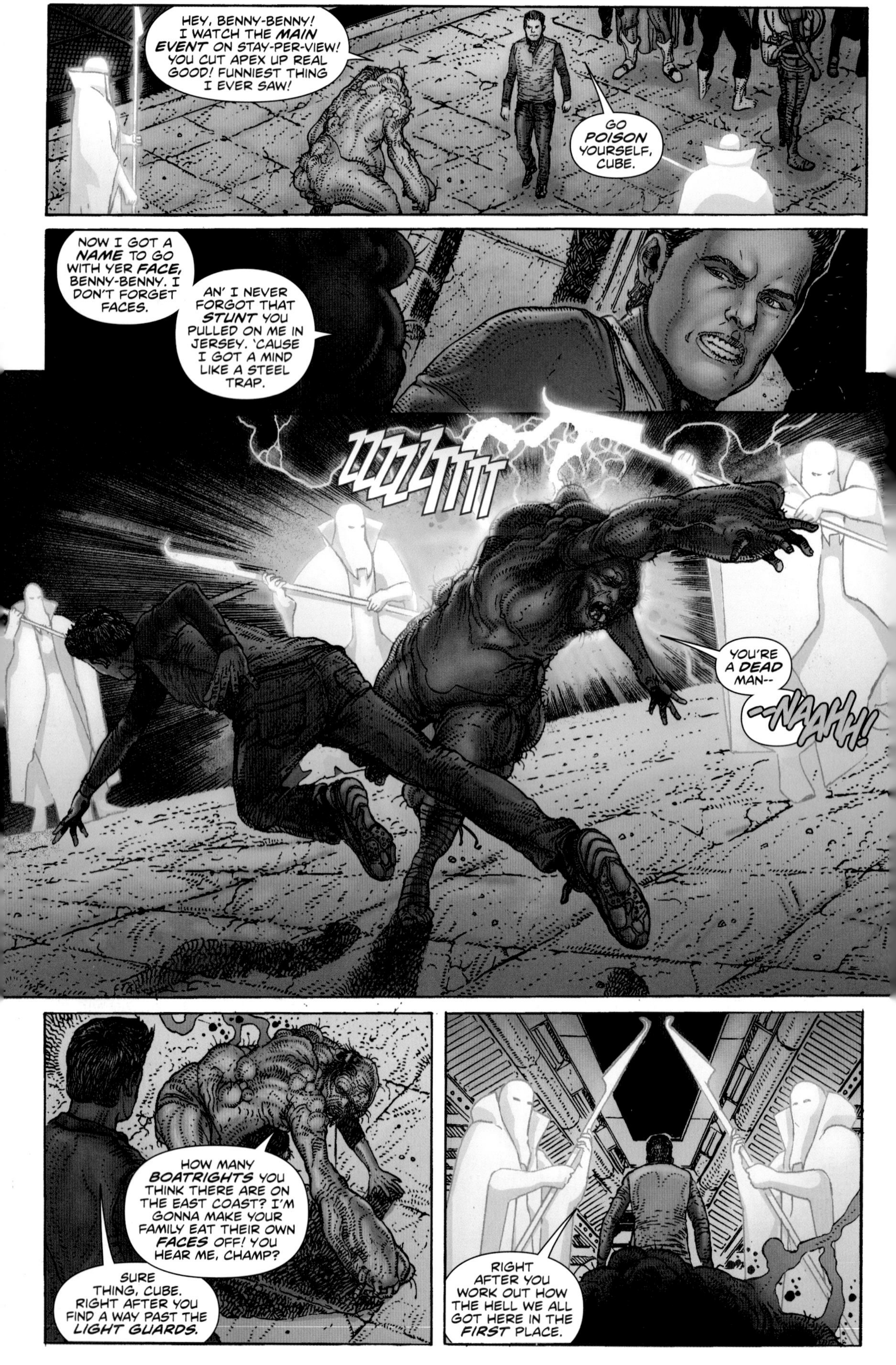
HEY, BENNY-BENNY! I WATCH THE MAIN EVENT ON STAY-PER-VIEW! YOU CUT APEX UP REAL GOOD! FUNNIEST THING I EVER SAW!
GO POISON YOURSELF, CUBE.
NOW I GOT A NAME TO GO WITH YER FACE, BENNY-BENNY. I DON'T FORGET FACES.
AN' I NEVER FORGOT THAT STUNT YOU PULLED ON ME IN JERSEY. 'CAUSE I GOT A MIND LIKE A STEEL TRAP.
ZZZZZTTTTT
YOU'RE A DEAD MAN--
--NAAHH!
HOW MANY BOATRIGHTS YOU THINK THERE ARE ON THE EAST COAST? I'M GONNA MAKE YOUR FAMILY EAT THEIR OWN FACES OFF! YOU HEAR ME, CHAMP?
SURE THING, CUBE. RIGHT AFTER YOU FIND A WAY PAST THE LIGHT GUARDS.
RIGHT AFTER YOU WORK OUT HOW THE HELL WE ALL GOT HERE IN THE FIRST PLACE.

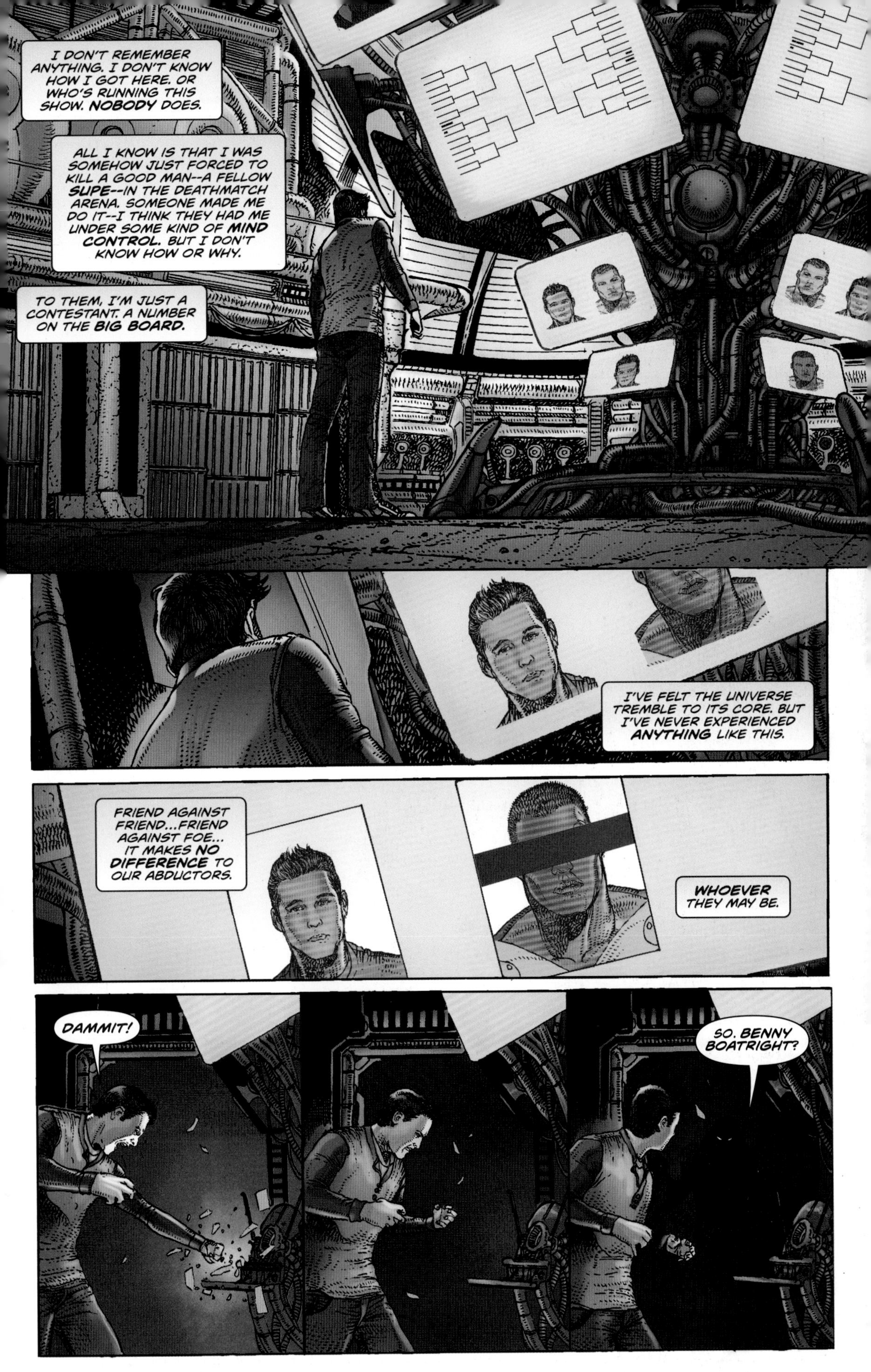
I DON'T REMEMBER ANYTHING. I DON'T KNOW HOW I GOT HERE. OR WHO'S RUNNING THIS SHOW. NOBODY DOES.
ALL I KNOW IS THAT I WAS SOMEHOW JUST FORCED TO KILL A GOOD MAN--A FELLOW SUPE--IN THE DEATHMATCH ARENA. SOMEONE MADE ME DO IT--I THINK THEY HAD ME UNDER SOME KIND OF MIND CONTROL. BUT I DON'T KNOW HOW OR WHY.
TO THEM, I'M JUST A CONTESTANT. A NUMBER ON THE BIG BOARD.
I'VE FELT THE UNIVERSE TREMBLE TO ITS CORE. BUT I'VE NEVER EXPERIENCED ANYTHING LIKE THIS.
FRIEND AGAINST FRIEND...FRIEND AGAINST FOE... IT MAKES NO DIFFERENCE TO OUR ABDUCTORS.
WHOEVER THEY MAY BE.
DAMMIT!
SO. BENNY BOATRIGHT?

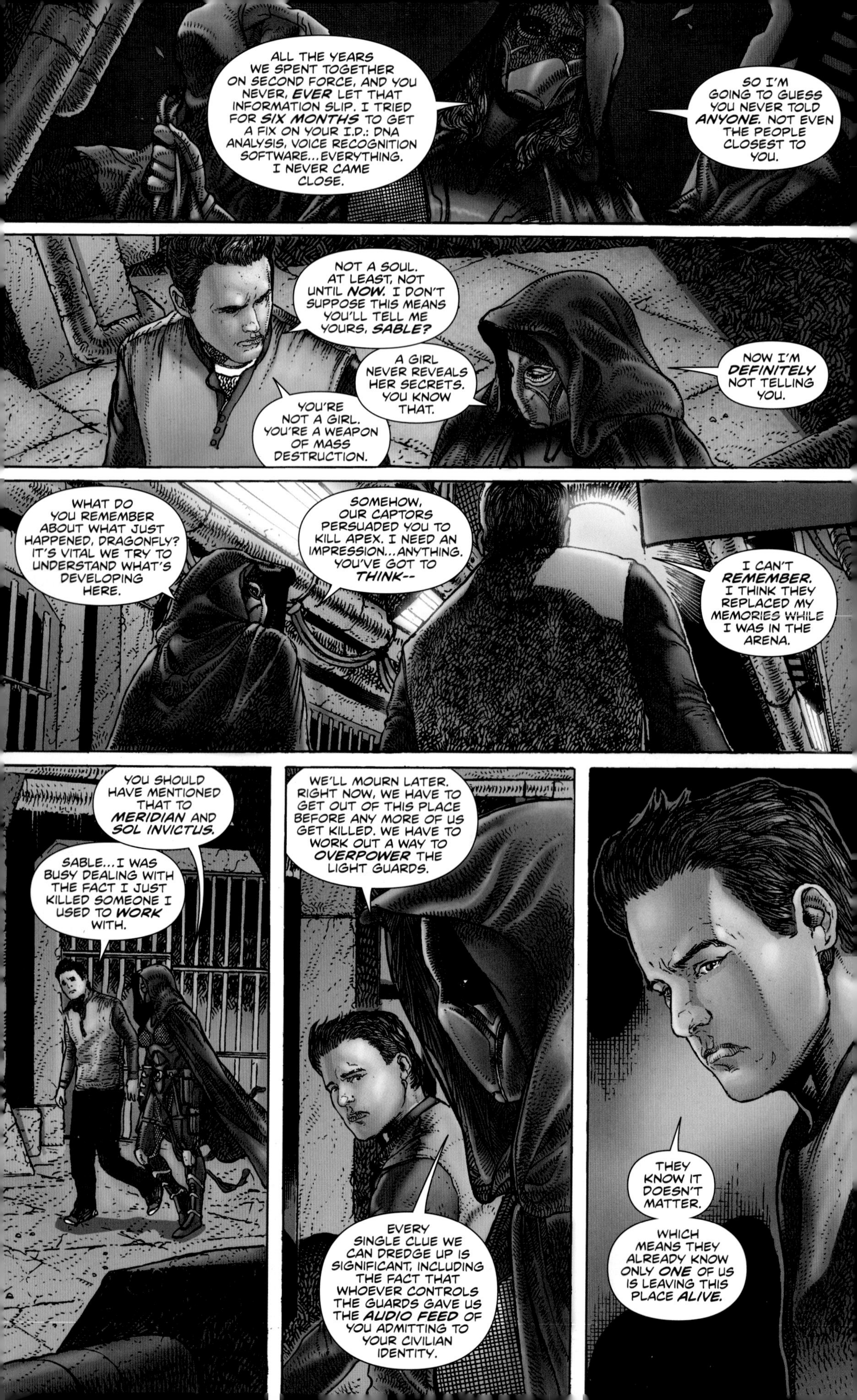
ALL THE YEARS WE SPENT TOGETHER ON SECOND FORCE, AND YOU NEVER, EVER LET THAT INFORMATION SLIP. I TRIED FOR SIX MONTHS TO GET A FIX ON YOUR I.D.: DNA ANALYSIS, VOICE RECOGNITION SOFTWARE...EVERYTHING. I NEVER CAME CLOSE.
SO I'M GOING TO GUESS YOU NEVER TOLD ANYONE. NOT EVEN THE PEOPLE CLOSEST TO YOU.
NOT A SOUL. AT LEAST, NOT UNTIL NOW. I DON'T SUPPOSE THIS MEANS YOU'LL TELL ME YOURS, SABLE?
A GIRL NEVER REVEALS HER SECRETS. YOU KNOW THAT.
YOU'RE NOT A GIRL. YOU'RE A WEAPON OF MASS DESTRUCTION.
NOW I'M DEFINITELY NOT TELLING YOU.
WHAT DO YOU REMEMBER ABOUT WHAT JUST HAPPENED, DRAGONFLY? IT'S VITAL WE TRY TO UNDERSTAND WHAT'S DEVELOPING HERE.
SOMEHOW, OUR CAPTORS PERSUADED YOU TO KILL APEX. I NEED AN IMPRESSION...ANYTHING. YOU'VE GOT TO THINK--
I CAN'T REMEMBER. I THINK THEY REPLACED MY MEMORIES WHILE I WAS IN THE ARENA.
YOU SHOULD HAVE MENTIONED THAT TO MERIDIAN AND SOL INVICTUS.
SABLE...I WAS BUSY DEALING WITH THE FACT I JUST KILLED SOMEONE I USED TO WORK WITH.
WE'LL MOURN LATER. RIGHT NOW, WE HAVE TO GET OUT OF THIS PLACE BEFORE ANY MORE OF US GET KILLED. WE HAVE TO WORK OUT A WAY TO OVERPOWER THE LIGHT GUARDS.
EVERY SINGLE CLUE WE CAN DREDGE UP IS SIGNIFICANT, INCLUDING THE FACT THAT WHOEVER CONTROLS THE GUARDS GAVE US THE AUDIO FEED OF YOU ADMITTING TO YOUR CIVILIAN IDENTITY.
THEY KNOW IT DOESN'T MATTER.
WHICH MEANS THEY ALREADY KNOW ONLY ONE OF US IS LEAVING THIS PLACE ALIVE.

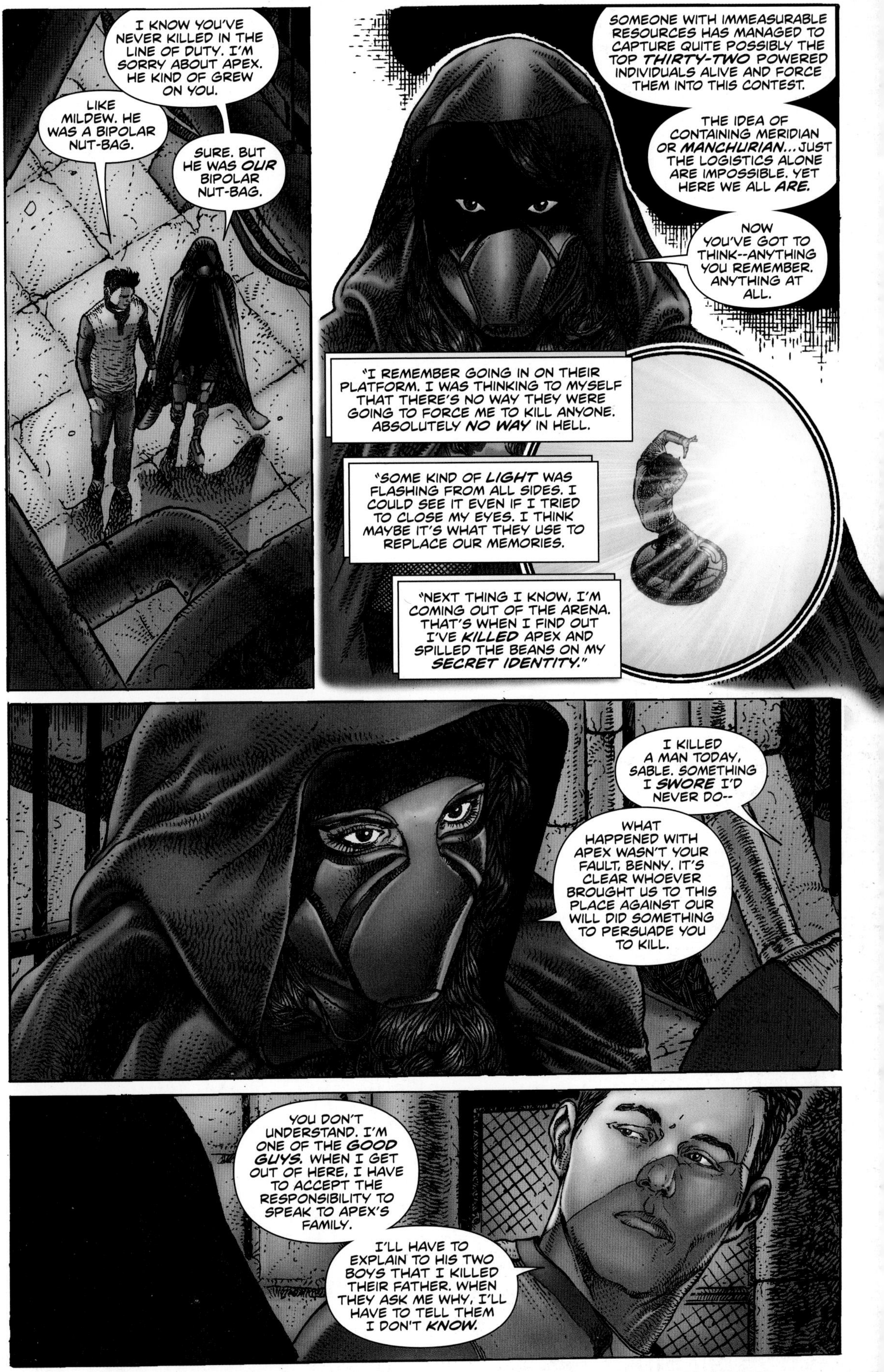
I KNOW YOU'VE NEVER KILLED IN THE LINE OF DUTY. I'M SORRY ABOUT APEX. HE KIND OF GREW ON YOU.
LIKE MILDEW. HE WAS A BIPOLAR NUT-BAG.
SURE. BUT HE WAS OUR BIPOLAR NUT-BAG.
SOMEONE WITH IMMEASURABLE RESOURCES HAS MANAGED TO CAPTURE QUITE POSSIBLY THE TOP THIRTY-TWO POWERED INDIVIDUALS ALIVE AND FORCE THEM INTO THIS CONTEST.
THE IDEA OF CONTAINING MERIDIAN OR MANCHURIAN... JUST THE LOGISTICS ALONE ARE IMPOSSIBLE. YET HERE WE ALL ARE.
NOW YOU'VE GOT TO THINK--ANYTHING YOU REMEMBER. ANYTHING AT ALL.
"I REMEMBER GOING IN ON THEIR PLATFORM. I WAS THINKING TO MYSELF THAT THERE'S NO WAY THEY WERE GOING TO FORCE ME TO KILL ANYONE. ABSOLUTELY NO WAY IN HELL.
"SOME KIND OF LIGHT WAS FLASHING FROM ALL SIDES. I COULD SEE IT EVEN IF I TRIED TO CLOSE MY EYES. I THINK MAYBE IT'S WHAT THEY USE TO REPLACE OUR MEMORIES.
"NEXT THING I KNOW, I'M COMING OUT OF THE ARENA. THAT'S WHEN I FIND OUT I'VE KILLED APEX AND SPILLED THE BEANS ON MY SECRET IDENTITY."
I KILLED A MAN TODAY, SABLE. SOMETHING I SWORE I'D NEVER DO--
WHAT HAPPENED WITH APEX WASN'T YOUR FAULT, BENNY. IT'S CLEAR WHOEVER BROUGHT US TO THIS PLACE AGAINST OUR WILL DID SOMETHING TO PERSUADE YOU TO KILL.
YOU DON'T UNDERSTAND. I'M ONE OF THE GOOD GUYS. WHEN I GET OUT OF HERE, I HAVE TO ACCEPT THE RESPONSIBILITY TO SPEAK TO APEX'S FAMILY.
I'LL HAVE TO EXPLAIN TO HIS TWO BOYS THAT I KILLED THEIR FATHER. WHEN THEY ASK ME WHY, I'LL HAVE TO TELL THEM I DON'T KNOW.

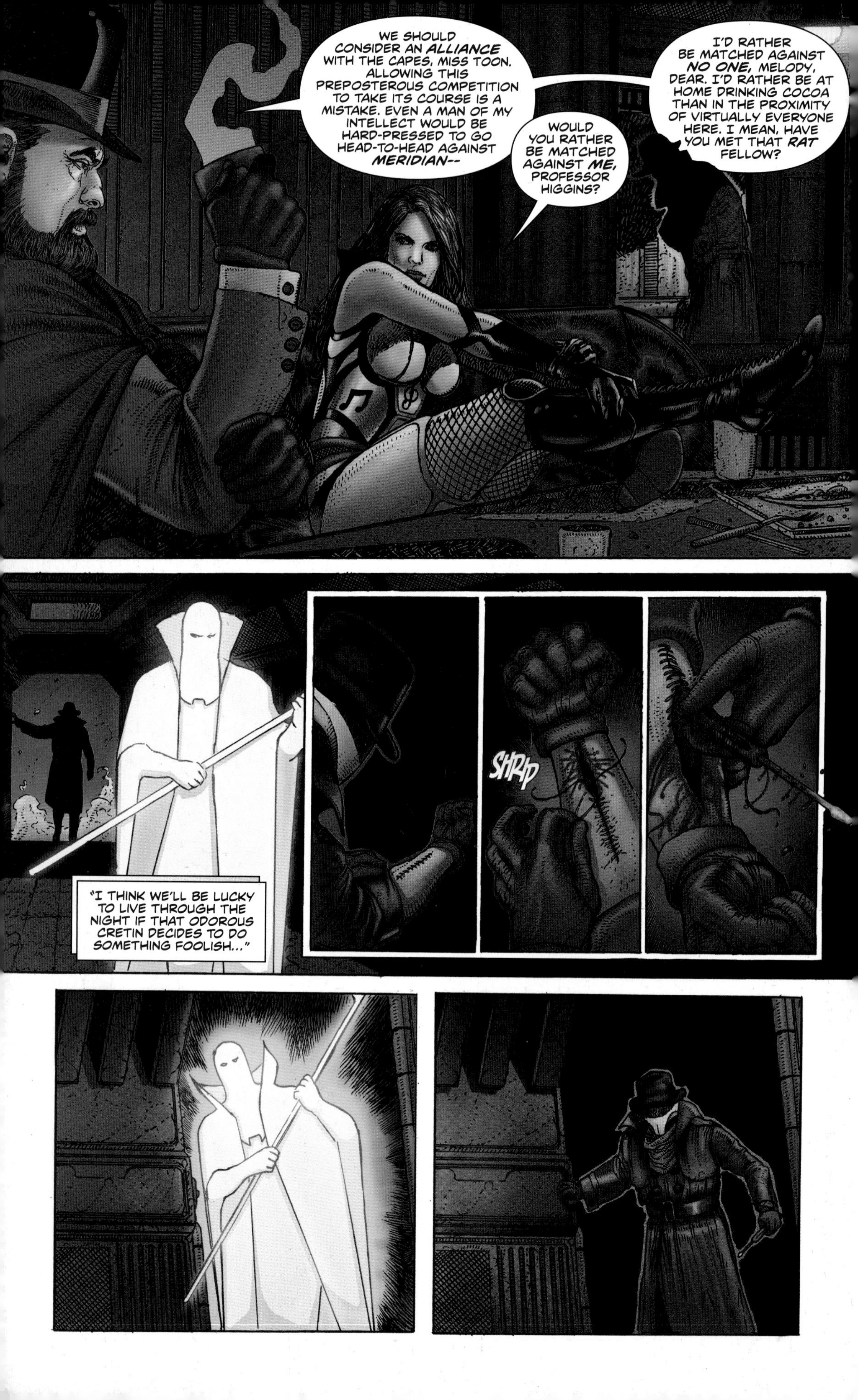
WE SHOULD CONSIDER AN ALLIANCE WITH THE CAPES, MISS TOON. ALLOWING THIS PREPOSTEROUS COMPETITION TO TAKE ITS COURSE IS A MISTAKE. EVEN A MAN OF MY INTELLECT WOULD BE HARD-PRESSED TO GO HEAD-TO-HEAD AGAINST MERIDIAN--
WOULD YOU RATHER BE MATCHED AGAINST ME, PROFESSOR HIGGINS?
I'D RATHER BE MATCHED AGAINST NO ONE, MELODY, DEAR. I'D RATHER BE AT HOME DRINKING COCOA THAN IN THE PROXIMITY OF VIRTUALLY EVERYONE HERE. I MEAN, HAVE YOU MET THAT RAT FELLOW?
"I THINK WE'LL BE LUCKY TO LIVE THROUGH THE NIGHT IF THAT ODOROUS CRETIN DECIDES TO DO SOMETHING FOOLISH..."
SHRIP

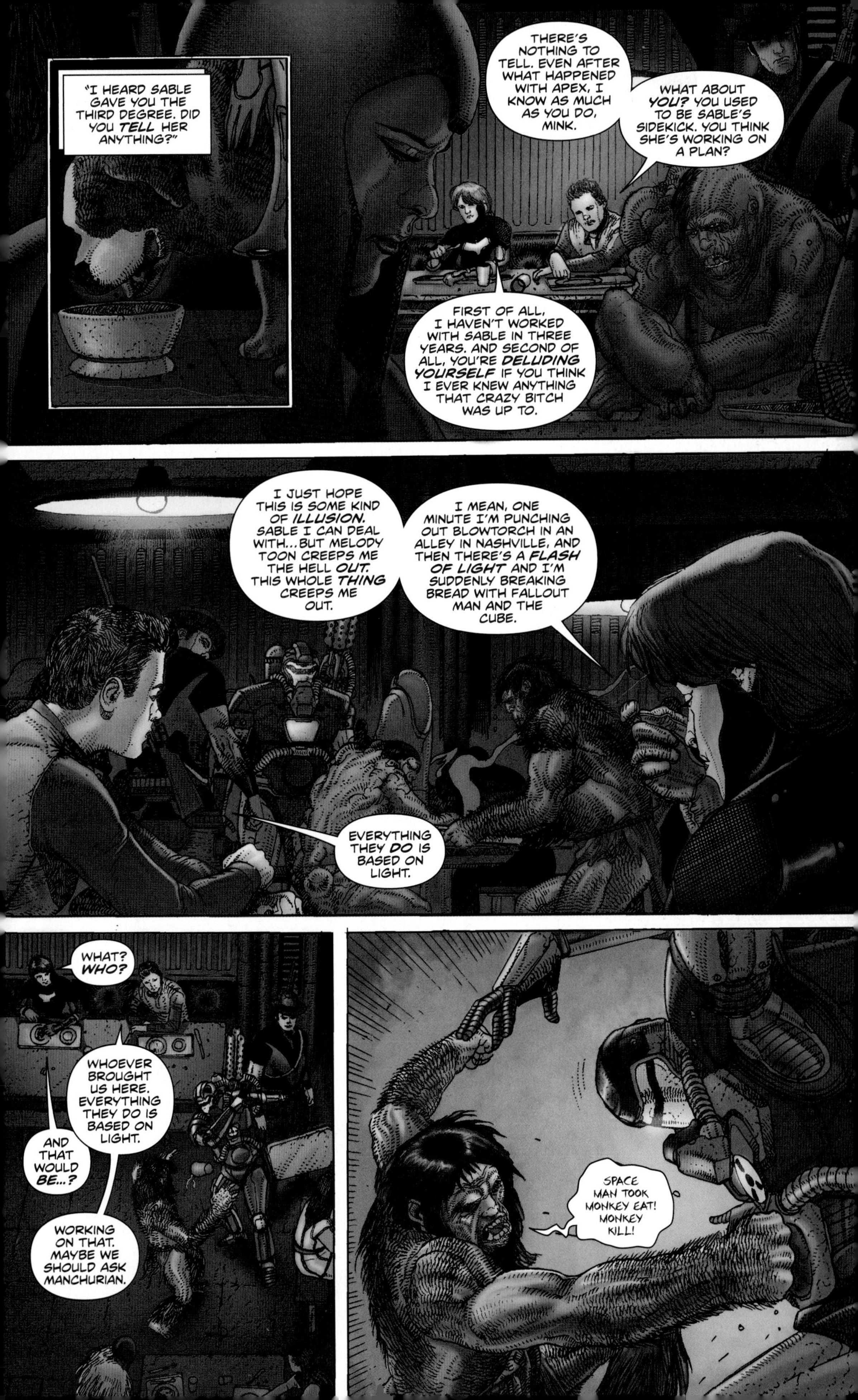
"I HEARD SABLE GAVE YOU THE THIRD DEGREE. DID YOU TELL HER ANYTHING?"
THERE'S NOTHING TO TELL. EVEN AFTER WHAT HAPPENED WITH APEX, I KNOW AS MUCH AS YOU DO, MINK.
WHAT ABOUT YOU? YOU USED TO BE SABLE'S SIDEKICK. YOU THINK SHE'S WORKING ON A PLAN?
FIRST OF ALL, I HAVEN'T WORKED WITH SABLE IN THREE YEARS. AND SECOND OF ALL, YOU'RE DELUDING YOURSELF IF YOU THINK I EVER KNEW ANYTHING THAT CRAZY BITCH WAS UP TO.
I JUST HOPE THIS IS SOME KIND OF ILLUSION. SABLE I CAN DEAL WITH... BUT MELODY TOON CREEPS ME THE HELL OUT. THIS WHOLE THING CREEPS ME OUT.
I MEAN, ONE MINUTE I'M PUNCHING OUT BLOWTORCH IN AN ALLEY IN NASHVILLE, AND THEN THERE'S A FLASH OF LIGHT AND I'M SUDDENLY BREAKING BREAD WITH FALLOUT MAN AND THE CUBE.
EVERYTHING THEY DO IS BASED ON LIGHT.
WHAT? WHO?
WHOEVER BROUGHT US HERE. EVERYTHING THEY DO IS BASED ON LIGHT.
AND THAT WOULD BE...?
WORKING ON THAT. MAYBE WE SHOULD ASK MANCHURIAN.
SPACE MAN TOOK MONKEY EAT! MONKEY KILL!

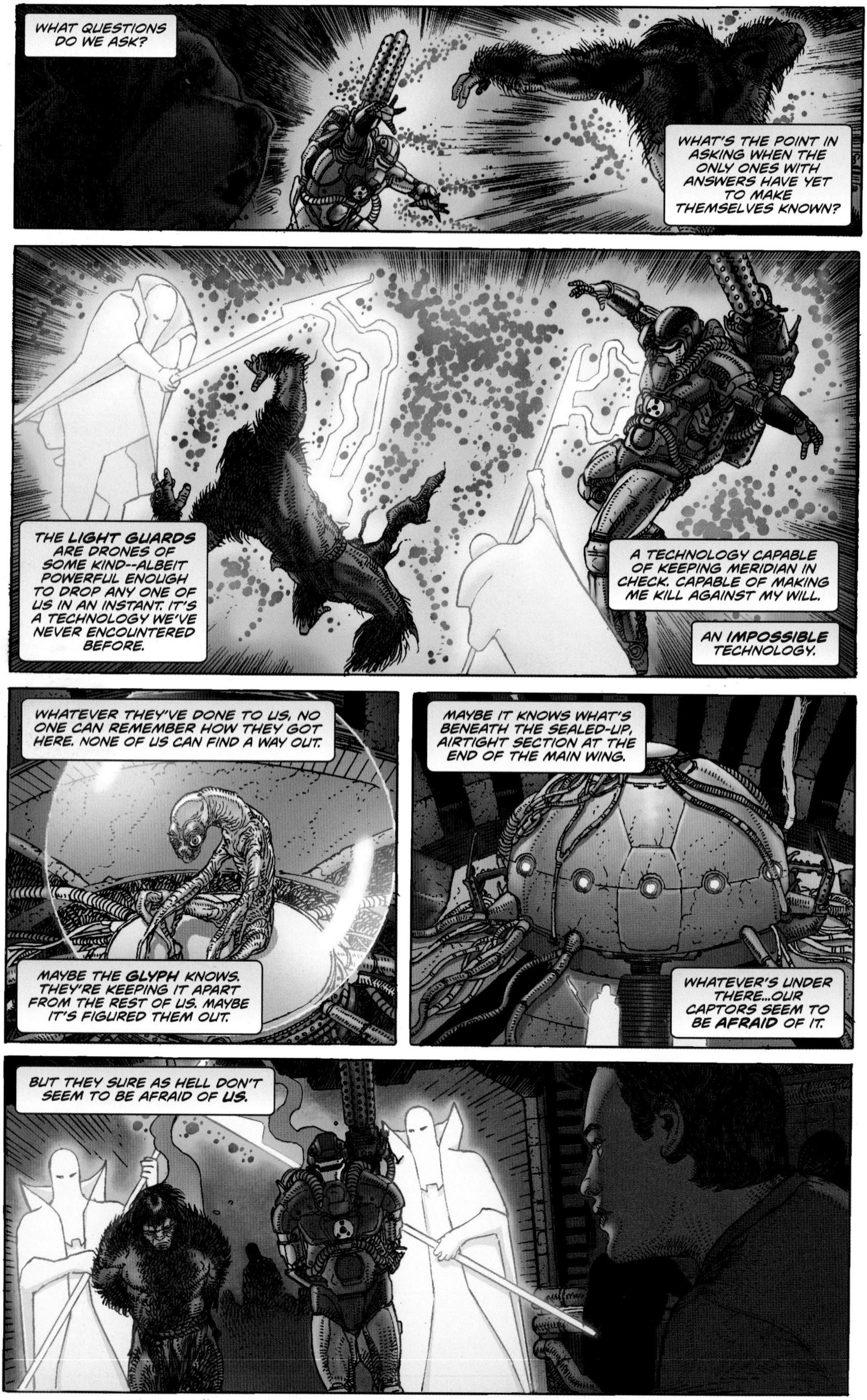
WHAT QUESTIONS DO WE ASK?
WHAT'S THE POINT IN ASKING WHEN THE ONLY ONES WITH ANSWERS HAVE YET TO MAKE THEMSELVES KNOWN?
THE LIGHT GUARDS ARE DRONES OF SOME KIND--ALBEIT POWERFUL ENOUGH TO DROP ANY ONE OF US IN AN INSTANT. IT'S A TECHNOLOGY WE'VE NEVER ENCOUNTERED BEFORE.
A TECHNOLOGY CAPABLE OF KEEPING MERIDIAN IN CHECK. CAPABLE OF MAKING ME KILL AGAINST MY WILL.
AN IMPOSSIBLE TECHNOLOGY.
WHATEVER THEY'VE DONE TO US, NO ONE CAN REMEMBER HOW THEY GOT HERE. NONE OF US CAN FIND A WAY OUT.
MAYBE THE GLYPH KNOWS. THEY'RE KEEPING IT APART FROM THE REST OF US. MAYBE IT'S FIGURED THEM OUT.
MAYBE IT KNOWS WHAT'S BENEATH THE SEALED-UP, AIRTIGHT SECTION AT THE END OF THE MAIN WING.
WHATEVER'S UNDER THERE...OUR CAPTORS SEEM TO BE AFRAID OF IT.
BUT THEY SURE AS HELL DON'T SEEM TO BE AFRAID OF US.

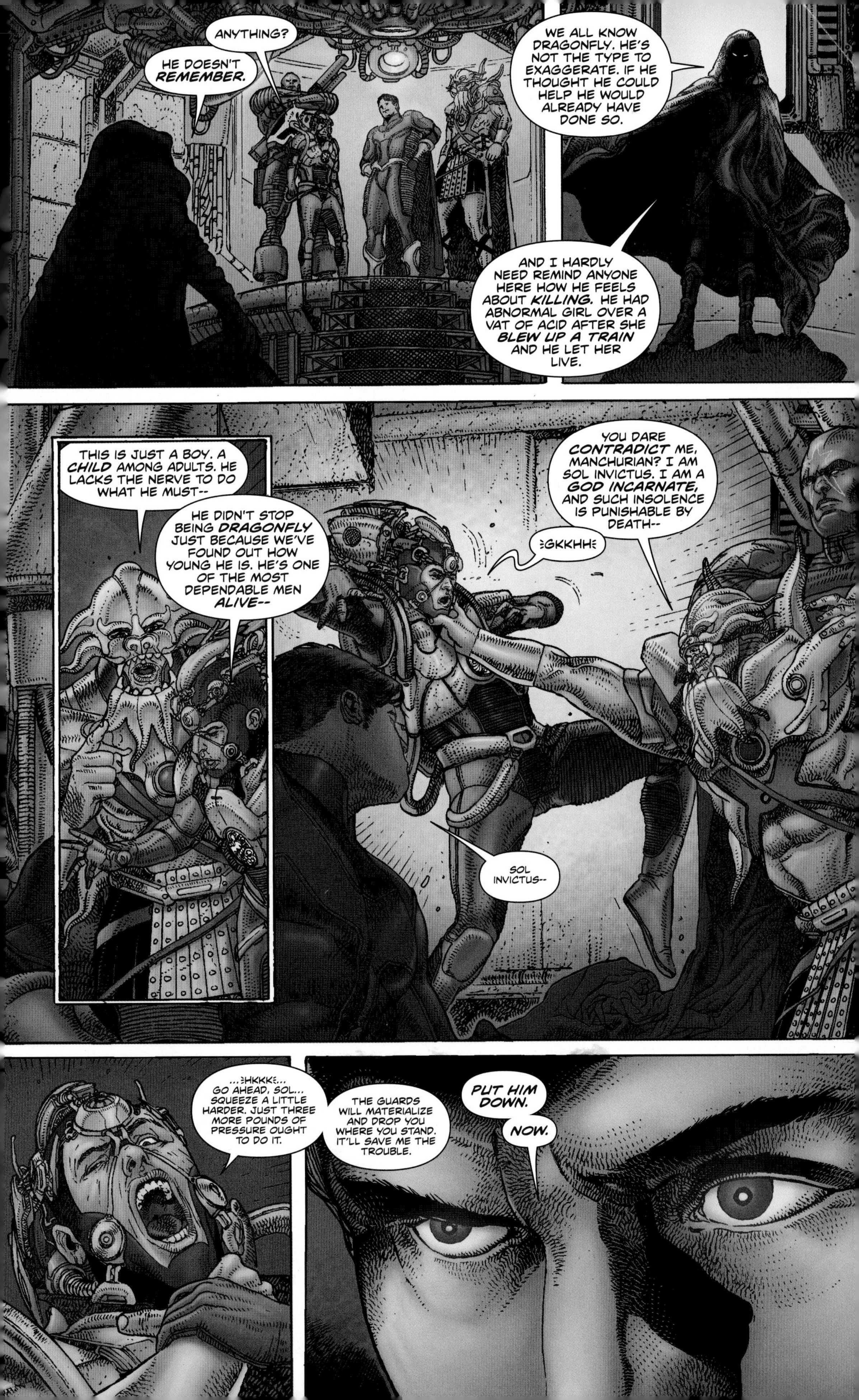

ANYTHING?
HE DOESN'T REMEMBER.
WE ALL KNOW DRAGONFLY. HE'S NOT THE TYPE TO EXAGGERATE. IF HE THOUGHT HE COULD HELP HE WOULD ALREADY HAVE DONE SO.
AND I HARDLY NEED REMIND ANYONE HERE HOW HE FEELS ABOUT KILLING. HE HAD ABNORMAL GIRL OVER A VAT OF ACID AFTER SHE BLEW UP A TRAIN AND HE LET HER LIVE.
THIS IS JUST A BOY. A CHILD AMONG ADULTS. HE LACKS THE NERVE TO DO WHAT HE MUST--
HE DIDN'T STOP BEING DRAGONFLY JUST BECAUSE WE'VE FOUND OUT HOW YOUNG HE IS. HE'S ONE OF THE MOST DEPENDABLE MEN ALIVE--
YOU DARE CONTRADICT ME, MANCHURIAN? I AM SOL INVICTUS. I AM A GOD INCARNATE, AND SUCH INSOLENCE IS PUNISHABLE BY DEATH--
GKKHH
SOL INVICTUS--
...HKKK... GO AHEAD, SOL... SQUEEZE A LITTLE HARDER. JUST THREE MORE POUNDS OF PRESSURE OUGHT TO DO IT.
THE GUARDS WILL MATERIALIZE AND DROP YOU WHERE YOU STAND. IT'LL SAVE ME THE TROUBLE.
PUT HIM DOWN.
NOW.

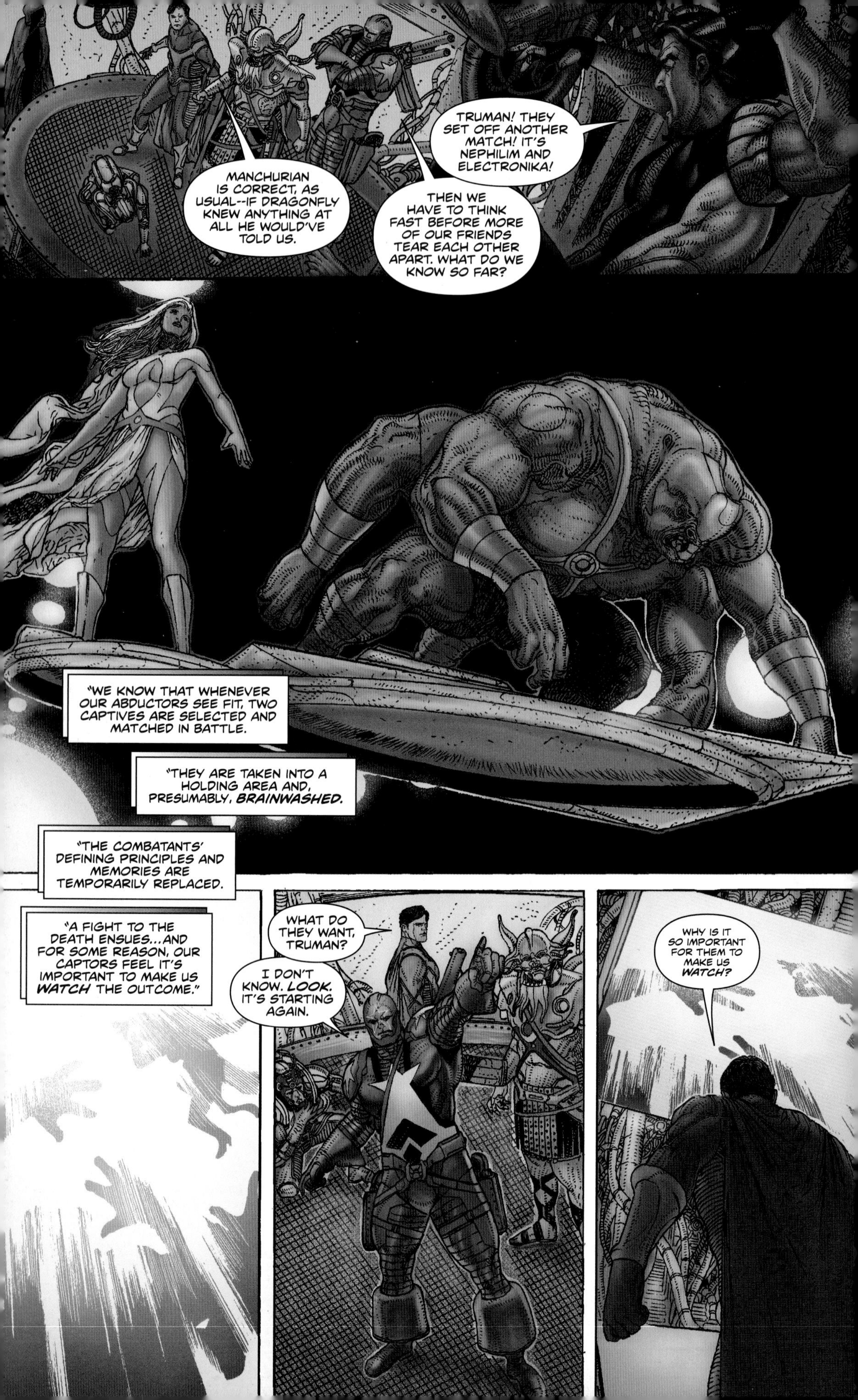
MANCHURIAN IS CORRECT, AS USUAL--IF DRAGONFLY KNEW ANYTHING AT ALL HE WOULD'VE TOLD US.
TRUMAN! THEY SET OFF ANOTHER MATCH! IT'S NEPHILIM AND ELECTRONIKA!
THEN WE HAVE TO THINK FAST BEFORE MORE OF OUR FRIENDS TEAR EACH OTHER APART. WHAT DO WE KNOW SO FAR?
"WE KNOW THAT WHENEVER OUR ABDUCTORS SEE FIT, TWO CAPTIVES ARE SELECTED AND MATCHED IN BATTLE.
"THEY ARE TAKEN INTO A HOLDING AREA AND, PRESUMABLY, BRAINWASHED.
"THE COMBATANTS' DEFINING PRINCIPLES AND MEMORIES ARE TEMPORARILY REPLACED.
"A FIGHT TO THE DEATH ENSUES...AND FOR SOME REASON, OUR CAPTORS FEEL IT'S IMPORTANT TO MAKE US WATCH THE OUTCOME."
WHAT DO THEY WANT, TRUMAN?
I DON'T KNOW. LOOK. IT'S STARTING AGAIN.
WHY IS IT SO IMPORTANT FOR THEM TO MAKE US WATCH?

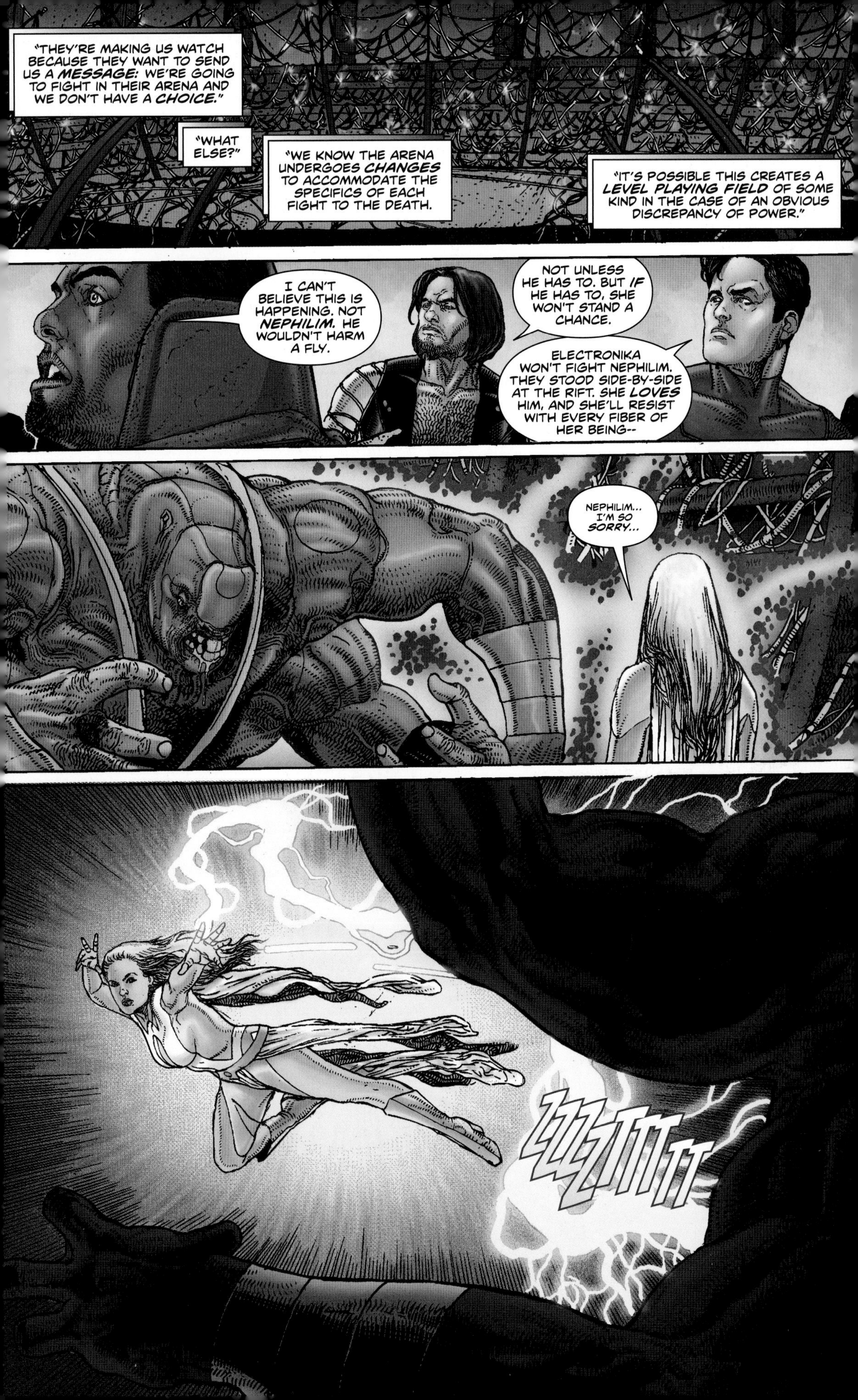
"THEY'RE MAKING US WATCH BECAUSE THEY WANT TO SEND US A MESSAGE: WE'RE GOING TO FIGHT IN THEIR ARENA AND WE DON'T HAVE A CHOICE."
"WHAT ELSE?"
"WE KNOW THE ARENA UNDERGOES CHANGES TO ACCOMMODATE THE SPECIFICS OF EACH FIGHT TO THE DEATH.
"IT'S POSSIBLE THIS CREATES A LEVEL PLAYING FIELD OF SOME KIND IN THE CASE OF AN OBVIOUS DISCREPANCY OF POWER."
I CAN'T BELIEVE THIS IS HAPPENING. NOT NEPHILIM. HE WOULDN'T HARM A FLY.
ELECTRONIKA WON'T FIGHT NEPHILIM. THEY STOOD SIDE-BY-SIDE AT THE RIFT. SHE LOVES HIM, AND SHE'LL RESIST WITH EVERY FIBER OF HER BEING--
NOT UNLESS HE HAS TO. BUT IF HE HAS TO, SHE WON'T STAND A CHANCE.
NEPHILIM... I'M SO SORRY...
ZZZZTTTTT

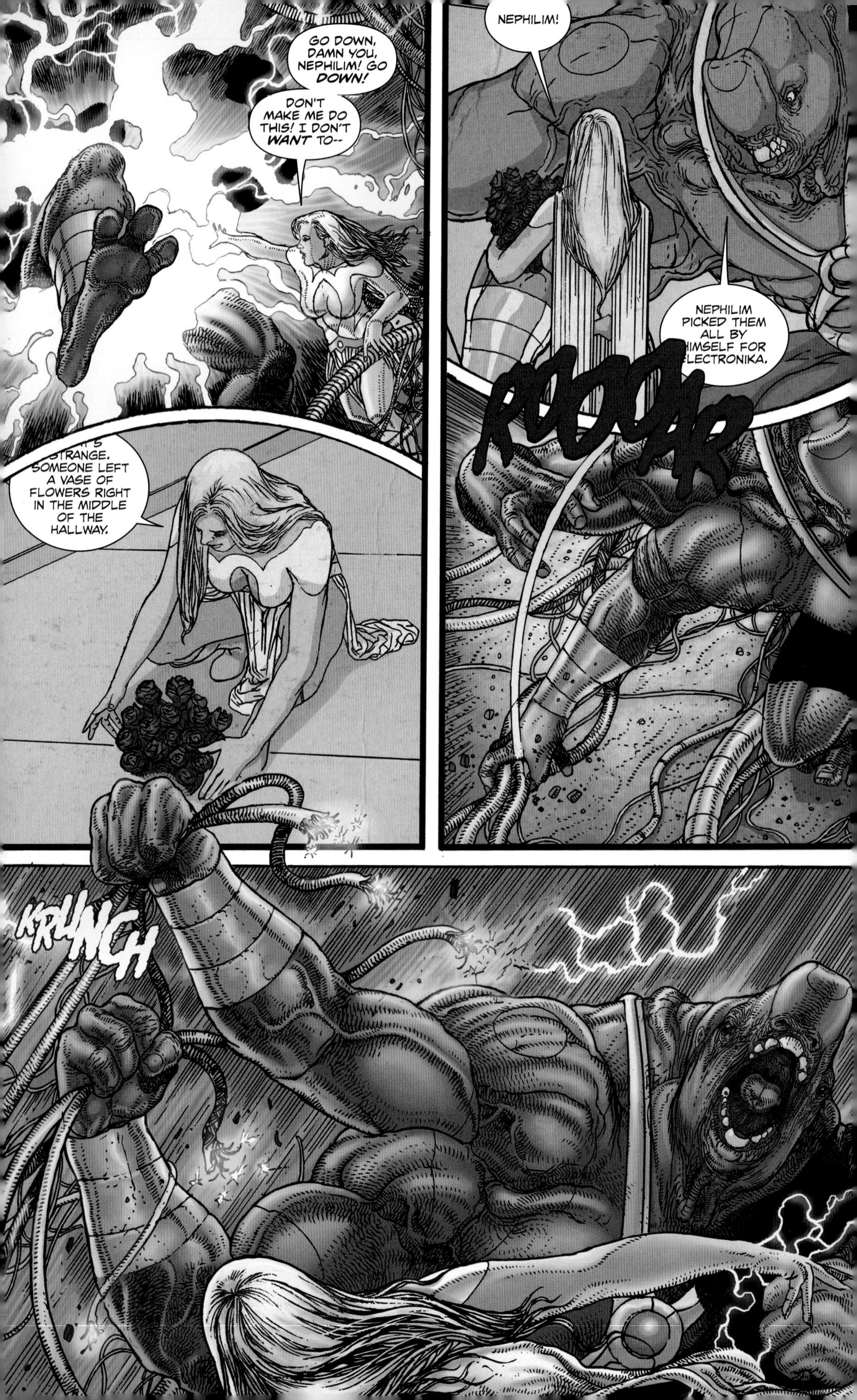
GO DOWN, DAMN YOU, NEPHILIM! GO DOWN!
DON'T MAKE ME DO THIS! I DON'T WANT TO--
NEPHILIM!
NEPHILIM PICKED THEM ALL BY HIMSELF FOR ELECTRONIKA.
STRANGE. SOMEONE LEFT A VASE OF FLOWERS RIGHT IN THE MIDDLE OF THE HALLWAY.
ROOOAR
KRUNCH

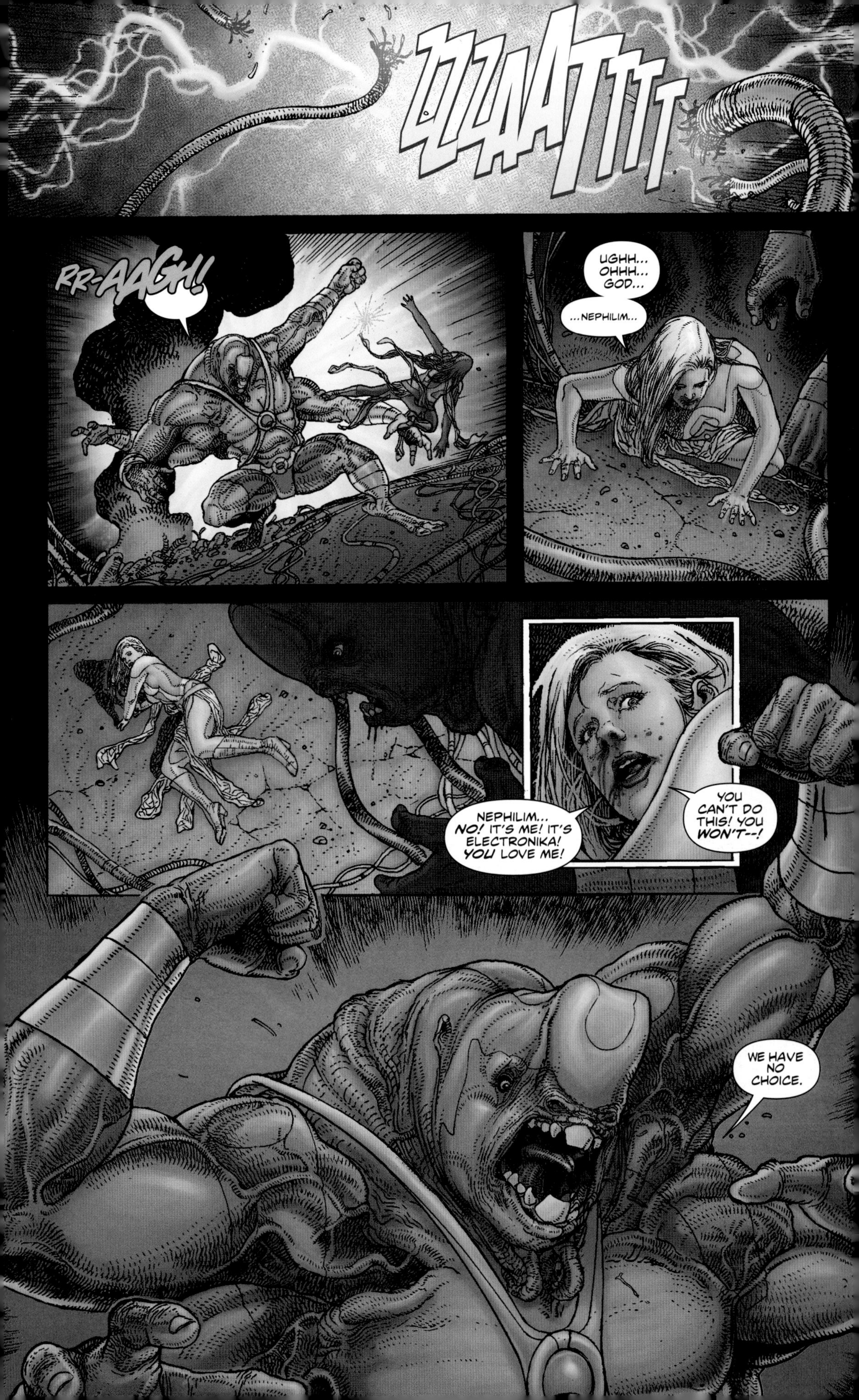
ZZZZAATTTTT
RR-AAGH!
UGHH... OHHH... GOD...
...NEPHILIM...
NEPHILIM... NO! IT'S ME! IT'S ELECTRONIKA! YOU LOVE ME!
YOU CAN'T DO THIS! YOU WON'T--!
WE HAVE NO CHOICE.

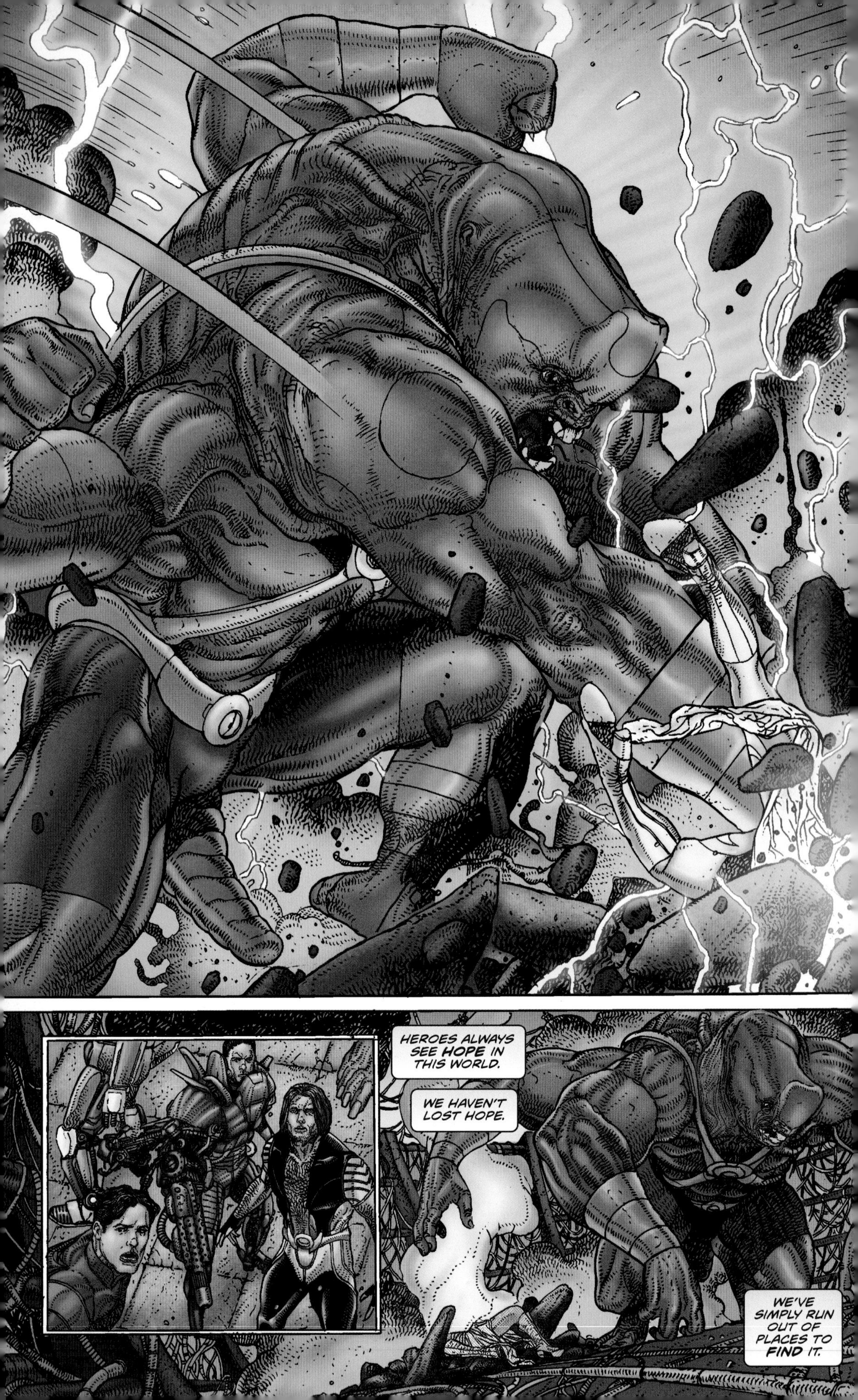
HEROES ALWAYS SEE HOPE IN THIS WORLD.
WE HAVEN'T LOST HOPE.
WE'VE SIMPLY RUN OUT OF PLACES TO FIND IT.

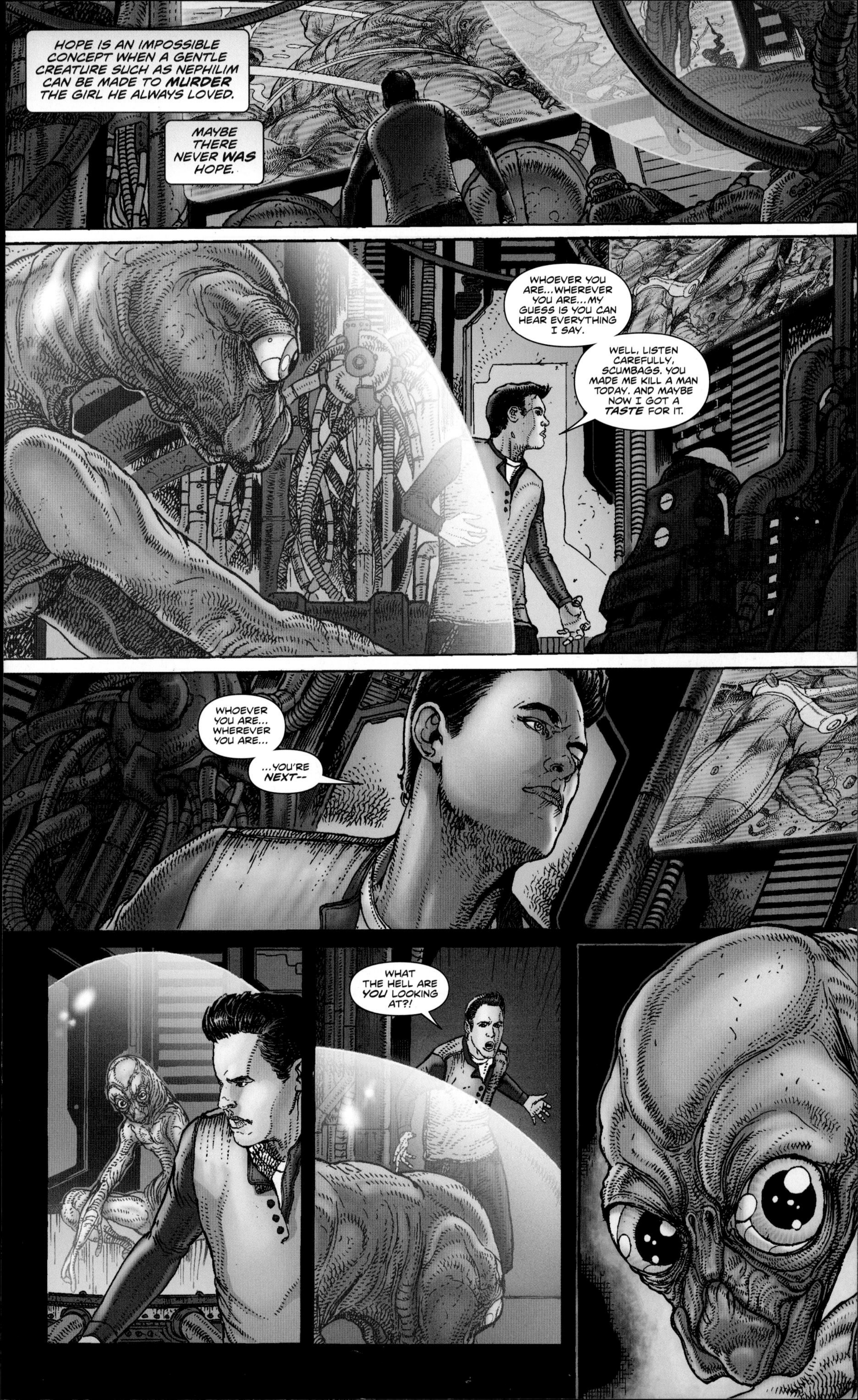
HOPE IS AN IMPOSSIBLE CONCEPT WHEN A GENTLE CREATURE SUCH AS NEPHILIM CAN BE MADE TO MURDER THE GIRL HE ALWAYS LOVED.
MAYBE THERE NEVER WAS HOPE.
WHOEVER YOU ARE...WHEREVER YOU ARE...MY GUESS IS YOU CAN HEAR EVERYTHING I SAY.
WELL, LISTEN CAREFULLY, SCUMBAGS. YOU MADE ME KILL A MAN TODAY. AND MAYBE NOW I GOT A TASTE FOR IT.
WHOEVER YOU ARE... WHEREVER YOU ARE...
...YOU'RE NEXT--
WHAT THE HELL ARE YOU LOOKING AT?!

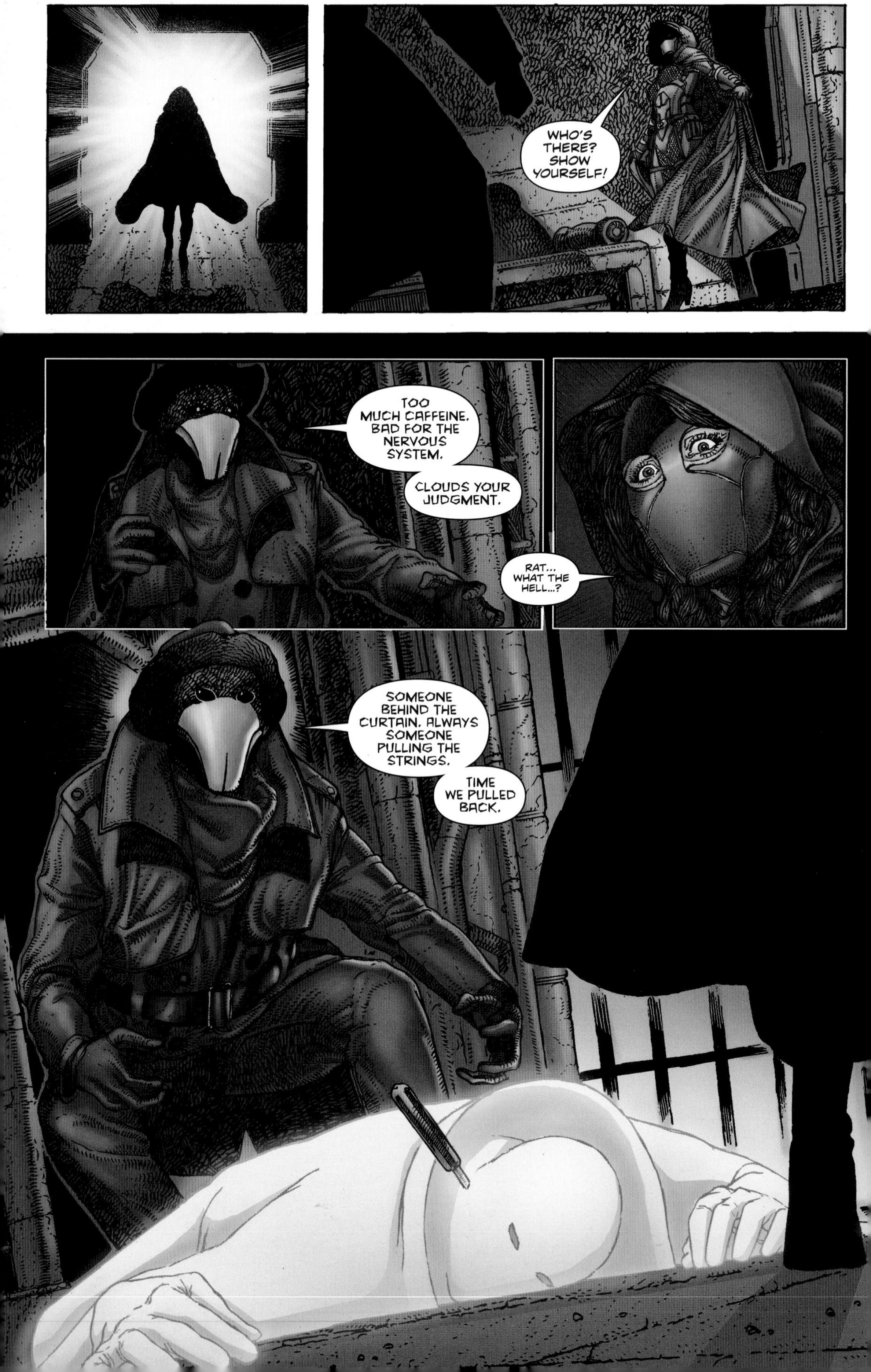
WHO'S THERE? SHOW YOURSELF!
TOO MUCH CAFFEINE. BAD FOR THE NERVOUS SYSTEM.
CLOUDS YOUR JUDGMENT.
RAT... WHAT THE HELL...?
SOMEONE BEHIND THE CURTAIN. ALWAYS SOMEONE PULLING THE STRINGS.
TIME WE PULLED BACK.

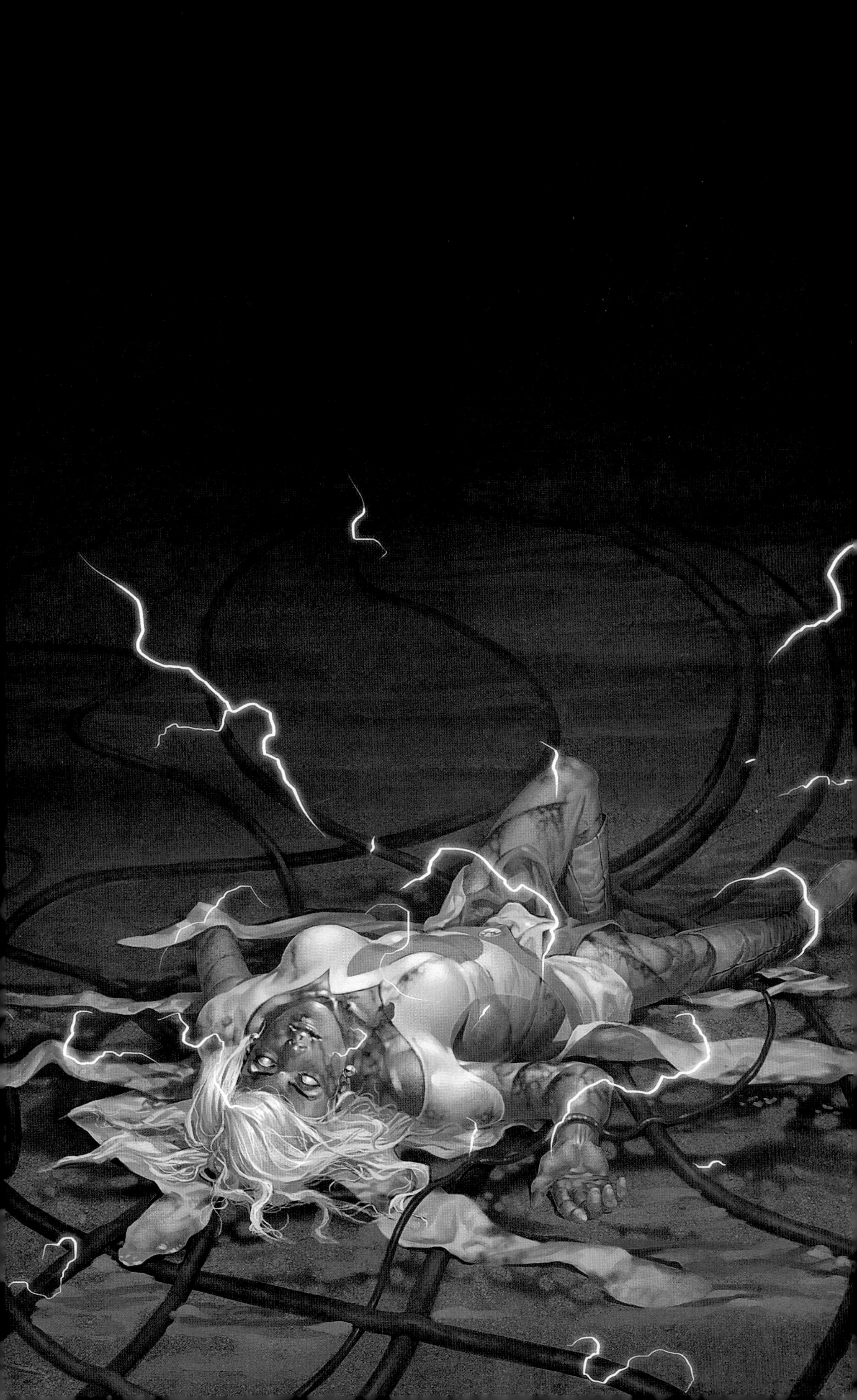

CHAPTER TWO

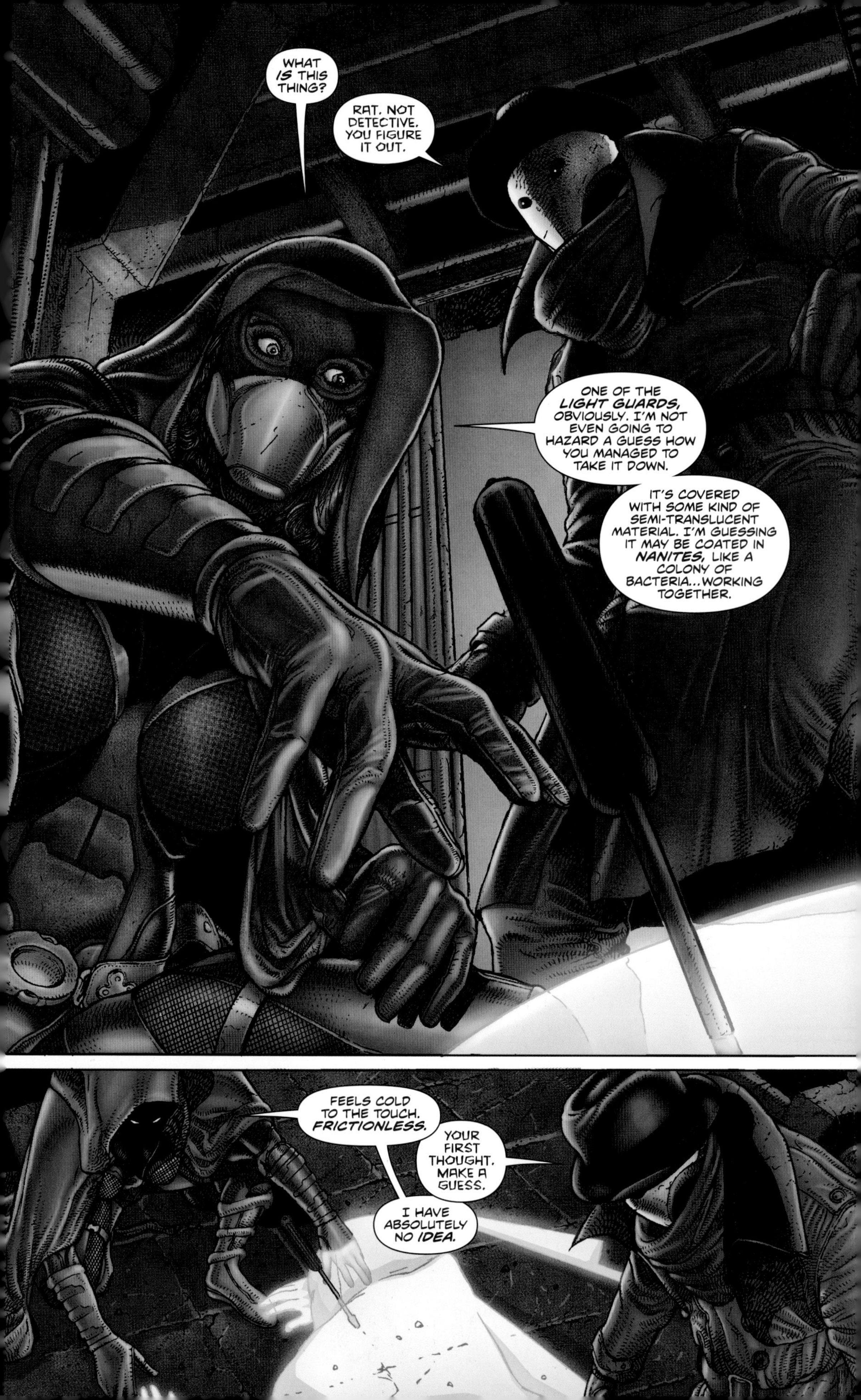
WHAT *IS* THIS THING?
RAT. NOT DETECTIVE. YOU FIGURE IT OUT.
ONE OF THE *LIGHT GUARDS,* OBVIOUSLY. I'M NOT EVEN GOING TO HAZARD A GUESS HOW YOU MANAGED TO TAKE IT DOWN.
IT'S COVERED WITH SOME KIND OF SEMI-TRANSLUCENT MATERIAL. I'M GUESSING IT MAY BE COATED IN *NANITES,* LIKE A COLONY OF BACTERIA...WORKING TOGETHER.
FEELS COLD TO THE TOUCH. *FRICTIONLESS.*
YOUR FIRST THOUGHT. MAKE A GUESS.
I HAVE ABSOLUTELY NO *IDEA.*

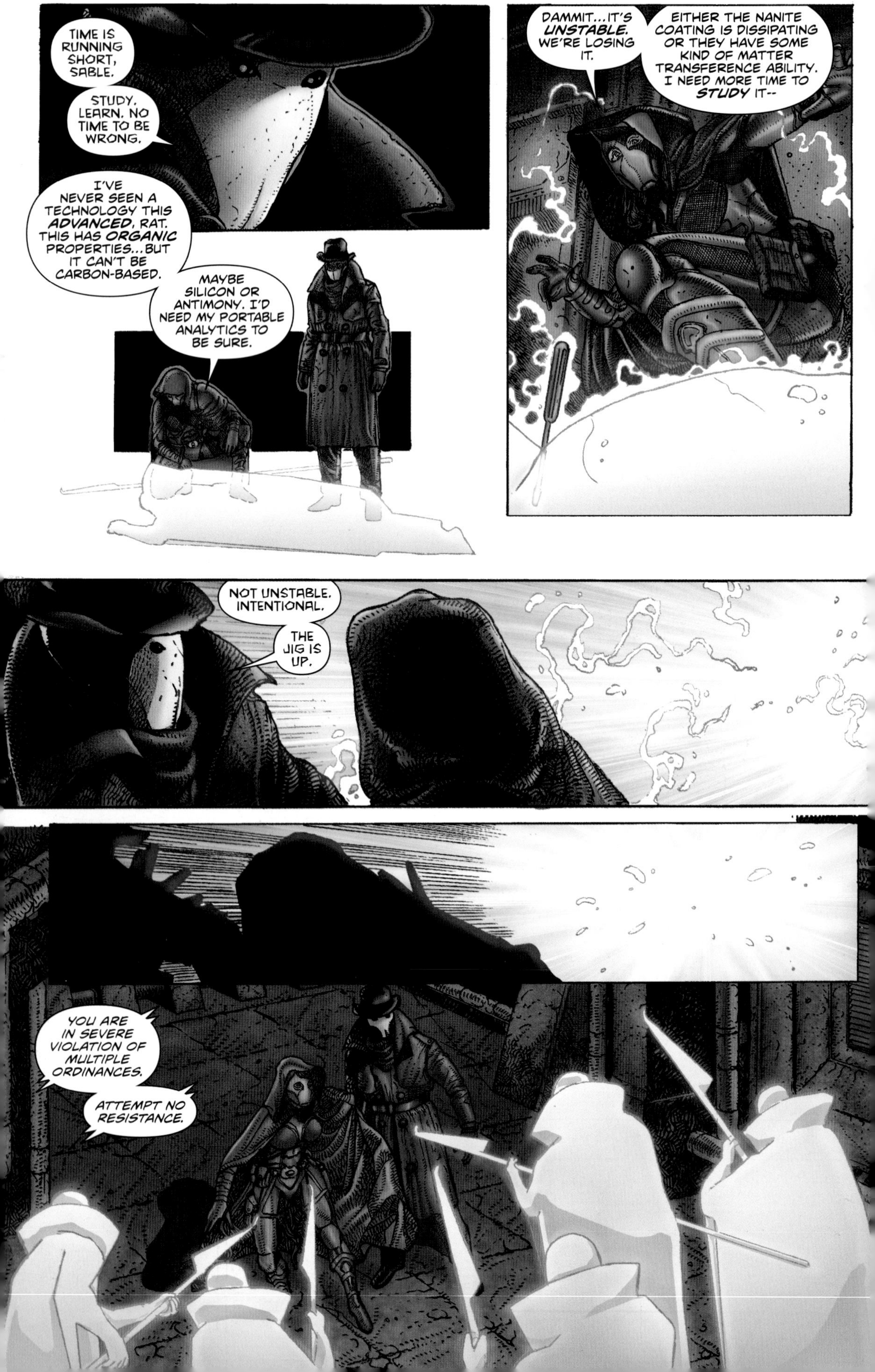
TIME IS RUNNING SHORT, SABLE.
STUDY. LEARN. NO TIME TO BE WRONG.
I'VE NEVER SEEN A TECHNOLOGY THIS ADVANCED, RAT. THIS HAS ORGANIC PROPERTIES...BUT IT CAN'T BE CARBON-BASED.
MAYBE SILICON OR ANTIMONY. I'D NEED MY PORTABLE ANALYTICS TO BE SURE.
DAMMIT...IT'S UNSTABLE. WE'RE LOSING IT.
EITHER THE NANITE COATING IS DISSIPATING OR THEY HAVE SOME KIND OF MATTER TRANSFERENCE ABILITY. I NEED MORE TIME TO STUDY IT--
NOT UNSTABLE. INTENTIONAL.
THE JIG IS UP.
YOU ARE IN SEVERE VIOLATION OF MULTIPLE ORDINANCES.
ATTEMPT NO RESISTANCE.

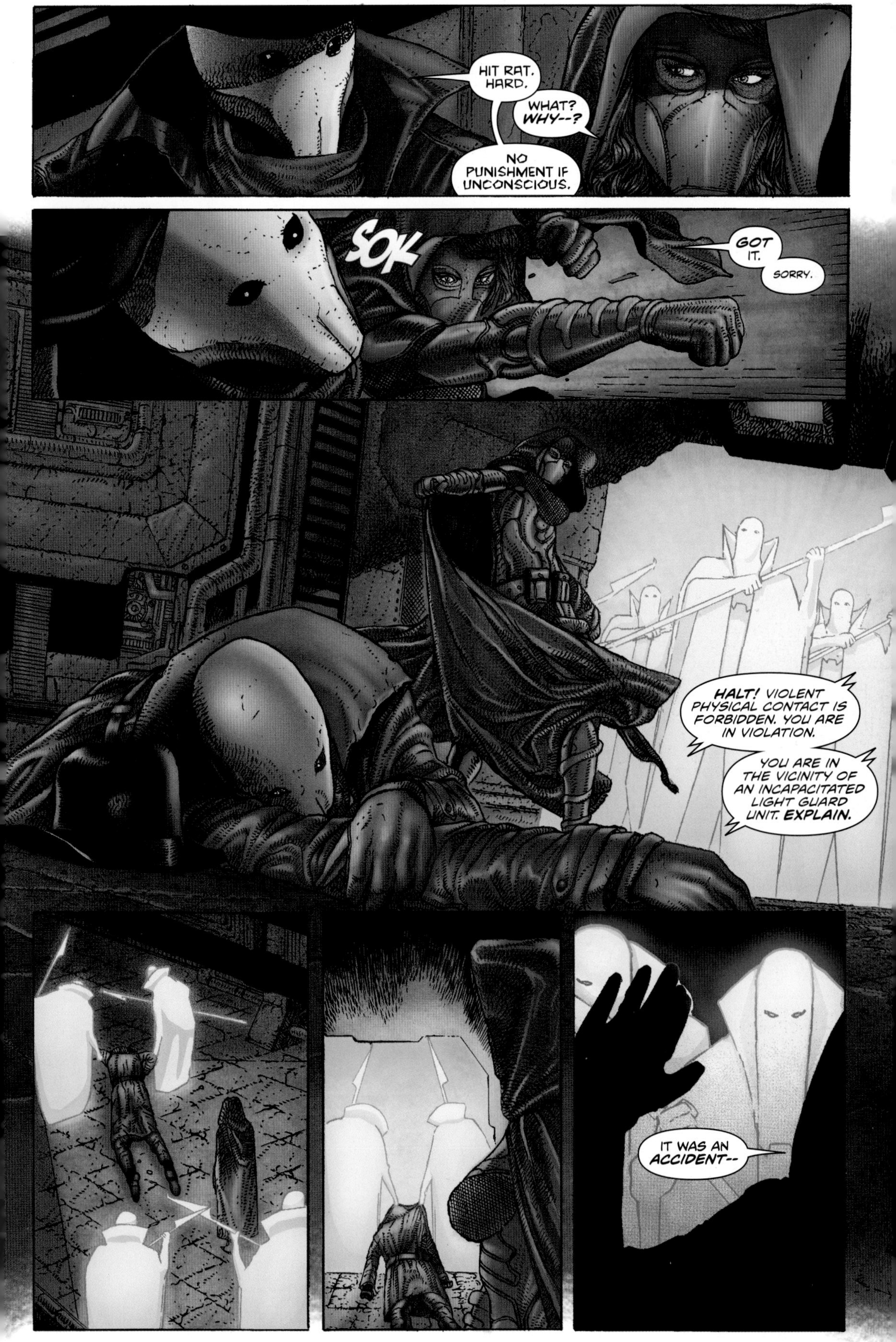
HIT RAT. HARD.
WHAT? WHY--?
NO PUNISHMENT IF UNCONSCIOUS.
SOK
GOT IT.
SORRY.
HALT! VIOLENT PHYSICAL CONTACT IS FORBIDDEN. YOU ARE IN VIOLATION.
YOU ARE IN THE VICINITY OF AN INCAPACITATED LIGHT GUARD UNIT. EXPLAIN.
IT WAS AN ACCIDENT--

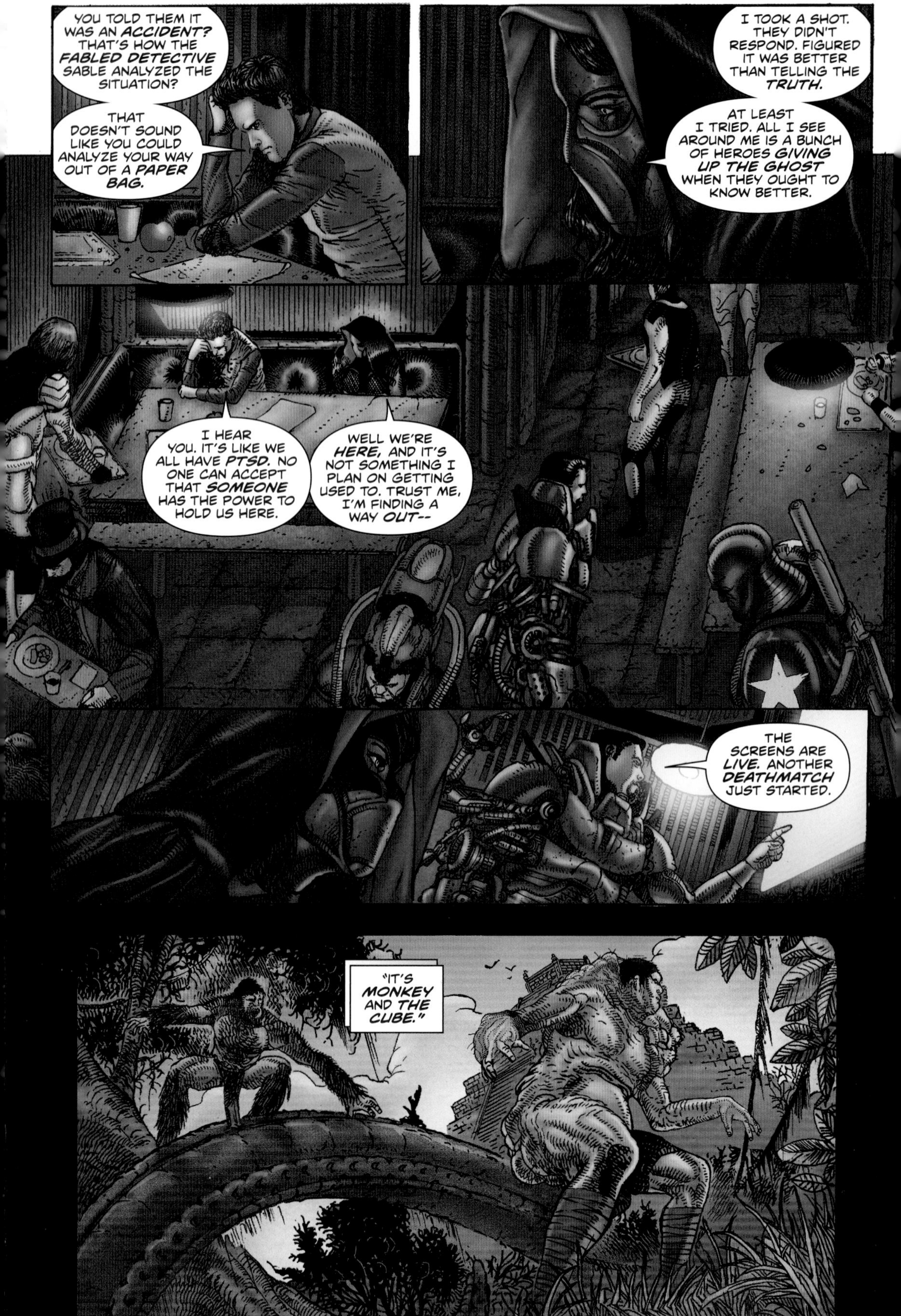
YOU TOLD THEM IT WAS AN ACCIDENT? THAT'S HOW THE FABLED DETECTIVE SABLE ANALYZED THE SITUATION?
THAT DOESN'T SOUND LIKE YOU COULD ANALYZE YOUR WAY OUT OF A PAPER BAG.
I TOOK A SHOT. THEY DIDN'T RESPOND. FIGURED IT WAS BETTER THAN TELLING THE TRUTH.
AT LEAST I TRIED. ALL I SEE AROUND ME IS A BUNCH OF HEROES GIVING UP THE GHOST WHEN THEY OUGHT TO KNOW BETTER.
I HEAR YOU. IT'S LIKE WE ALL HAVE PTSD. NO ONE CAN ACCEPT THAT SOMEONE HAS THE POWER TO HOLD US HERE.
WELL WE'RE HERE, AND IT'S NOT SOMETHING I PLAN ON GETTING USED TO. TRUST ME, I'M FINDING A WAY OUT--
THE SCREENS ARE LIVE. ANOTHER DEATHMATCH JUST STARTED.
"IT'S MONKEY AND THE CUBE."

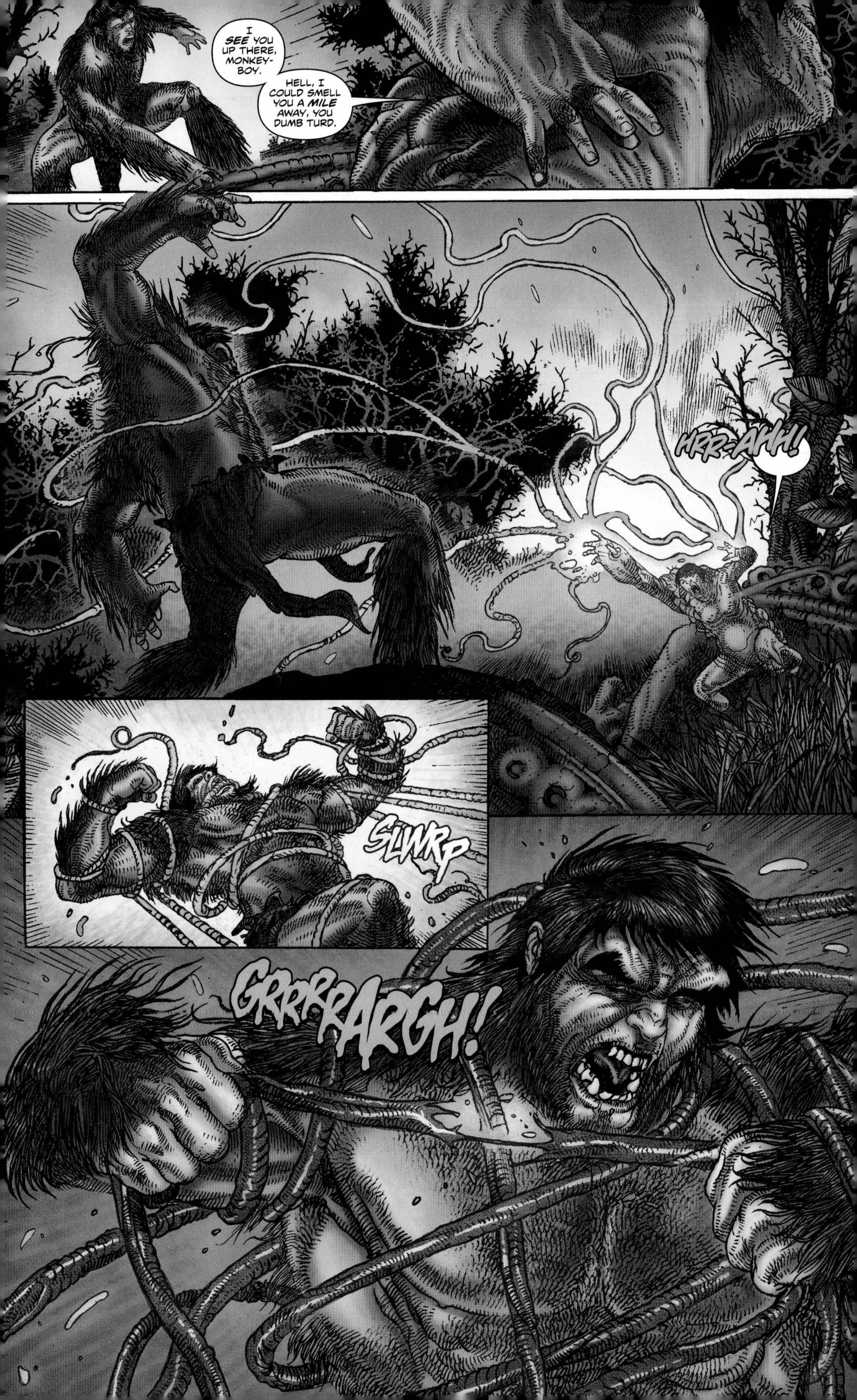
I SEE YOU UP THERE, MONKEY-BOY.
HELL, I COULD SMELL YOU A MILE AWAY, YOU DUMB TURD.
HRR-AHH!
SLWRP
GRRRRARGH!

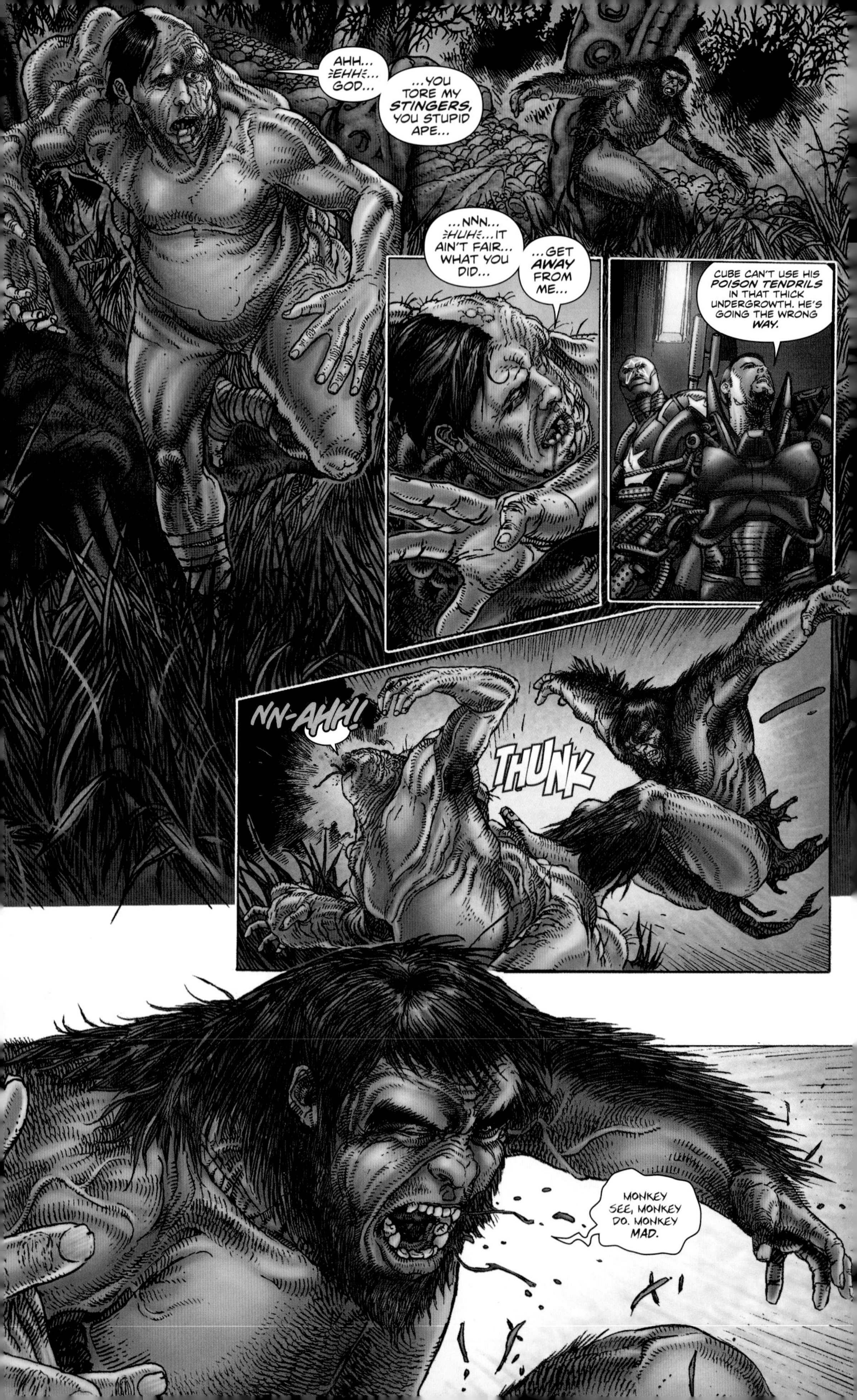
AHH... EHH... GOD...
...YOU TORE MY STINGERS, YOU STUPID APE...
...NNN... HUH...IT AIN'T FAIR... WHAT YOU DID...
...GET AWAY FROM ME...
CUBE CAN'T USE HIS POISON TENDRILS IN THAT THICK UNDERGROWTH. HE'S GOING THE WRONG WAY.
NN-AHH!
THUNK
MONKEY SEE, MONKEY DO. MONKEY MAD.

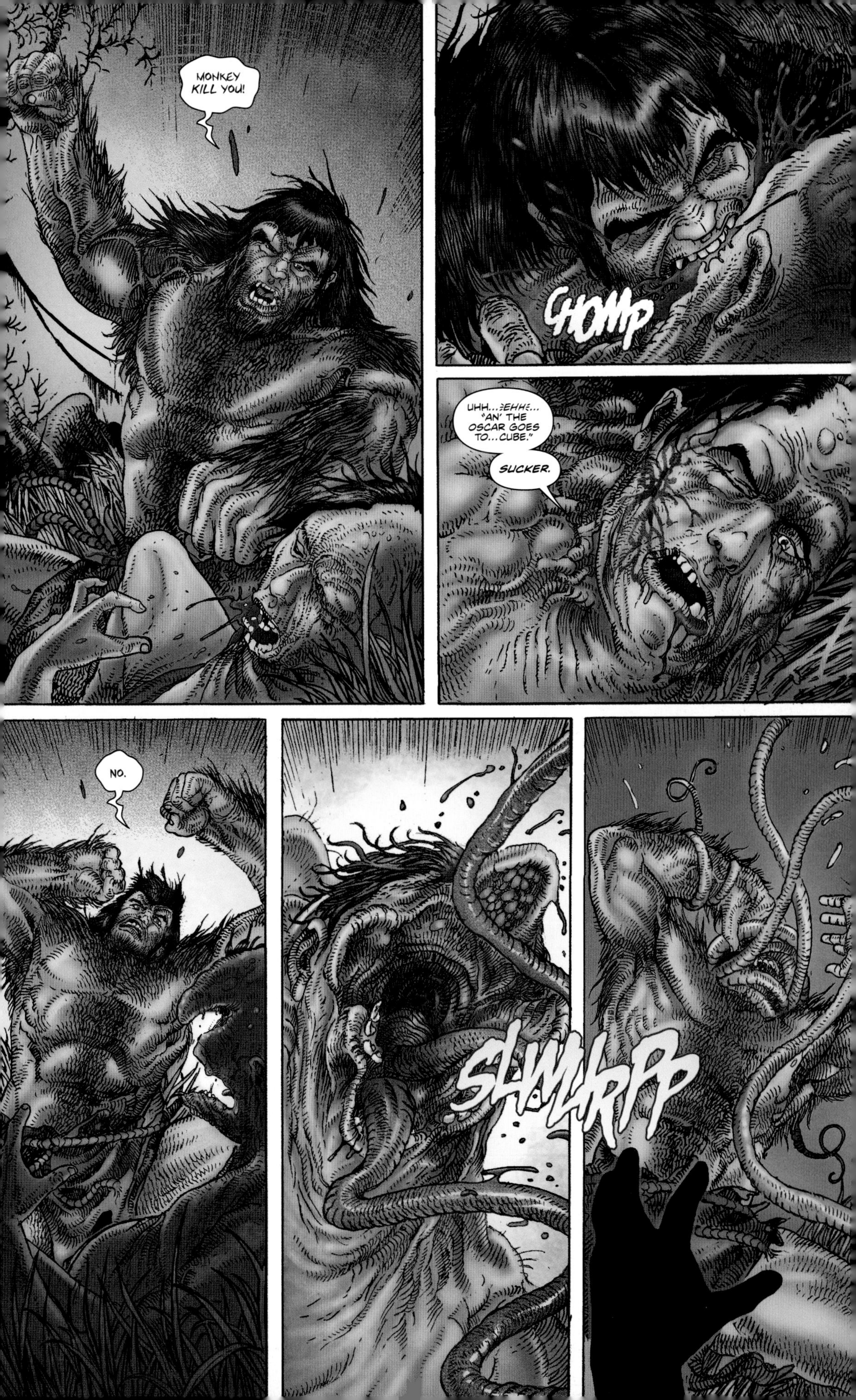
MONKEY KILL YOU!
CHOMP
UHH...EHH... "AN' THE OSCAR GOES TO...CUBE."
SUCKER.
NO.
SLWURPP

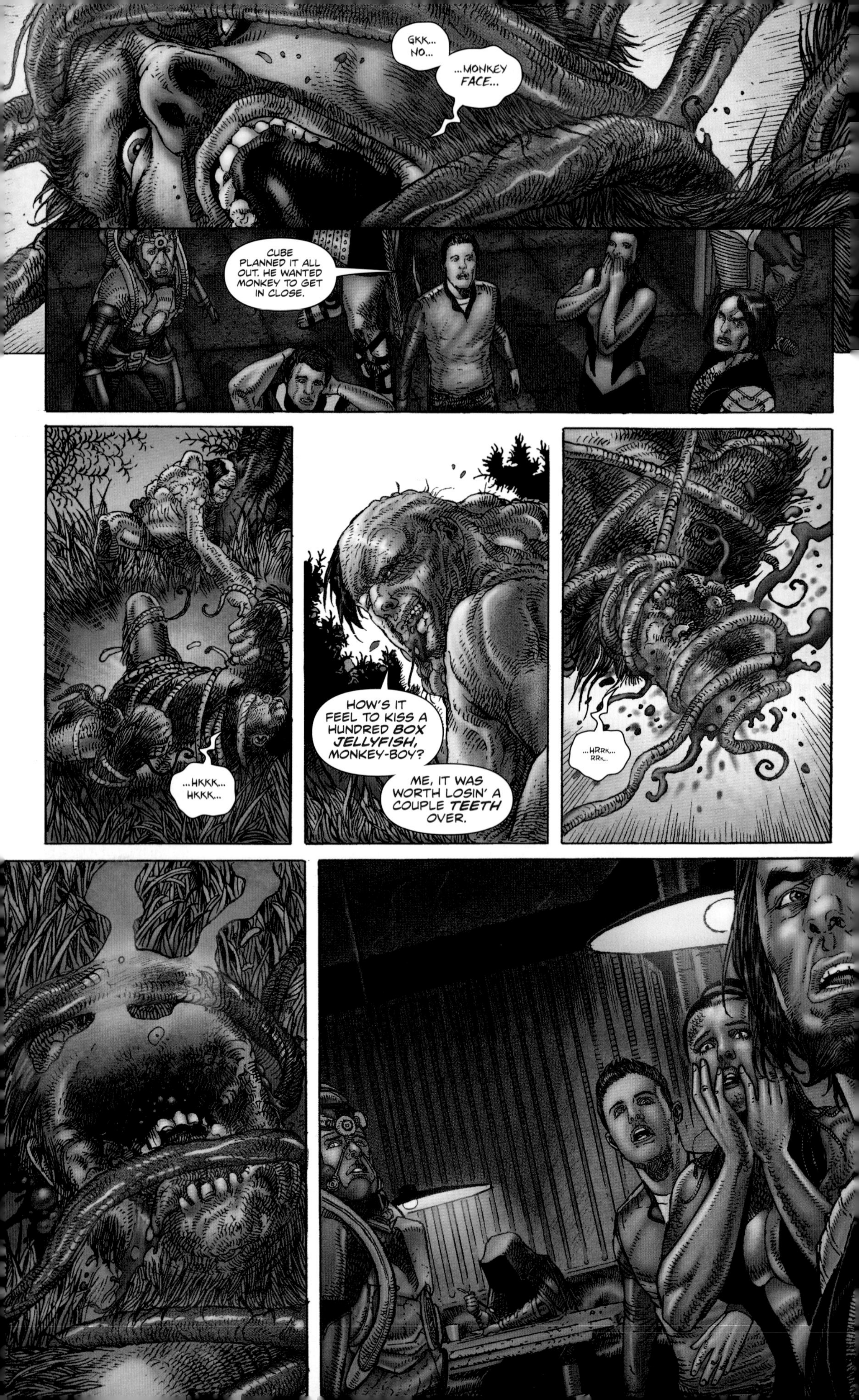
GKK... NO...
...MONKEY FACE...
CUBE PLANNED IT ALL OUT. HE WANTED MONKEY TO GET IN CLOSE.
...HKKK... HKKK...
HOW'S IT FEEL TO KISS A HUNDRED BOX JELLYFISH, MONKEY-BOY?
ME, IT WAS WORTH LOSIN' A COUPLE TEETH OVER.
...HRRK... RRK...

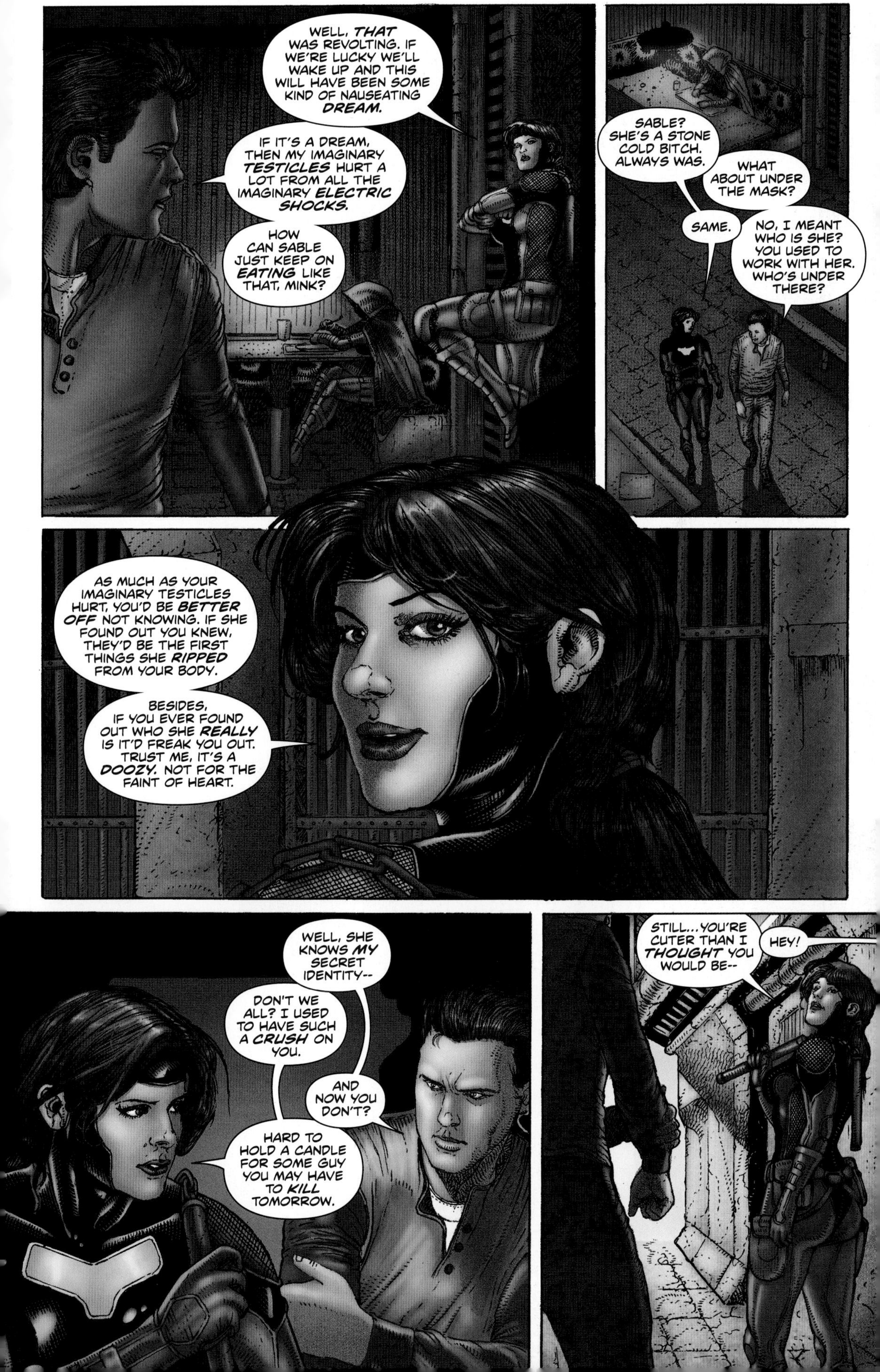
WELL, THAT WAS REVOLTING. IF WE'RE LUCKY WE'LL WAKE UP AND THIS WILL HAVE BEEN SOME KIND OF NAUSEATING DREAM.
IF IT'S A DREAM, THEN MY IMAGINARY TESTICLES HURT A LOT FROM ALL THE IMAGINARY ELECTRIC SHOCKS.
HOW CAN SABLE JUST KEEP ON EATING LIKE THAT, MINK?
SABLE? SHE'S A STONE COLD BITCH. ALWAYS WAS.
WHAT ABOUT UNDER THE MASK?
SAME.
NO, I MEANT WHO IS SHE? YOU USED TO WORK WITH HER. WHO'S UNDER THERE?
AS MUCH AS YOUR IMAGINARY TESTICLES HURT, YOU'D BE BETTER OFF NOT KNOWING. IF SHE FOUND OUT YOU KNEW, THEY'D BE THE FIRST THINGS SHE RIPPED FROM YOUR BODY.
BESIDES, IF YOU EVER FOUND OUT WHO SHE REALLY IS IT'D FREAK YOU OUT. TRUST ME, IT'S A DOOZY. NOT FOR THE FAINT OF HEART.
WELL, SHE KNOWS MY SECRET IDENTITY--
DON'T WE ALL? I USED TO HAVE SUCH A CRUSH ON YOU.
AND NOW YOU DON'T?
HARD TO HOLD A CANDLE FOR SOME GUY YOU MAY HAVE TO KILL TOMORROW.
STILL... YOU'RE CUTER THAN I THOUGHT YOU WOULD BE--
HEY!

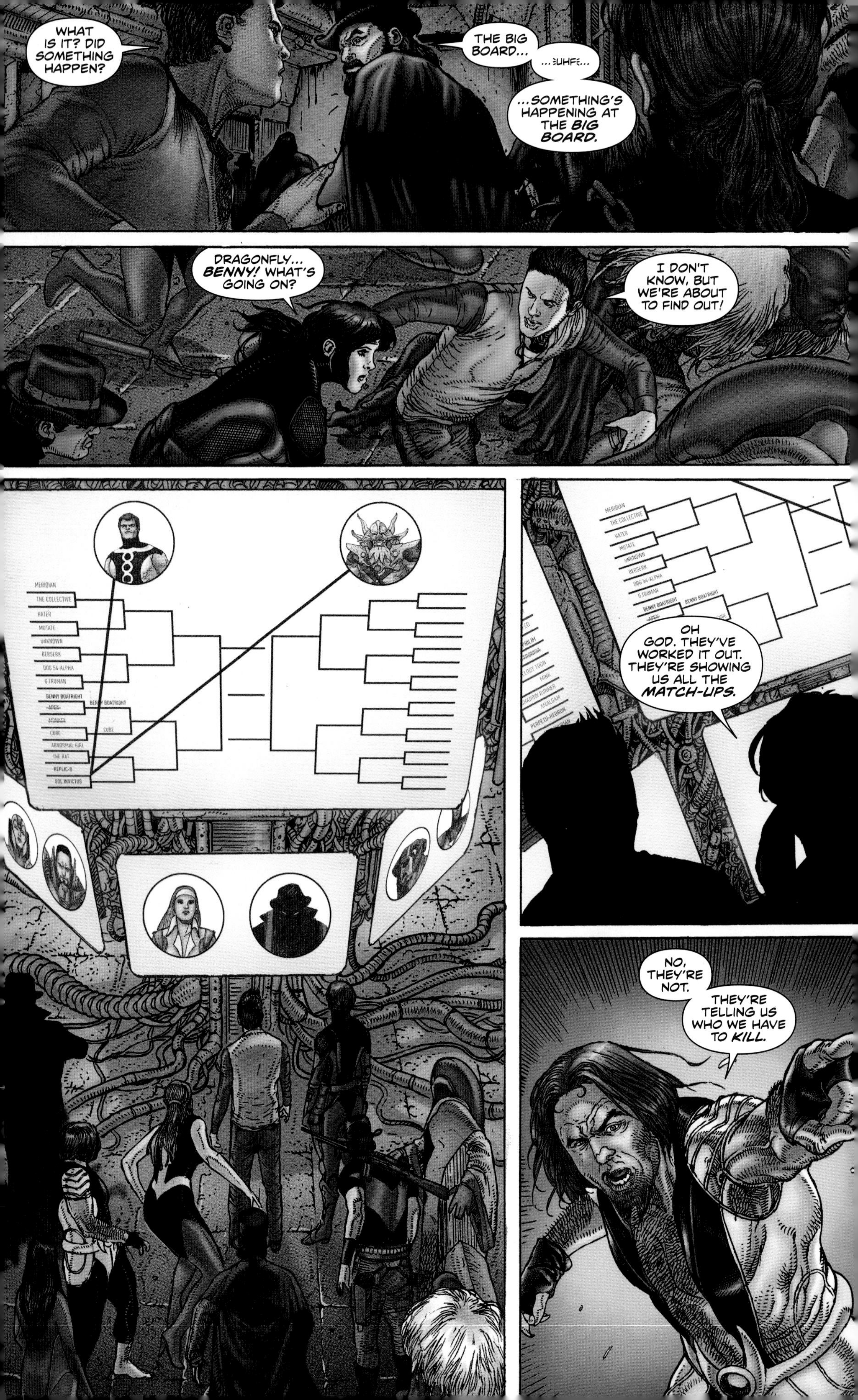
WHAT IS IT? DID SOMETHING HAPPEN?
THE BIG BOARD...
...UHF...
...SOMETHING'S HAPPENING AT THE BIG BOARD.
DRAGONFLY... BENNY! WHAT'S GOING ON?
I DON'T KNOW, BUT WE'RE ABOUT TO FIND OUT!
MERIDIAN
THE COLLECTIVE
HATER
MUTATE
UNKNOWN
BERSERK
DOG 54-ALPHA
G.TRUMAN
BENNY BOATRIGHT
BENNY BOATRIGHT
CUBE
CUBE
ABNORMAL GIRL
THE RAT
REPLIC-8
SOL INVICTUS
OH GOD. THEY'VE WORKED IT OUT. THEY'RE SHOWING US ALL THE MATCH-UPS.
NO, THEY'RE NOT.
THEY'RE TELLING US WHO WE HAVE TO KILL.

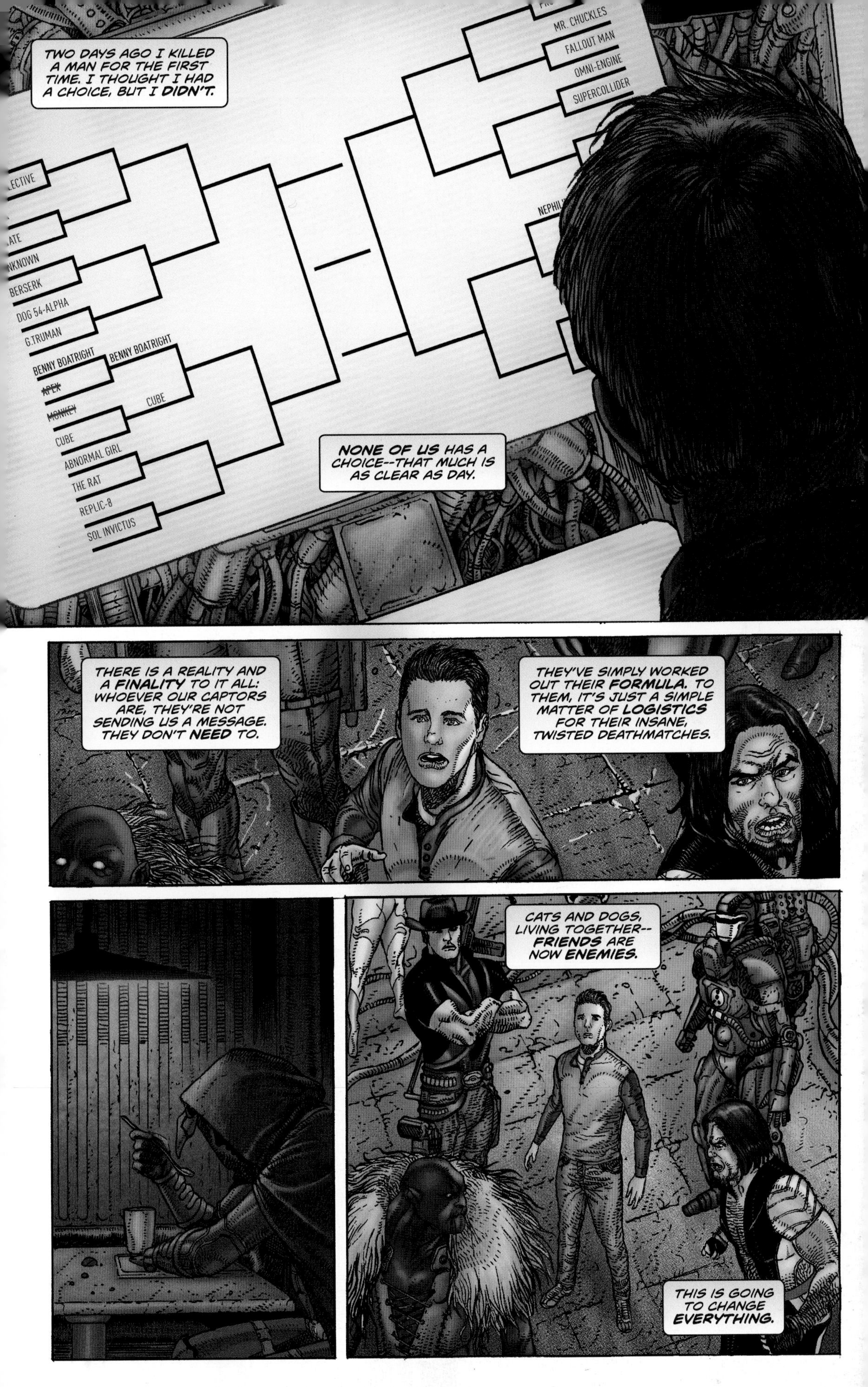
TWO DAYS AGO I KILLED A MAN FOR THE FIRST TIME. I THOUGHT I HAD A CHOICE, BUT I DIDN'T.
MR. CHUCKLES
FALLOUT MAN
OMNI-ENGINE
SUPERCOLLIDER
BERSERK
DOG 54-ALPHA
G.TRUMAN
BENNY BOATRIGHT
APEX
MONKEY
CUBE
ABNORMAL GIRL
THE RAT
REPLIC-8
SOL INVICTUS
BENNY BOATRIGHT
CUBE
NONE OF US HAS A CHOICE--THAT MUCH IS AS CLEAR AS DAY.
THERE IS A REALITY AND A FINALITY TO IT ALL: WHOEVER OUR CAPTORS ARE, THEY'RE NOT SENDING US A MESSAGE. THEY DON'T NEED TO.
THEY'VE SIMPLY WORKED OUT THEIR FORMULA. TO THEM, IT'S JUST A SIMPLE MATTER OF LOGISTICS FOR THEIR INSANE, TWISTED DEATHMATCHES.
CATS AND DOGS, LIVING TOGETHER-- FRIENDS ARE NOW ENEMIES.
THIS IS GOING TO CHANGE EVERYTHING.

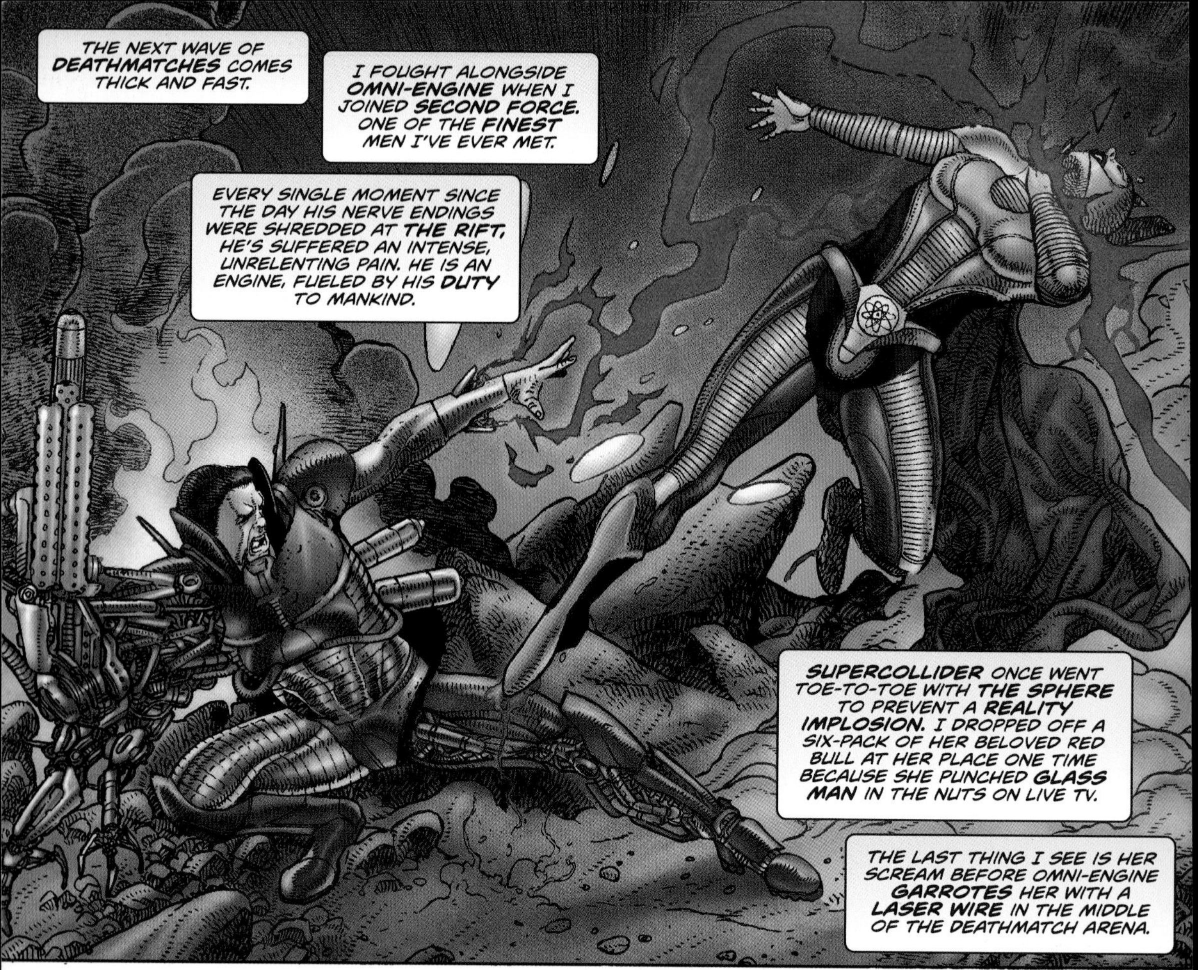
THE NEXT WAVE OF DEATHMATCHES COMES THICK AND FAST.
I FOUGHT ALONGSIDE OMNI-ENGINE WHEN I JOINED SECOND FORCE. ONE OF THE FINEST MEN I'VE EVER MET.
EVERY SINGLE MOMENT SINCE THE DAY HIS NERVE ENDINGS WERE SHREDDED AT THE RIFT, HE'S SUFFERED AN INTENSE, UNRELENTING PAIN. HE IS AN ENGINE, FUELED BY HIS DUTY TO MANKIND.
SUPERCOLLIDER ONCE WENT TOE-TO-TOE WITH THE SPHERE TO PREVENT A REALITY IMPLOSION. I DROPPED OFF A SIX-PACK OF HER BELOVED RED BULL AT HER PLACE ONE TIME BECAUSE SHE PUNCHED GLASS MAN IN THE NUTS ON LIVE TV.
THE LAST THING I SEE IS HER SCREAM BEFORE OMNI-ENGINE GARROTES HER WITH A LASER WIRE IN THE MIDDLE OF THE DEATHMATCH ARENA.

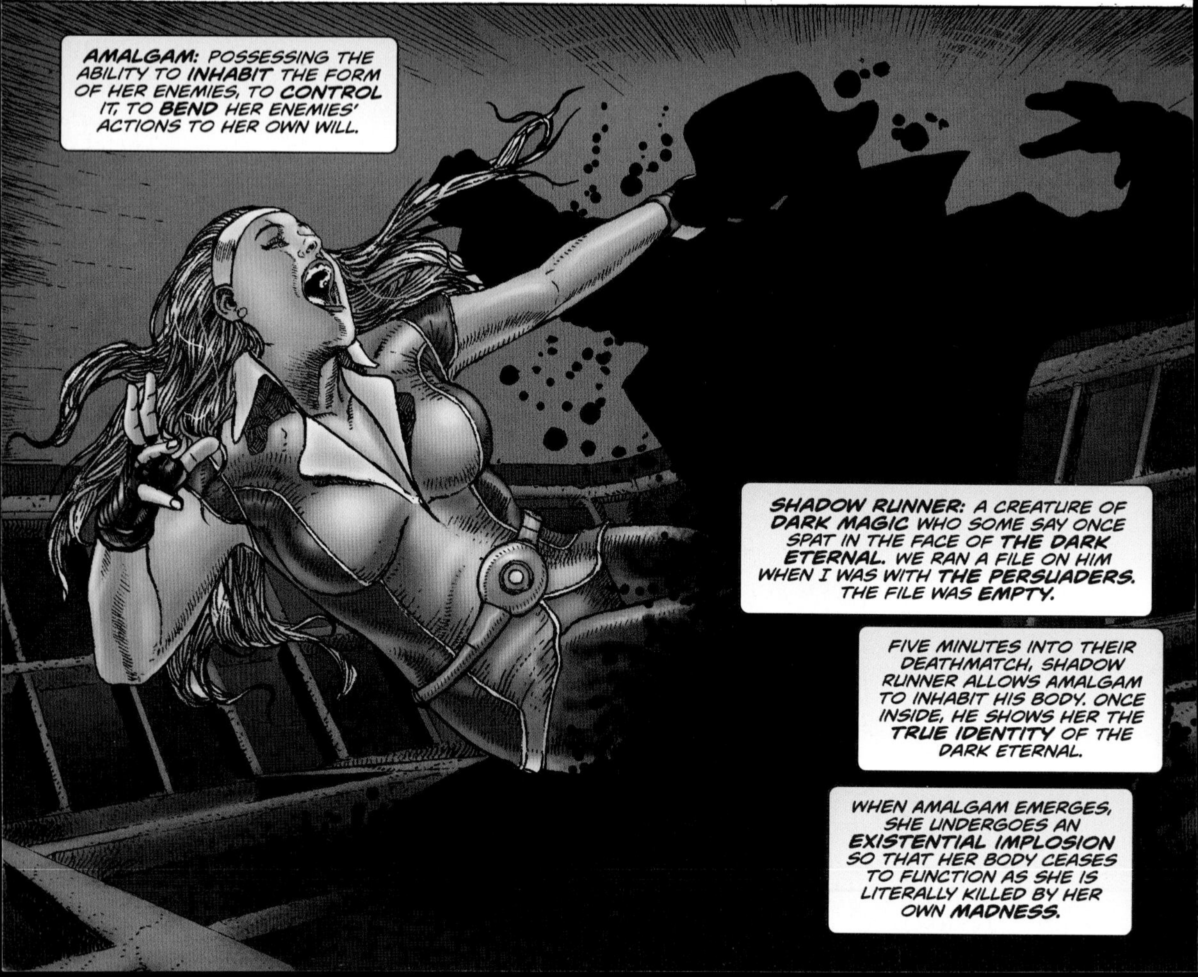
AMALGAM: POSSESSING THE ABILITY TO INHABIT THE FORM OF HER ENEMIES, TO CONTROL IT, TO BEND HER ENEMIES' ACTIONS TO HER OWN WILL.
SHADOW RUNNER: A CREATURE OF DARK MAGIC WHO SOME SAY ONCE SPAT IN THE FACE OF THE DARK ETERNAL. WE RAN A FILE ON HIM WHEN I WAS WITH THE PERSUADERS. THE FILE WAS EMPTY.
FIVE MINUTES INTO THEIR DEATHMATCH, SHADOW RUNNER ALLOWS AMALGAM TO INHABIT HIS BODY. ONCE INSIDE, HE SHOWS HER THE TRUE IDENTITY OF THE DARK ETERNAL.
WHEN AMALGAM EMERGES, SHE UNDERGOES AN EXISTENTIAL IMPLOSION SO THAT HER BODY CEASES TO FUNCTION AS SHE IS LITERALLY KILLED BY HER OWN MADNESS.

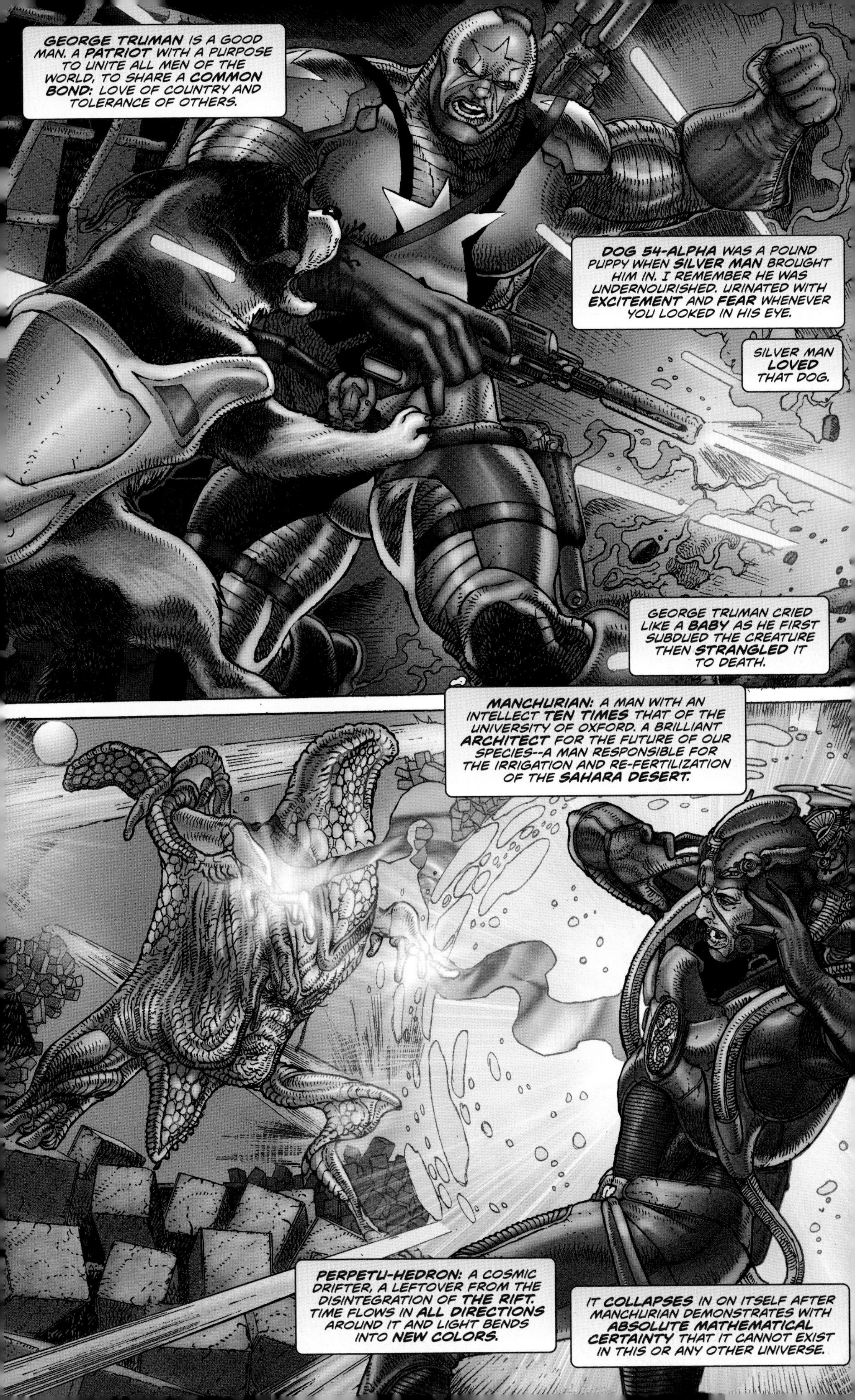
GEORGE TRUMAN IS A GOOD MAN. A PATRIOT WITH A PURPOSE TO UNITE ALL MEN OF THE WORLD, TO SHARE A COMMON BOND: LOVE OF COUNTRY AND TOLERANCE OF OTHERS.
DOG 54-ALPHA WAS A POUND PUPPY WHEN SILVER MAN BROUGHT HIM IN. I REMEMBER HE WAS UNDERNOURISHED. URINATED WITH EXCITEMENT AND FEAR WHENEVER YOU LOOKED IN HIS EYE.
SILVER MAN LOVED THAT DOG.
GEORGE TRUMAN CRIED LIKE A BABY AS HE FIRST SUBDUED THE CREATURE THEN STRANGLED IT TO DEATH.
MANCHURIAN: A MAN WITH AN INTELLECT TEN TIMES THAT OF THE UNIVERSITY OF OXFORD. A BRILLIANT ARCHITECT FOR THE FUTURE OF OUR SPECIES--A MAN RESPONSIBLE FOR THE IRRIGATION AND RE-FERTILIZATION OF THE SAHARA DESERT.
PERPETU-HEDRON: A COSMIC DRIFTER, A LEFTOVER FROM THE DISINTEGRATION OF THE RIFT. TIME FLOWS IN ALL DIRECTIONS AROUND IT AND LIGHT BENDS INTO NEW COLORS.
IT COLLAPSES IN ON ITSELF AFTER MANCHURIAN DEMONSTRATES WITH ABSOLUTE MATHEMATICAL CERTAINTY THAT IT CANNOT EXIST IN THIS OR ANY OTHER UNIVERSE.

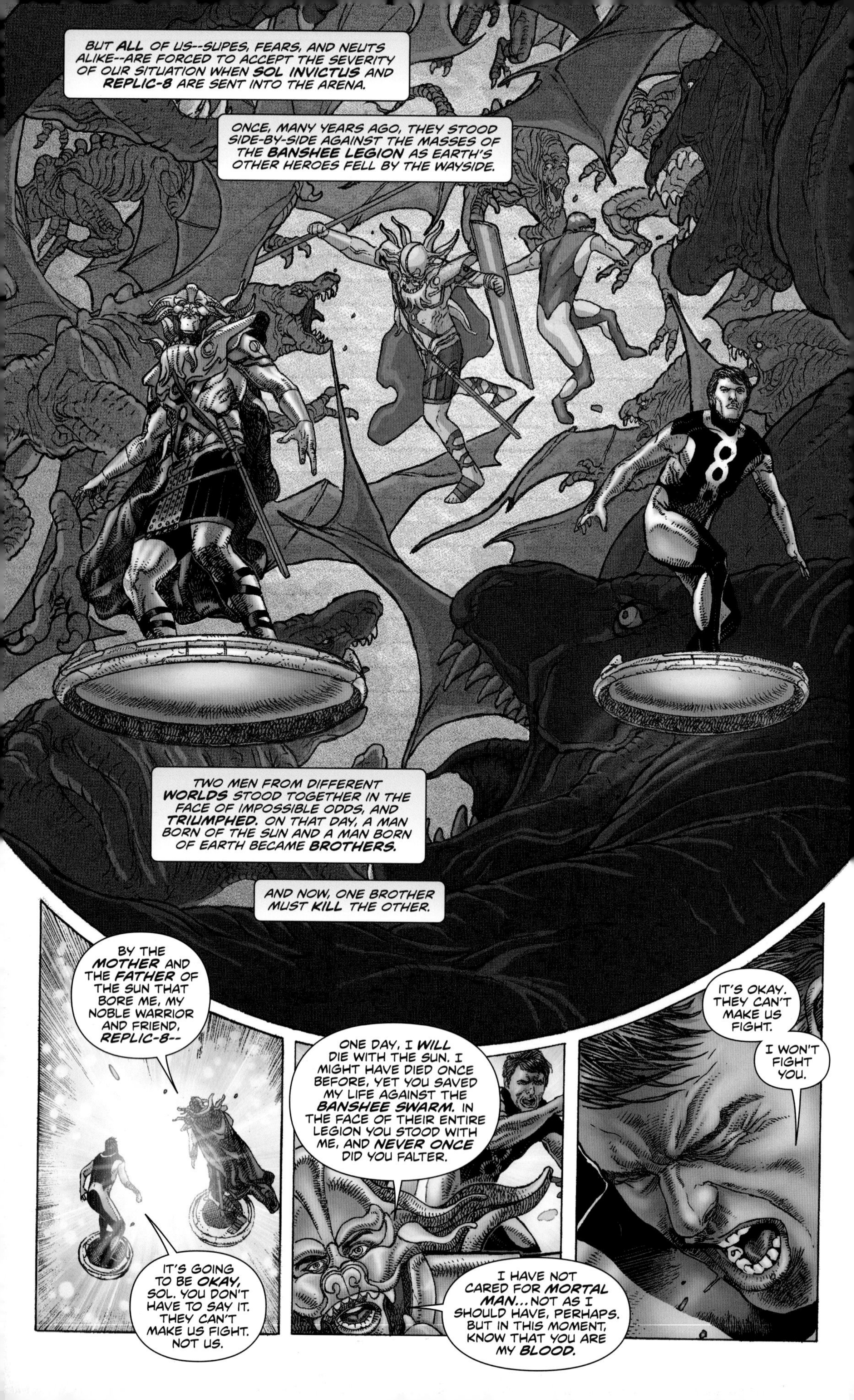
BUT ALL OF US--SUPES, FEARS, AND NEUTS ALIKE--ARE FORCED TO ACCEPT THE SEVERITY OF OUR SITUATION WHEN SOL INVICTUS AND REPLIC-8 ARE SENT INTO THE ARENA.
ONCE, MANY YEARS AGO, THEY STOOD SIDE-BY-SIDE AGAINST THE MASSES OF THE BANSHEE LEGION AS EARTH'S OTHER HEROES FELL BY THE WAYSIDE.
TWO MEN FROM DIFFERENT WORLDS STOOD TOGETHER IN THE FACE OF IMPOSSIBLE ODDS, AND TRIUMPHED. ON THAT DAY, A MAN BORN OF THE SUN AND A MAN BORN OF EARTH BECAME BROTHERS.
AND NOW, ONE BROTHER MUST KILL THE OTHER.
BY THE MOTHER AND THE FATHER OF THE SUN THAT BORE ME, MY NOBLE WARRIOR AND FRIEND, REPLIC-8--
IT'S GOING TO BE OKAY, SOL. YOU DON'T HAVE TO SAY IT. THEY CAN'T MAKE US FIGHT. NOT US.
ONE DAY, I WILL DIE WITH THE SUN. I MIGHT HAVE DIED ONCE BEFORE, YET YOU SAVED MY LIFE AGAINST THE BANSHEE SWARM. IN THE FACE OF THEIR ENTIRE LEGION YOU STOOD WITH ME, AND NEVER ONCE DID YOU FALTER.
I HAVE NOT CARED FOR MORTAL MAN... NOT AS I SHOULD HAVE, PERHAPS. BUT IN THIS MOMENT, KNOW THAT YOU ARE MY BLOOD.
IT'S OKAY. THEY CAN'T MAKE US FIGHT.
I WON'T FIGHT YOU.

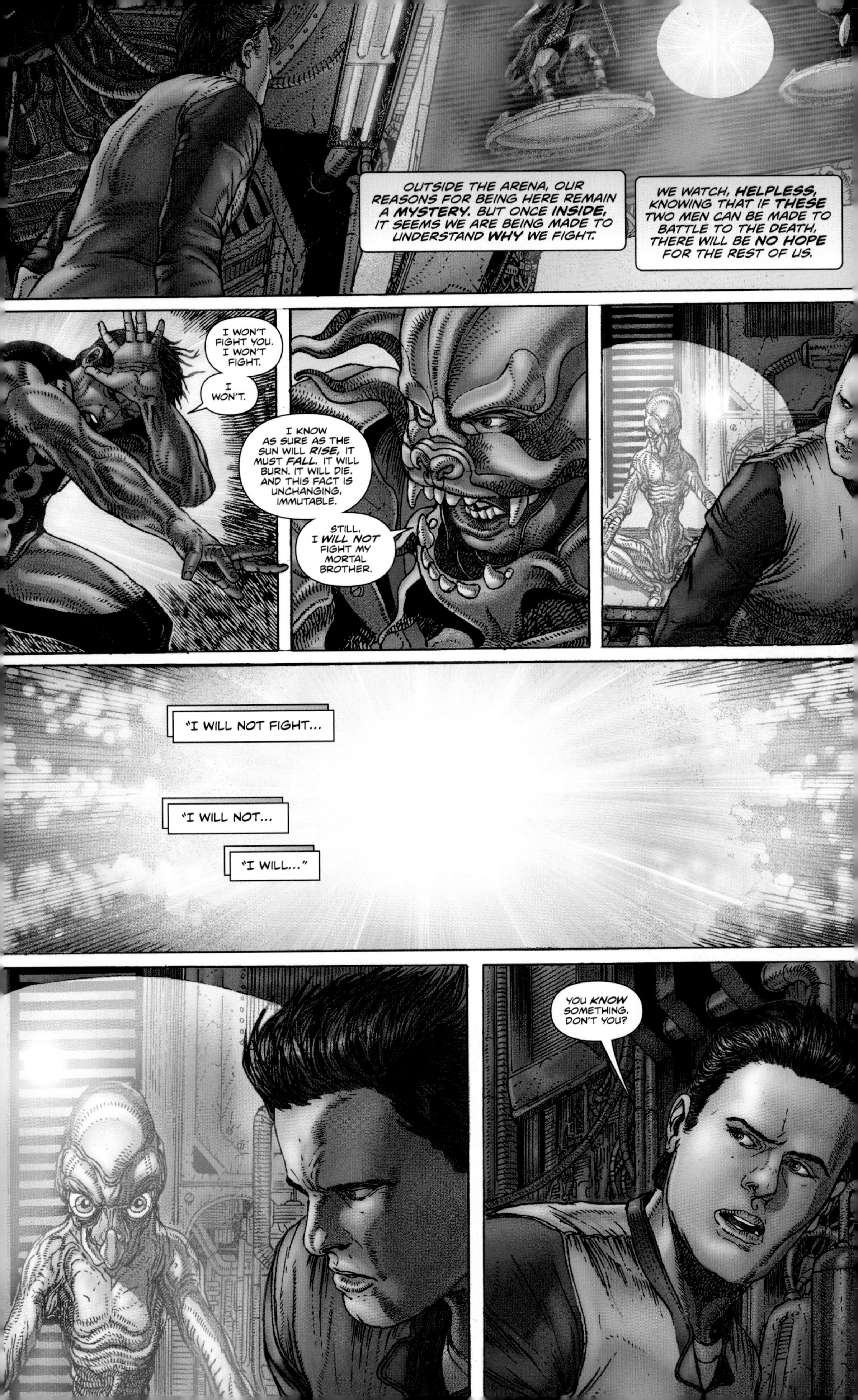
OUTSIDE THE ARENA, OUR REASONS FOR BEING HERE REMAIN A MYSTERY. BUT ONCE INSIDE, IT SEEMS WE ARE BEING MADE TO UNDERSTAND WHY WE FIGHT.
WE WATCH, HELPLESS, KNOWING THAT IF THESE TWO MEN CAN BE MADE TO BATTLE TO THE DEATH, THERE WILL BE NO HOPE FOR THE REST OF US.
I WON'T FIGHT YOU. I WON'T FIGHT.
I WON'T.
I KNOW AS SURE AS THE SUN WILL RISE, IT MUST FALL. IT WILL BURN. IT WILL DIE. AND THIS FACT IS UNCHANGING, IMMUTABLE.
STILL, I WILL NOT FIGHT MY MORTAL BROTHER.
"I WILL NOT FIGHT...
"I WILL NOT...
"I WILL..."
YOU KNOW SOMETHING, DON'T YOU?

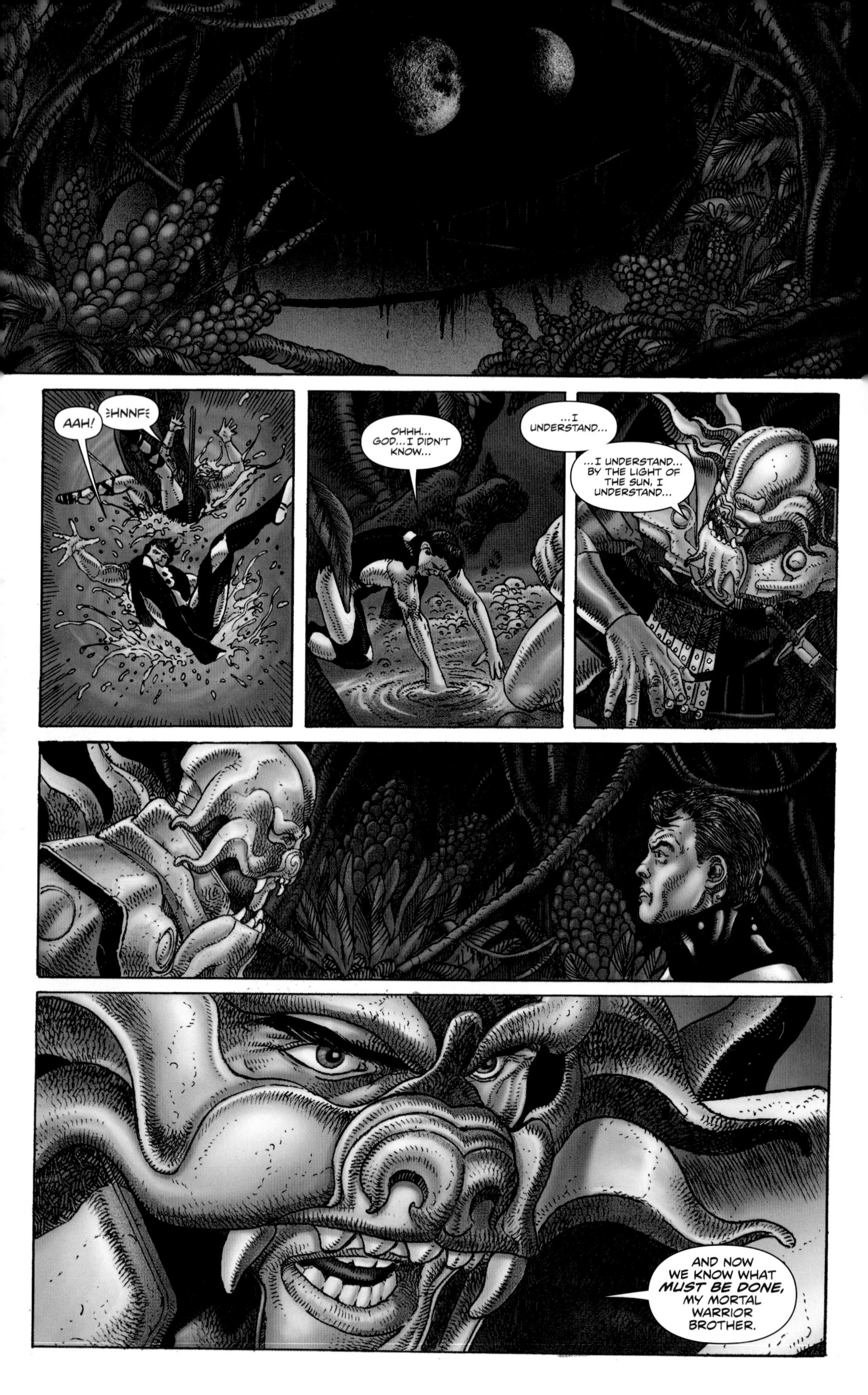
AAH!
HNNF
OHHH... GOD...I DIDN'T KNOW...
...I UNDERSTAND...
...I UNDERSTAND... BY THE LIGHT OF THE SUN, I UNDERSTAND...
AND NOW WE KNOW WHAT MUST BE DONE, MY MORTAL WARRIOR BROTHER.

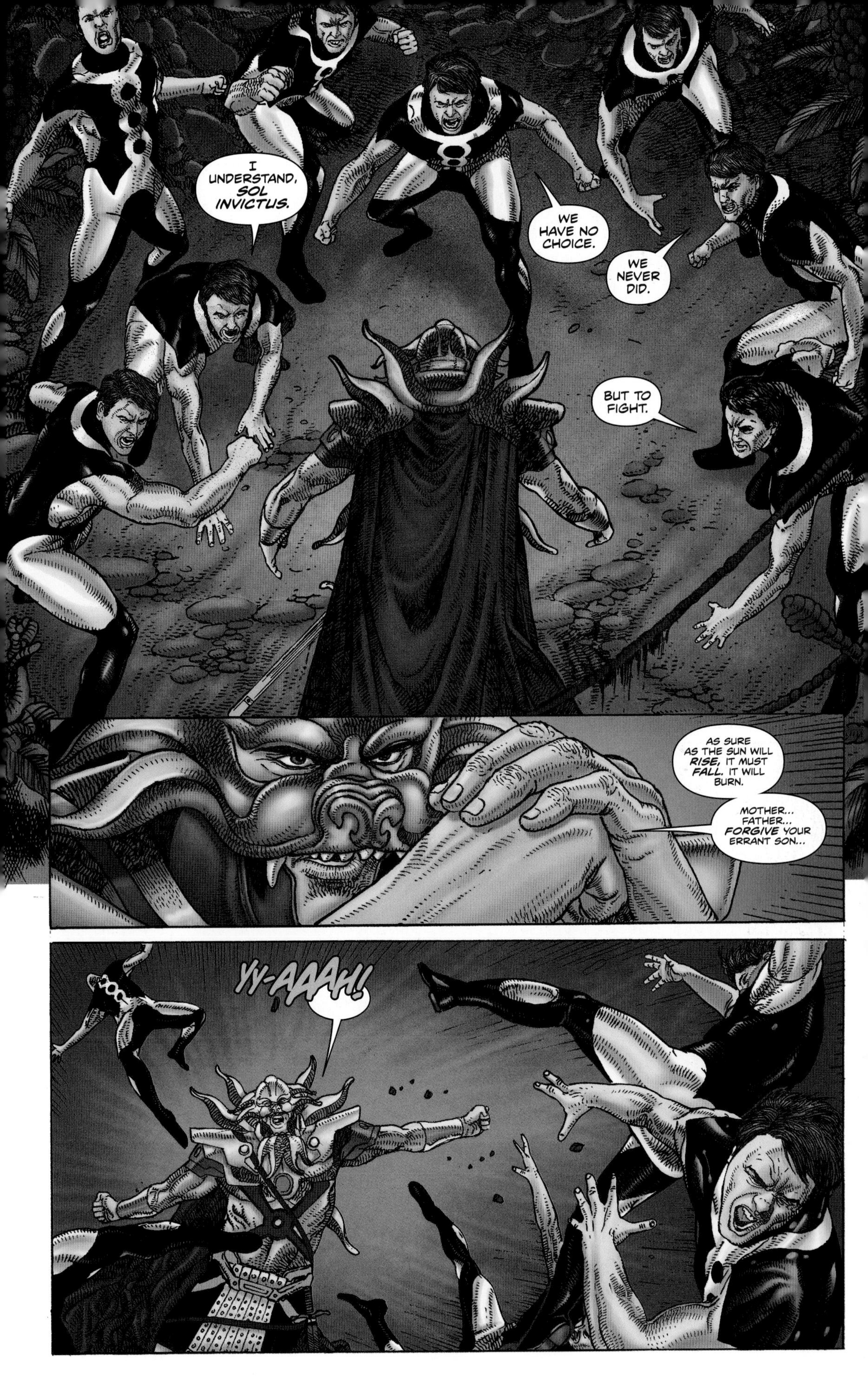
I UNDERSTAND, SOL INVICTUS.
WE HAVE NO CHOICE.
WE NEVER DID.
BUT TO FIGHT.
AS SURE AS THE SUN WILL RISE, IT MUST FALL. IT WILL BURN.
MOTHER... FATHER... FORGIVE YOUR ERRANT SON...
YY-AAAH!

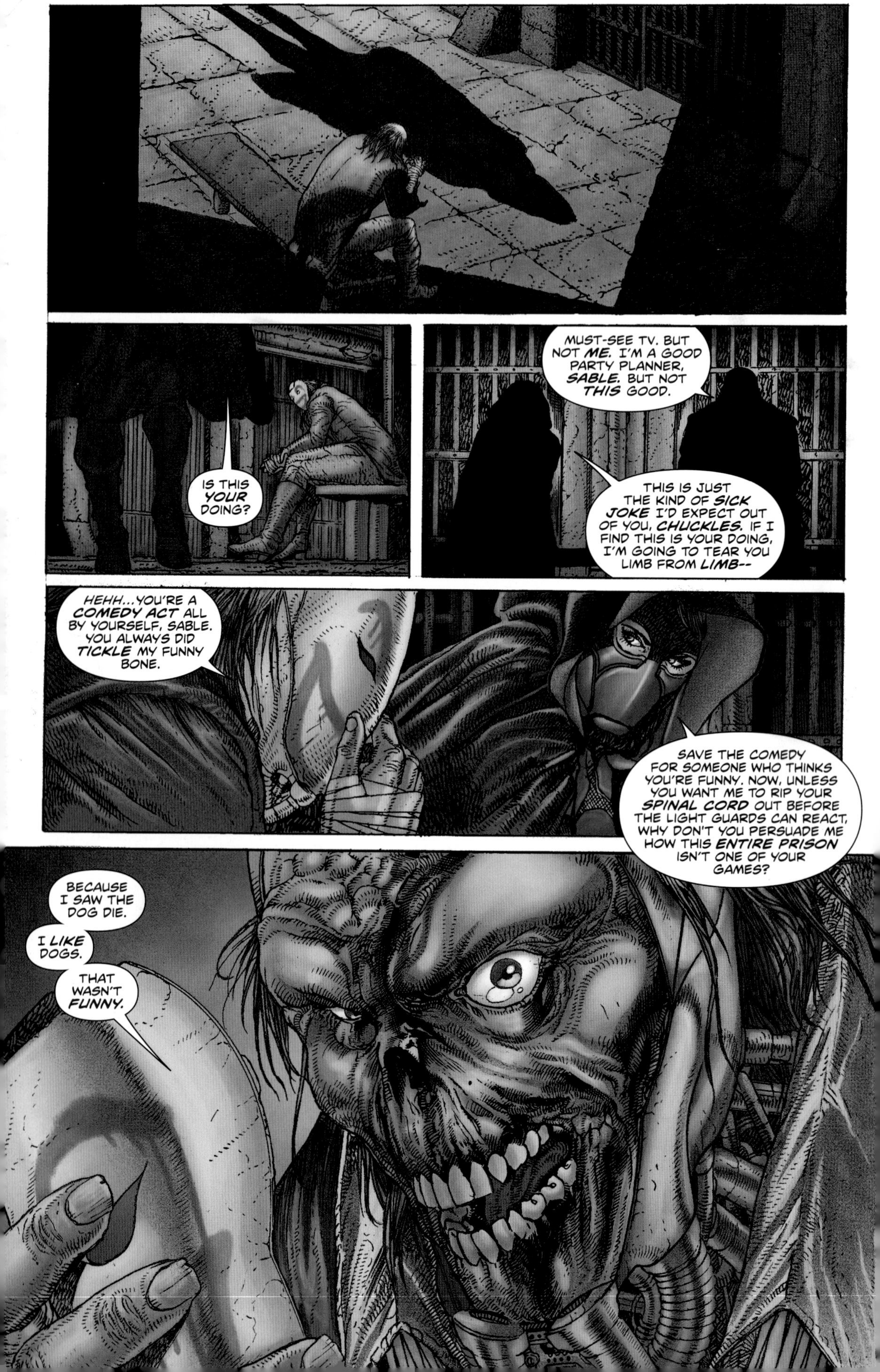

IS THIS YOUR DOING?
MUST-SEE TV. BUT NOT ME. I'M A GOOD PARTY PLANNER, SABLE. BUT NOT THIS GOOD.
THIS IS JUST THE KIND OF SICK JOKE I'D EXPECT OUT OF YOU, CHUCKLES. IF I FIND THIS IS YOUR DOING, I'M GOING TO TEAR YOU LIMB FROM LIMB--
HEHH...YOU'RE A COMEDY ACT ALL BY YOURSELF, SABLE. YOU ALWAYS DID TICKLE MY FUNNY BONE.
SAVE THE COMEDY FOR SOMEONE WHO THINKS YOU'RE FUNNY. NOW, UNLESS YOU WANT ME TO RIP YOUR SPINAL CORD OUT BEFORE THE LIGHT GUARDS CAN REACT, WHY DON'T YOU PERSUADE ME HOW THIS ENTIRE PRISON ISN'T ONE OF YOUR GAMES?
BECAUSE I SAW THE DOG DIE.
I LIKE DOGS.
THAT WASN'T FUNNY.

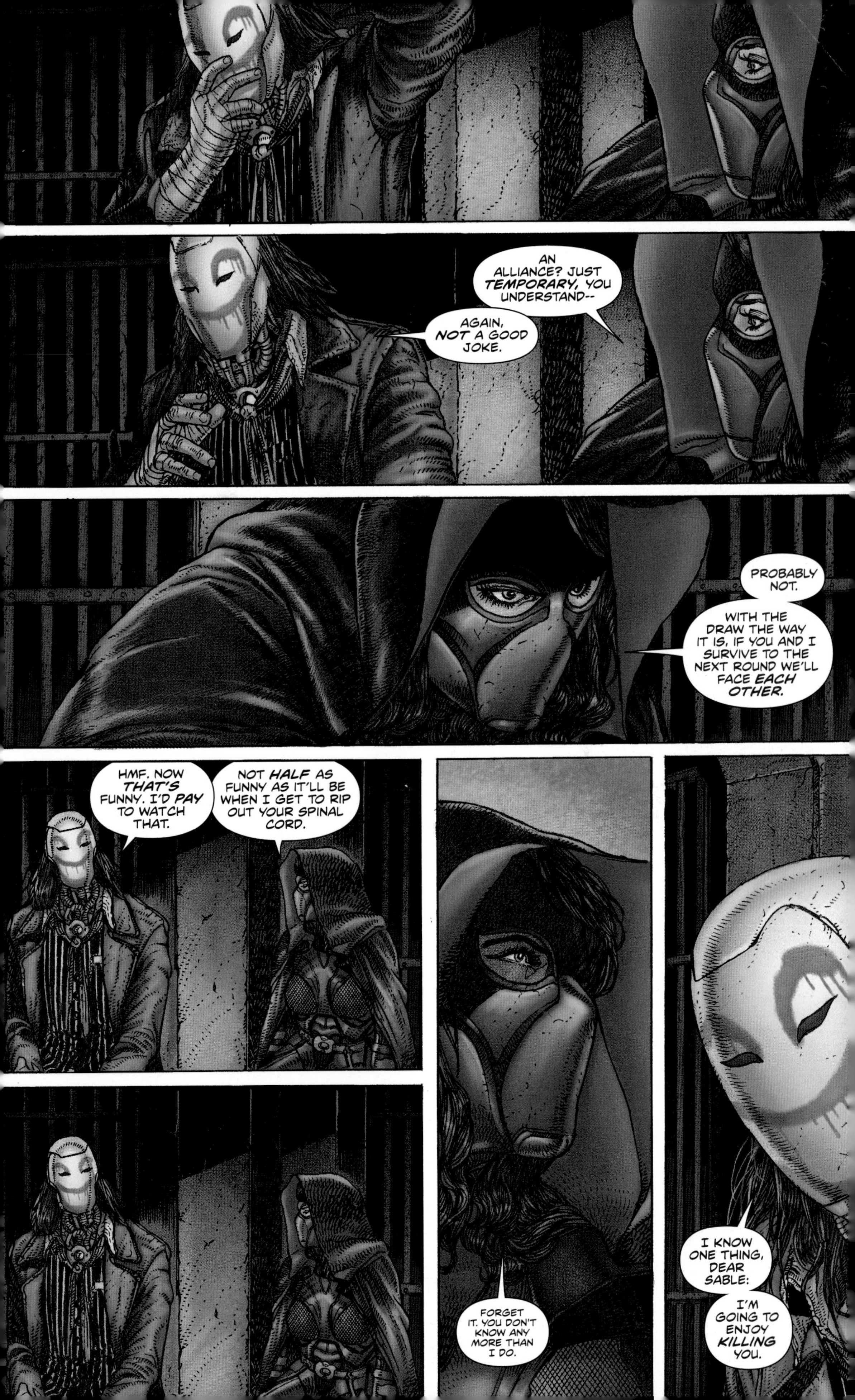
AN ALLIANCE? JUST TEMPORARY, YOU UNDERSTAND--
AGAIN, NOT A GOOD JOKE.
PROBABLY NOT.
WITH THE DRAW THE WAY IT IS, IF YOU AND I SURVIVE TO THE NEXT ROUND WE'LL FACE EACH OTHER.
HMF. NOW THAT'S FUNNY. I'D PAY TO WATCH THAT.
NOT HALF AS FUNNY AS IT'LL BE WHEN I GET TO RIP OUT YOUR SPINAL CORD.
FORGET IT. YOU DON'T KNOW ANY MORE THAN I DO.
I KNOW ONE THING, DEAR SABLE:
I'M GOING TO ENJOY KILLING YOU.

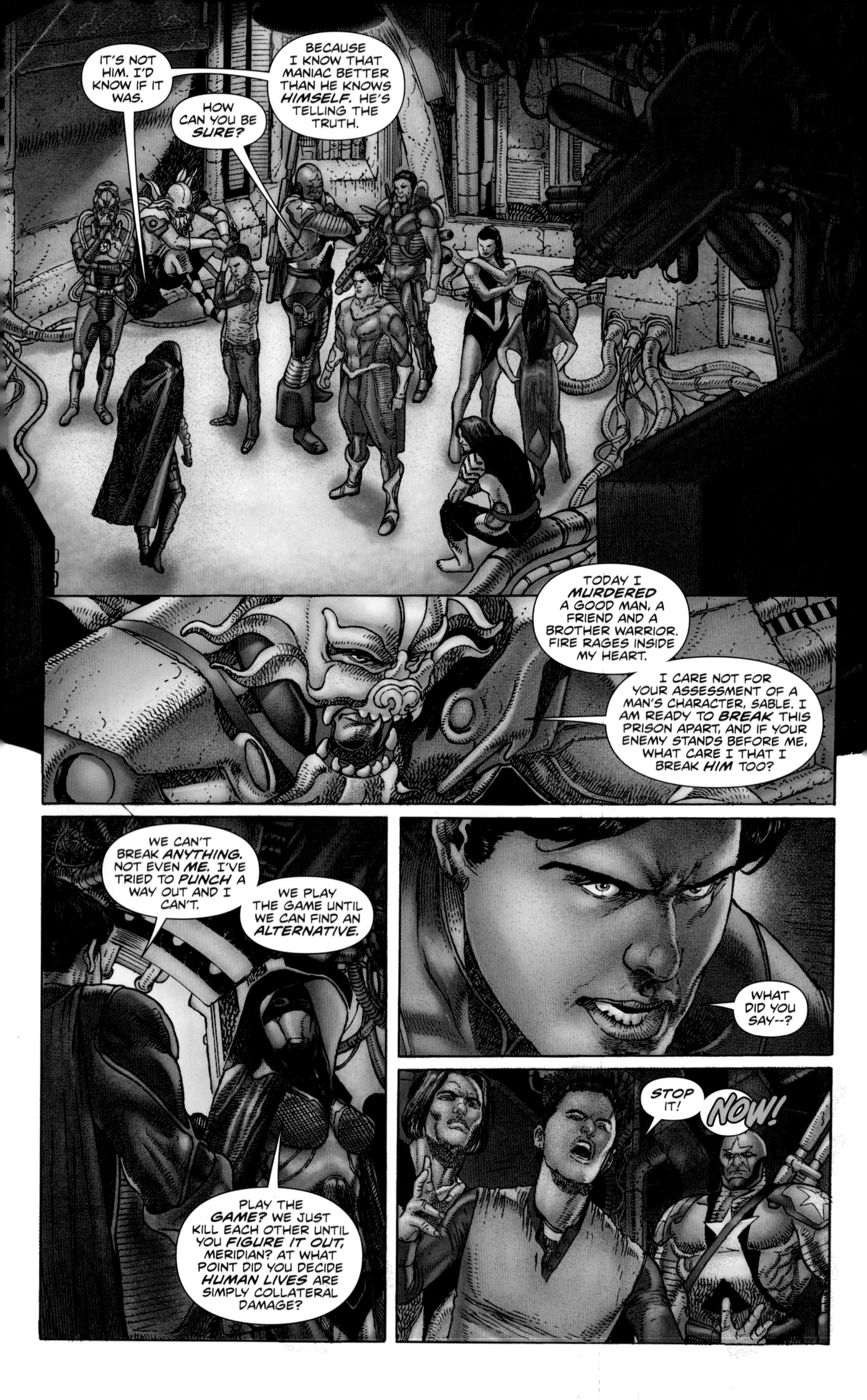
IT'S NOT HIM. I'D KNOW IF IT WAS.
HOW CAN YOU BE SURE?
BECAUSE I KNOW THAT MANIAC BETTER THAN HE KNOWS HIMSELF. HE'S TELLING THE TRUTH.
TODAY I MURDERED A GOOD MAN, A FRIEND AND A BROTHER WARRIOR. FIRE RAGES INSIDE MY HEART.
I CARE NOT FOR YOUR ASSESSMENT OF A MAN'S CHARACTER, SABLE. I AM READY TO BREAK THIS PRISON APART, AND IF YOUR ENEMY STANDS BEFORE ME, WHAT CARE I THAT I BREAK HIM TOO?
WE CAN'T BREAK ANYTHING. NOT EVEN ME. I'VE TRIED TO PUNCH A WAY OUT AND I CAN'T.
WE PLAY THE GAME UNTIL WE CAN FIND AN ALTERNATIVE.
PLAY THE GAME? WE JUST KILL EACH OTHER UNTIL YOU FIGURE IT OUT, MERIDIAN? AT WHAT POINT DID YOU DECIDE HUMAN LIVES ARE SIMPLY COLLATERAL DAMAGE?
WHAT DID YOU SAY--?
STOP IT!
NOW!

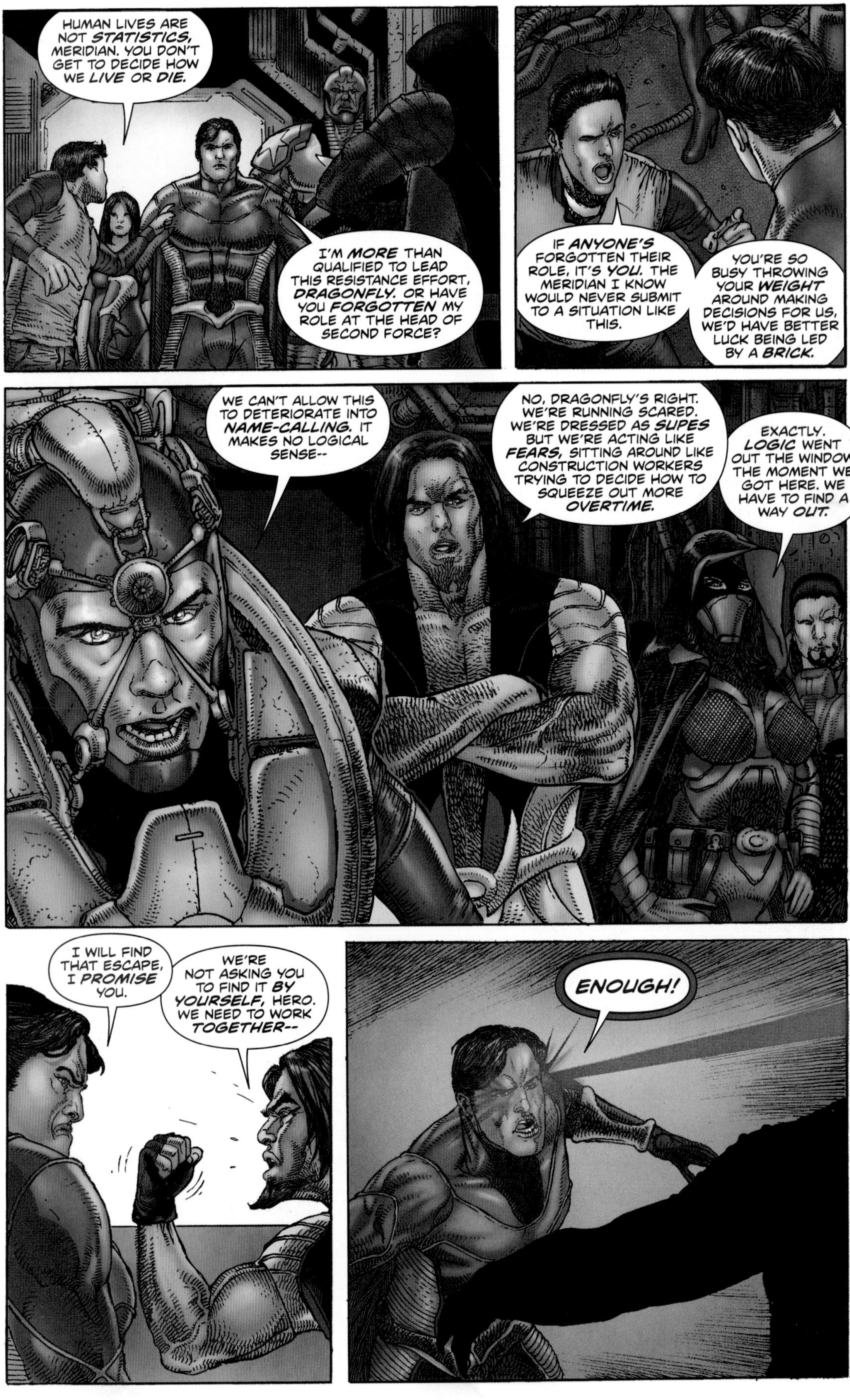
HUMAN LIVES ARE NOT *STATISTICS*, MERIDIAN. YOU DON'T GET TO DECIDE HOW WE *LIVE* OR *DIE*.
I'M **MORE** THAN QUALIFIED TO LEAD THIS RESISTANCE EFFORT, **DRAGONFLY.** OR HAVE YOU **FORGOTTEN** MY ROLE AT THE HEAD OF SECOND FORCE?
IF **ANYONE'S** FORGOTTEN THEIR ROLE, IT'S **YOU.** THE MERIDIAN I KNOW WOULD NEVER SUBMIT TO A SITUATION LIKE THIS.
YOU'RE SO BUSY THROWING YOUR **WEIGHT** AROUND MAKING DECISIONS FOR US, WE'D HAVE BETTER LUCK BEING LED BY A **BRICK.**
WE CAN'T ALLOW THIS TO DETERIORATE INTO **NAME-CALLING.** IT MAKES NO LOGICAL SENSE--
NO, DRAGONFLY'S RIGHT. WE'RE RUNNING SCARED. WE'RE DRESSED AS **SUPES** BUT WE'RE ACTING LIKE **FEARS,** SITTING AROUND LIKE CONSTRUCTION WORKERS TRYING TO DECIDE HOW TO SQUEEZE OUT MORE **OVERTIME.**
EXACTLY. **LOGIC** WENT OUT THE WINDOW THE MOMENT WE GOT HERE. WE HAVE TO FIND A WAY **OUT.**
I WILL FIND THAT ESCAPE, I *PROMISE* YOU.
WE'RE NOT ASKING YOU TO FIND IT **BY YOURSELF,** HERO. WE NEED TO WORK **TOGETHER--**
ENOUGH!

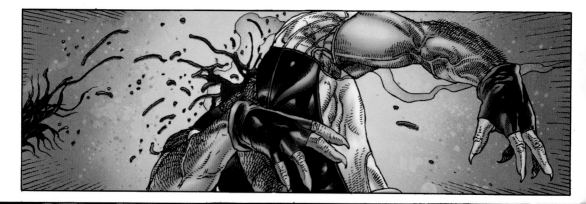

OHMYGOD--

--NO.

MERIDIAN... YOU *KILLED* HIM. YOU KILLED *BERSERK.*

WHAT THE HELL DID YOU JUST *DO?*

I...
I DON'T *KNOW.*

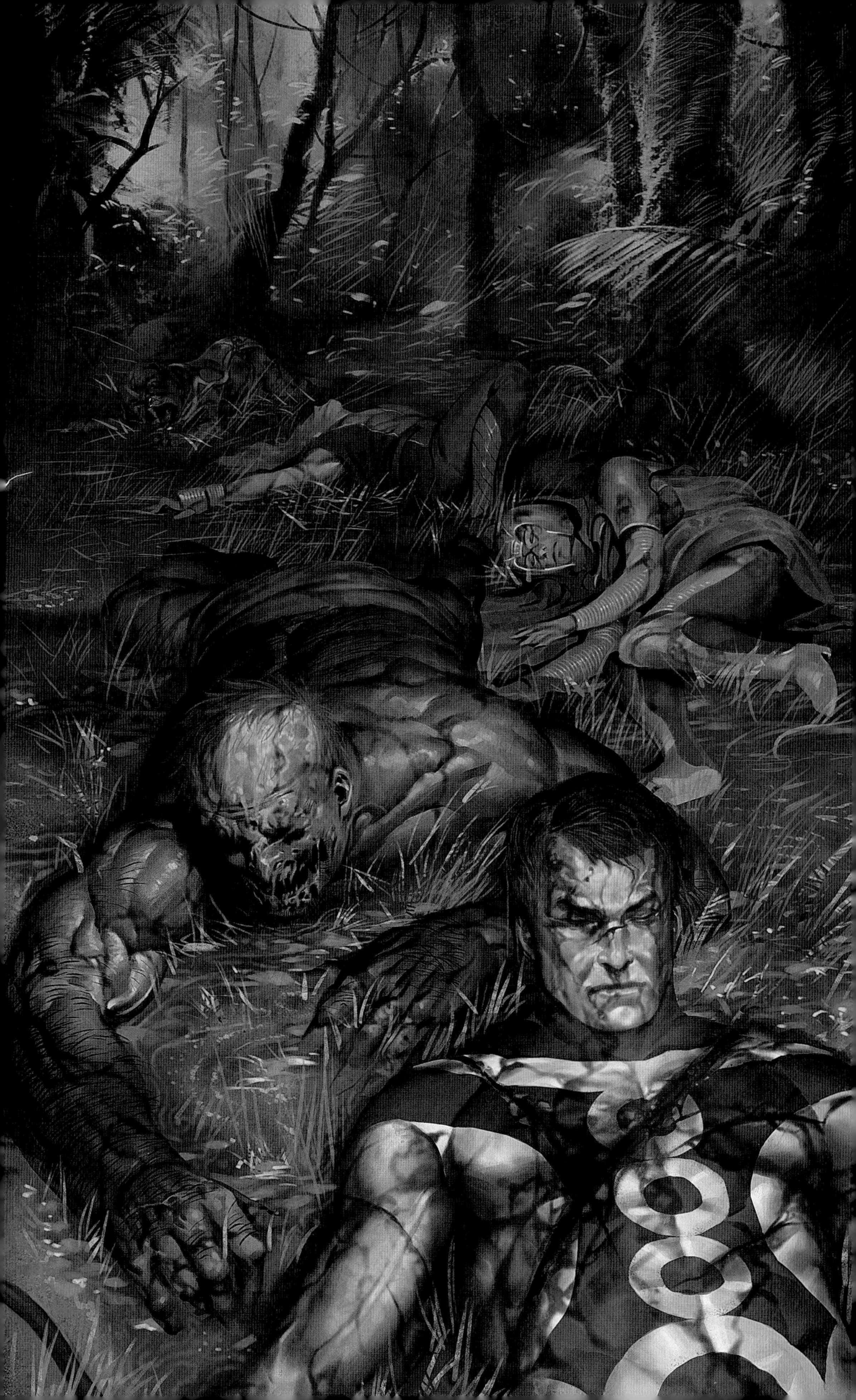

CHAPTER THREE

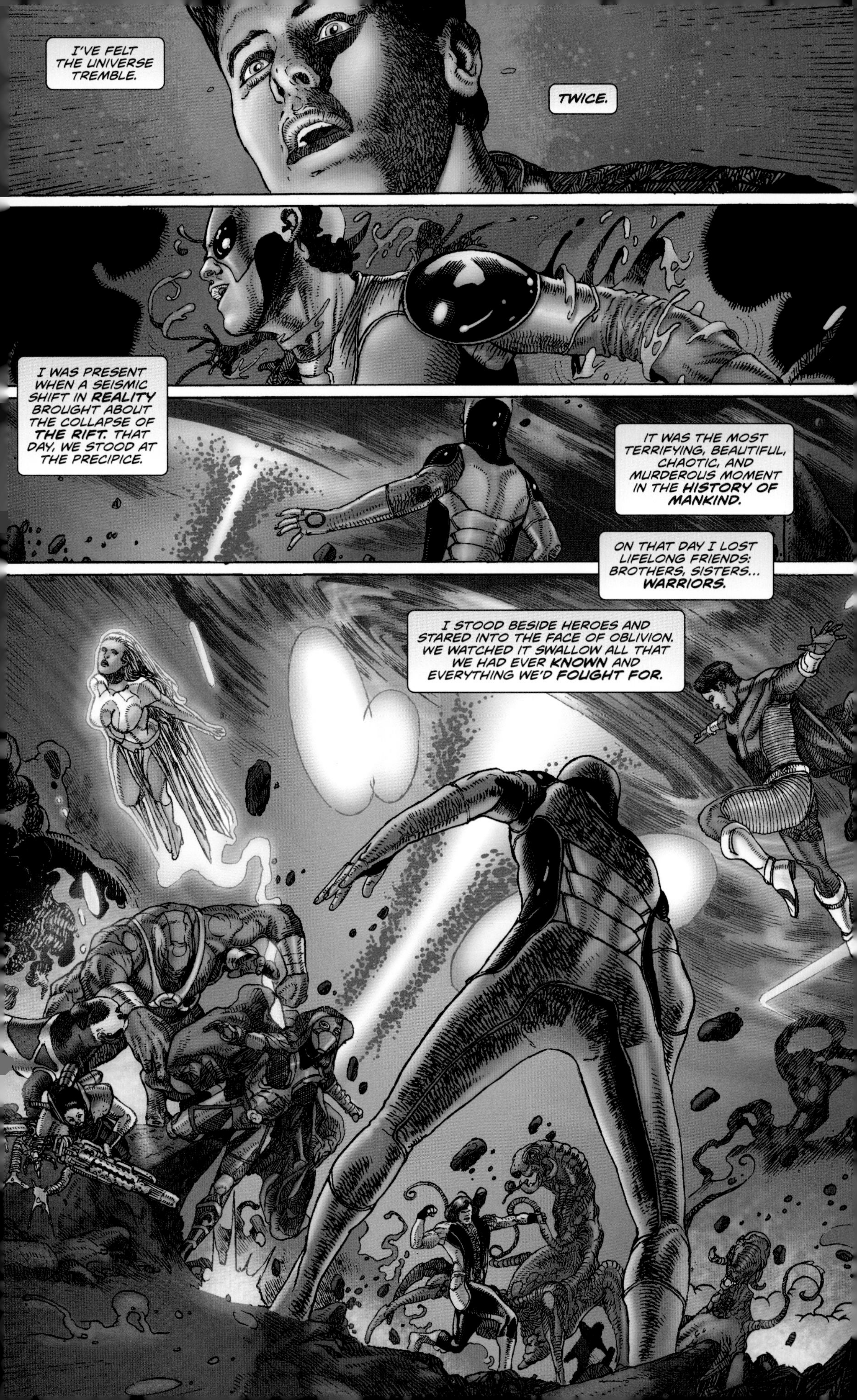
I'VE FELT THE UNIVERSE TREMBLE.
TWICE.
I WAS PRESENT WHEN A SEISMIC SHIFT IN REALITY BROUGHT ABOUT THE COLLAPSE OF THE RIFT. THAT DAY, WE STOOD AT THE PRECIPICE.
IT WAS THE MOST TERRIFYING, BEAUTIFUL, CHAOTIC, AND MURDEROUS MOMENT IN THE HISTORY OF MANKIND.
ON THAT DAY I LOST LIFELONG FRIENDS: BROTHERS, SISTERS... WARRIORS.
I STOOD BESIDE HEROES AND STARED INTO THE FACE OF OBLIVION. WE WATCHED IT SWALLOW ALL THAT WE HAD EVER KNOWN AND EVERYTHING WE'D FOUGHT FOR.

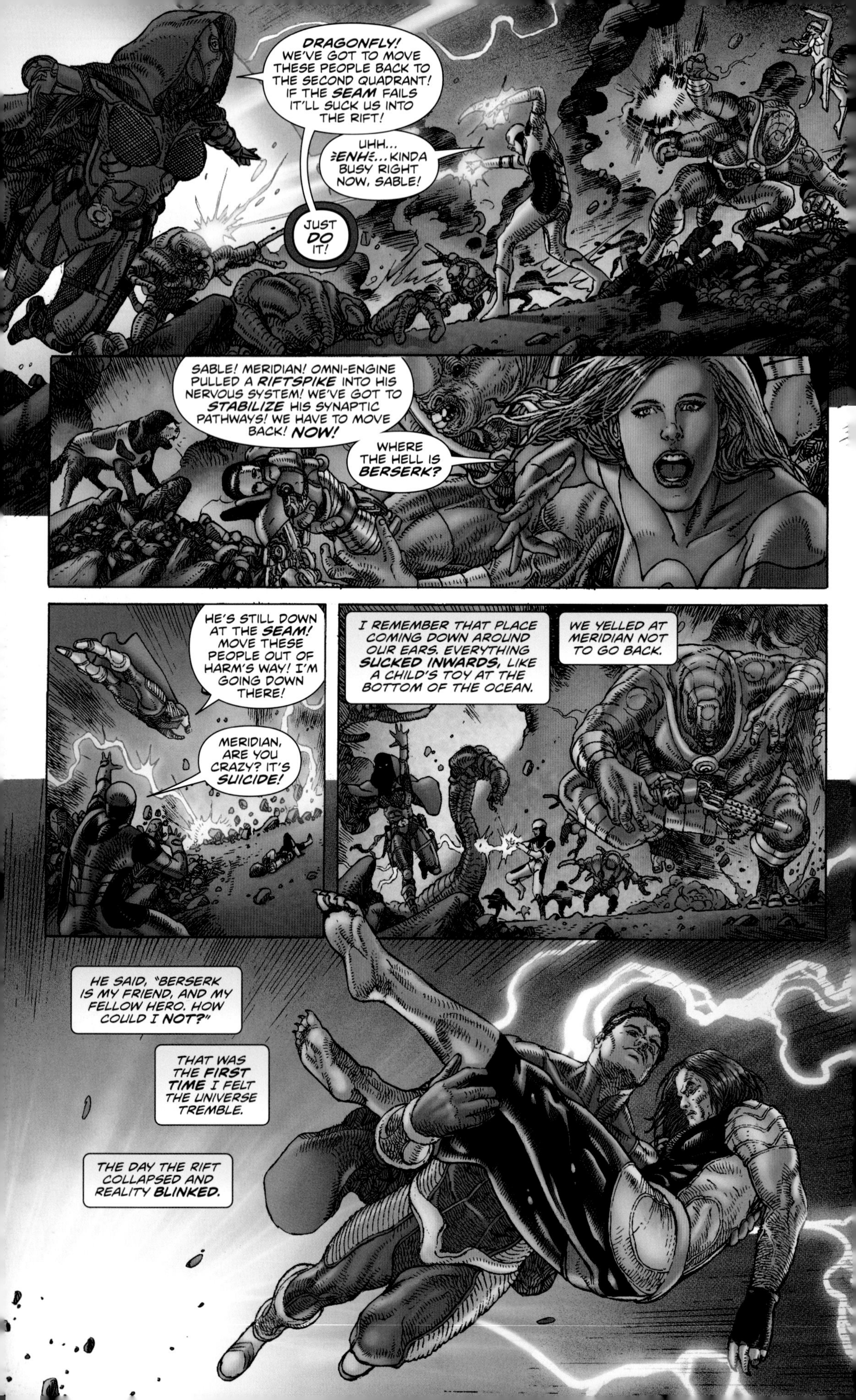
DRAGONFLY! WE'VE GOT TO MOVE THESE PEOPLE BACK TO THE SECOND QUADRANT! IF THE SEAM FAILS IT'LL SUCK US INTO THE RIFT!
UHH... ENH... KINDA BUSY RIGHT NOW, SABLE!
JUST DO IT!
SABLE! MERIDIAN! OMNI-ENGINE PULLED A RIFTSPIKE INTO HIS NERVOUS SYSTEM! WE'VE GOT TO STABILIZE HIS SYNAPTIC PATHWAYS! WE HAVE TO MOVE BACK! NOW!
WHERE THE HELL IS BERSERK?
HE'S STILL DOWN AT THE SEAM! MOVE THESE PEOPLE OUT OF HARM'S WAY! I'M GOING DOWN THERE!
MERIDIAN, ARE YOU CRAZY? IT'S SUICIDE!
I REMEMBER THAT PLACE COMING DOWN AROUND OUR EARS. EVERYTHING SUCKED INWARDS, LIKE A CHILD'S TOY AT THE BOTTOM OF THE OCEAN.
WE YELLED AT MERIDIAN NOT TO GO BACK.
HE SAID, "BERSERK IS MY FRIEND, AND MY FELLOW HERO. HOW COULD I NOT?"
THAT WAS THE FIRST TIME I FELT THE UNIVERSE TREMBLE.
THE DAY THE RIFT COLLAPSED AND REALITY BLINKED.

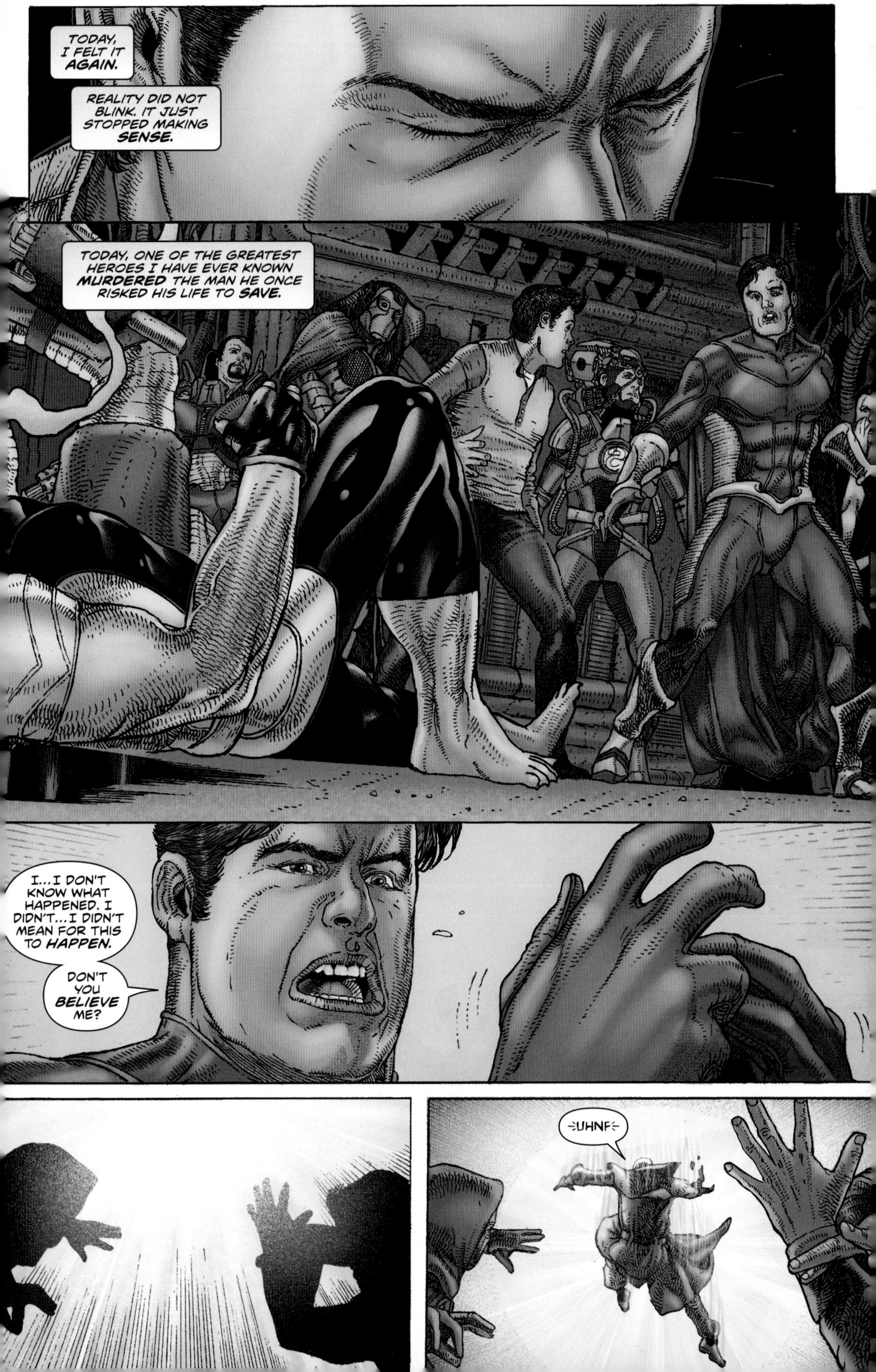
TODAY, I FELT IT AGAIN.
REALITY DID NOT BLINK. IT JUST STOPPED MAKING SENSE.
TODAY, ONE OF THE GREATEST HEROES I HAVE EVER KNOWN MURDERED THE MAN HE ONCE RISKED HIS LIFE TO SAVE.
I...I DON'T KNOW WHAT HAPPENED. I DIDN'T...I DIDN'T MEAN FOR THIS TO HAPPEN.
DON'T YOU BELIEVE ME?
UHNF

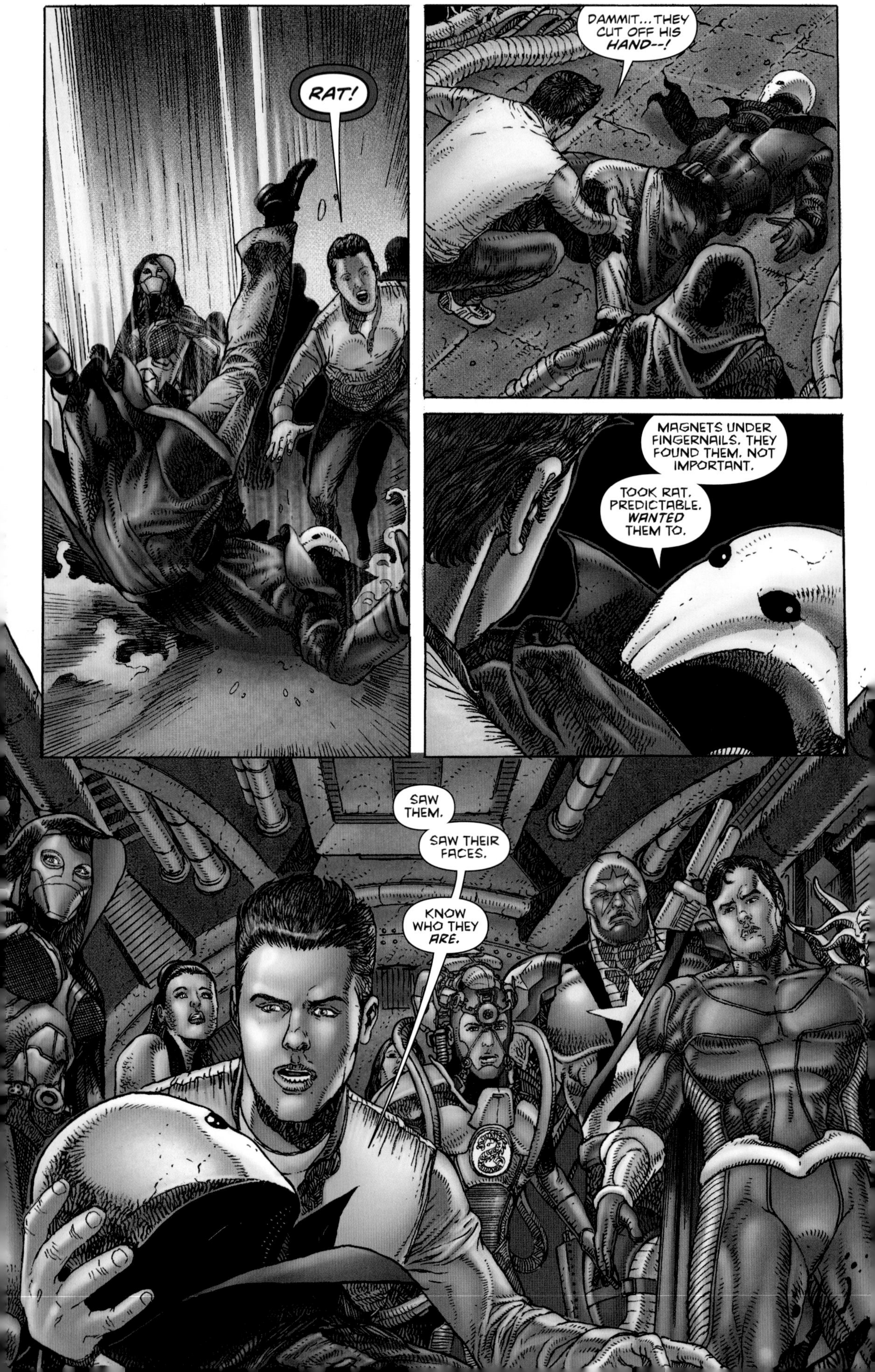
RAT!
DAMMIT...THEY CUT OFF HIS *HAND*--!
MAGNETS UNDER FINGERNAILS. THEY FOUND THEM. NOT IMPORTANT.
TOOK RAT. PREDICTABLE. *WANTED* THEM TO.
SAW THEM.
SAW THEIR FACES.
KNOW WHO THEY *ARE*.

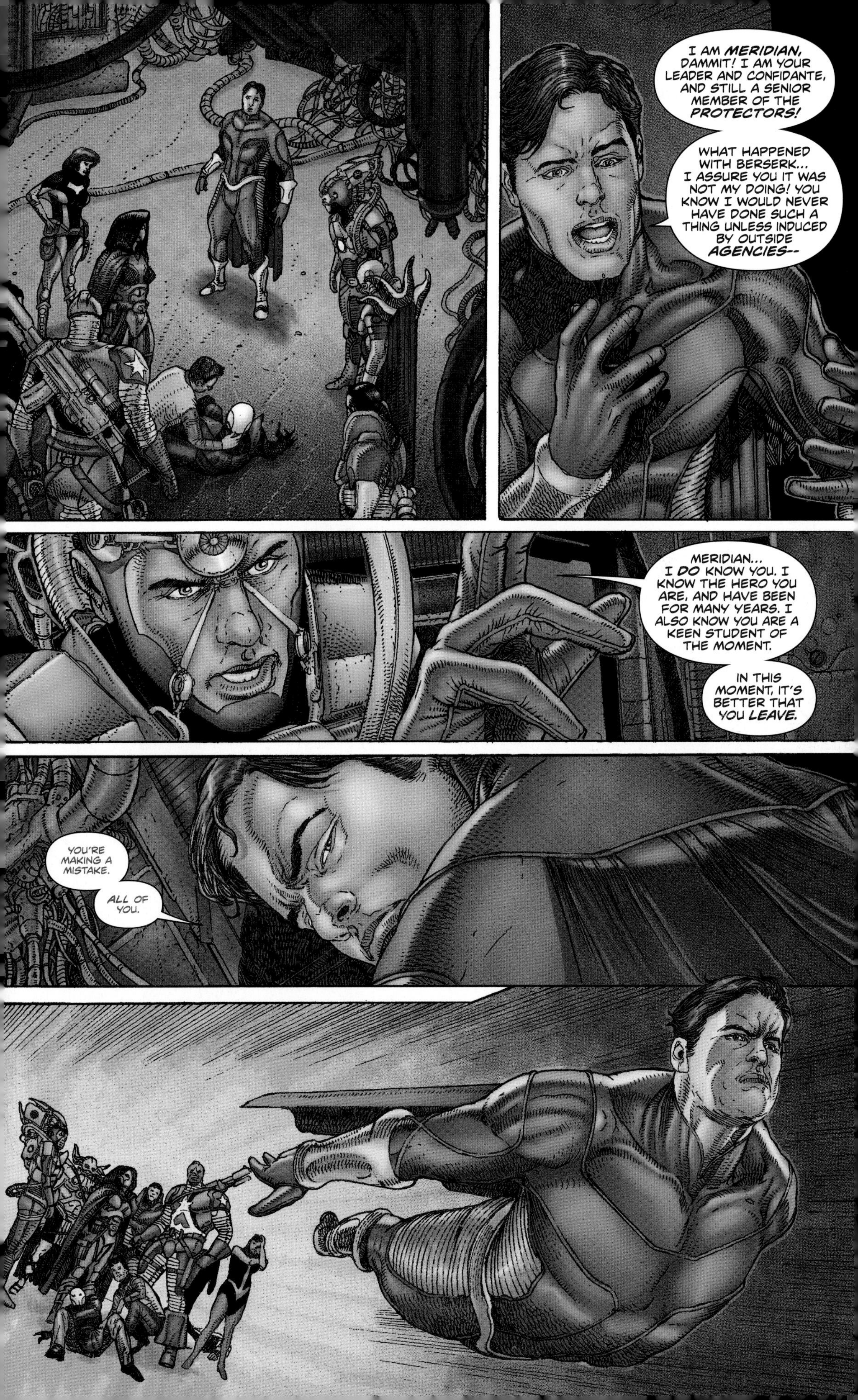

I AM MERIDIAN, DAMMIT! I AM YOUR LEADER AND CONFIDANTE, AND STILL A SENIOR MEMBER OF THE PROTECTORS!
WHAT HAPPENED WITH BERSERK... I ASSURE YOU IT WAS NOT MY DOING! YOU KNOW I WOULD NEVER HAVE DONE SUCH A THING UNLESS INDUCED BY OUTSIDE AGENCIES--
MERIDIAN... I DO KNOW YOU. I KNOW THE HERO YOU ARE, AND HAVE BEEN FOR MANY YEARS. I ALSO KNOW YOU ARE A KEEN STUDENT OF THE MOMENT.
IN THIS MOMENT, IT'S BETTER THAT YOU LEAVE.
YOU'RE MAKING A MISTAKE.
ALL OF YOU.

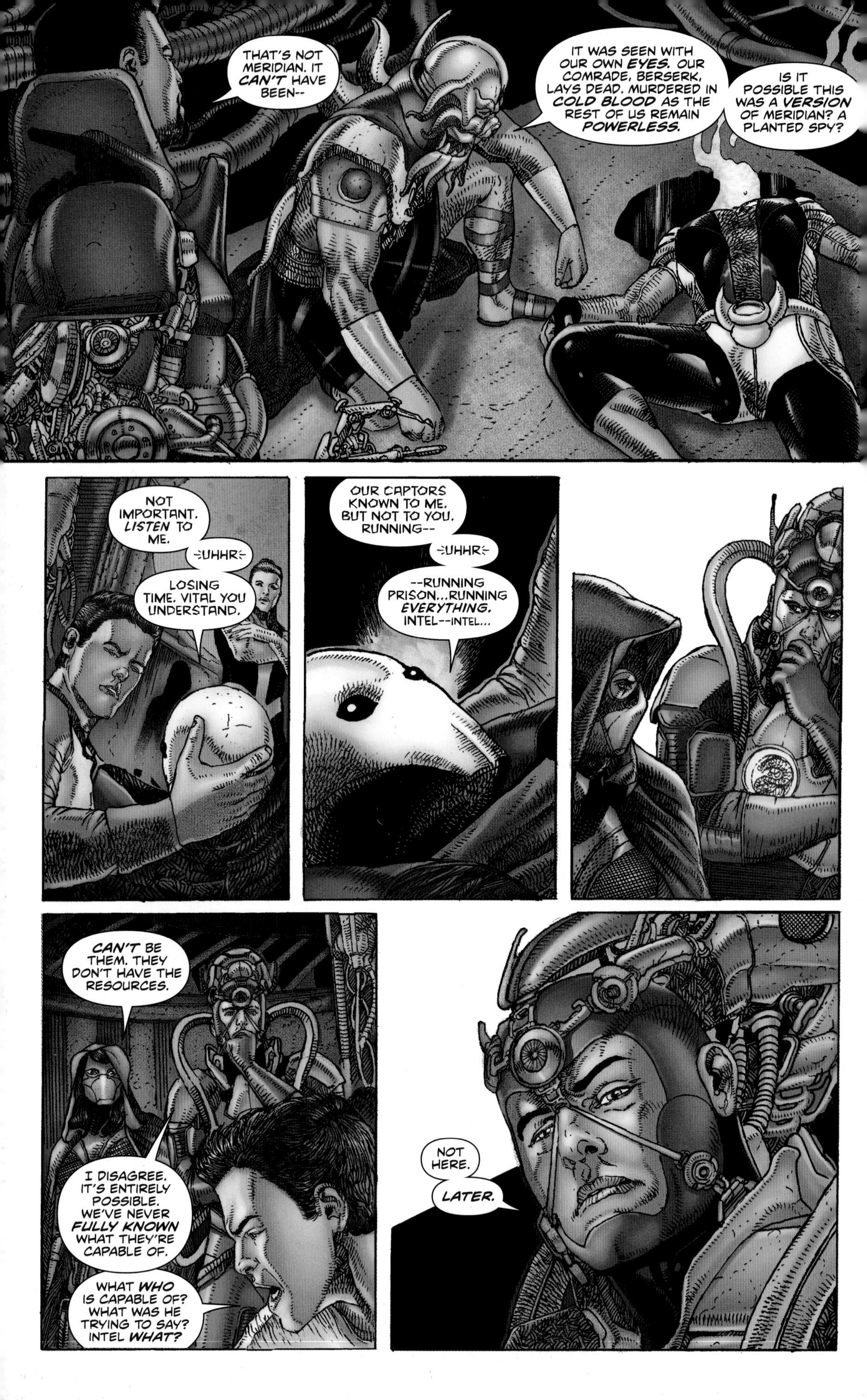
THAT'S NOT MERIDIAN. IT CAN'T HAVE BEEN--
IT WAS SEEN WITH OUR OWN EYES. OUR COMRADE, BERSERK, LAYS DEAD. MURDERED IN COLD BLOOD AS THE REST OF US REMAIN POWERLESS.
IS IT POSSIBLE THIS WAS A VERSION OF MERIDIAN? A PLANTED SPY?
NOT IMPORTANT. LISTEN TO ME.
UHHR
LOSING TIME. VITAL YOU UNDERSTAND.
OUR CAPTORS KNOWN TO ME. BUT NOT TO YOU. RUNNING--
UHHR
--RUNNING PRISON...RUNNING EVERYTHING. INTEL--INTEL...
CAN'T BE THEM. THEY DON'T HAVE THE RESOURCES.
I DISAGREE. IT'S ENTIRELY POSSIBLE. WE'VE NEVER FULLY KNOWN WHAT THEY'RE CAPABLE OF.
WHAT WHO IS CAPABLE OF? WHAT WAS HE TRYING TO SAY? INTEL WHAT?
NOT HERE.
LATER.

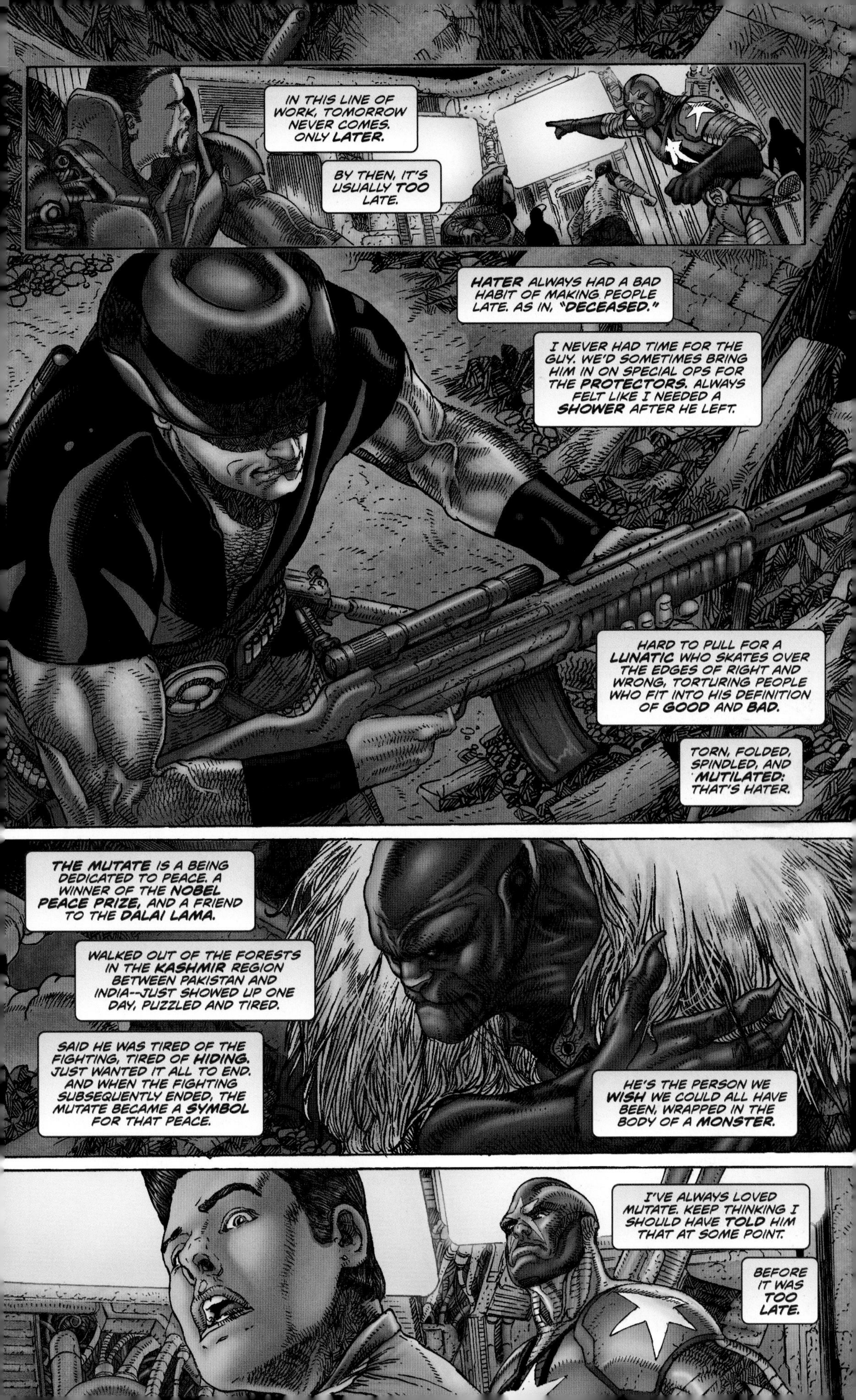

IN THIS LINE OF WORK, TOMORROW NEVER COMES. ONLY LATER.
BY THEN, IT'S USUALLY TOO LATE.
HATER ALWAYS HAD A BAD HABIT OF MAKING PEOPLE LATE. AS IN, "DECEASED."
I NEVER HAD TIME FOR THE GUY. WE'D SOMETIMES BRING HIM IN ON SPECIAL OPS FOR THE PROTECTORS. ALWAYS FELT LIKE I NEEDED A SHOWER AFTER HE LEFT.
HARD TO PULL FOR A LUNATIC WHO SKATES OVER THE EDGES OF RIGHT AND WRONG, TORTURING PEOPLE WHO FIT INTO HIS DEFINITION OF GOOD AND BAD.
TORN, FOLDED, SPINDLED, AND MUTILATED: THAT'S HATER.
THE MUTATE IS A BEING DEDICATED TO PEACE. A WINNER OF THE NOBEL PEACE PRIZE, AND A FRIEND TO THE DALAI LAMA.
WALKED OUT OF THE FORESTS IN THE KASHMIR REGION BETWEEN PAKISTAN AND INDIA--JUST SHOWED UP ONE DAY, PUZZLED AND TIRED.
SAID HE WAS TIRED OF THE FIGHTING, TIRED OF HIDING. JUST WANTED IT ALL TO END. AND WHEN THE FIGHTING SUBSEQUENTLY ENDED, THE MUTATE BECAME A SYMBOL FOR THAT PEACE.
HE'S THE PERSON WE WISH WE COULD ALL HAVE BEEN, WRAPPED IN THE BODY OF A MONSTER.
I'VE ALWAYS LOVED MUTATE. KEEP THINKING I SHOULD HAVE TOLD HIM THAT AT SOME POINT.
BEFORE IT WAS TOO LATE.

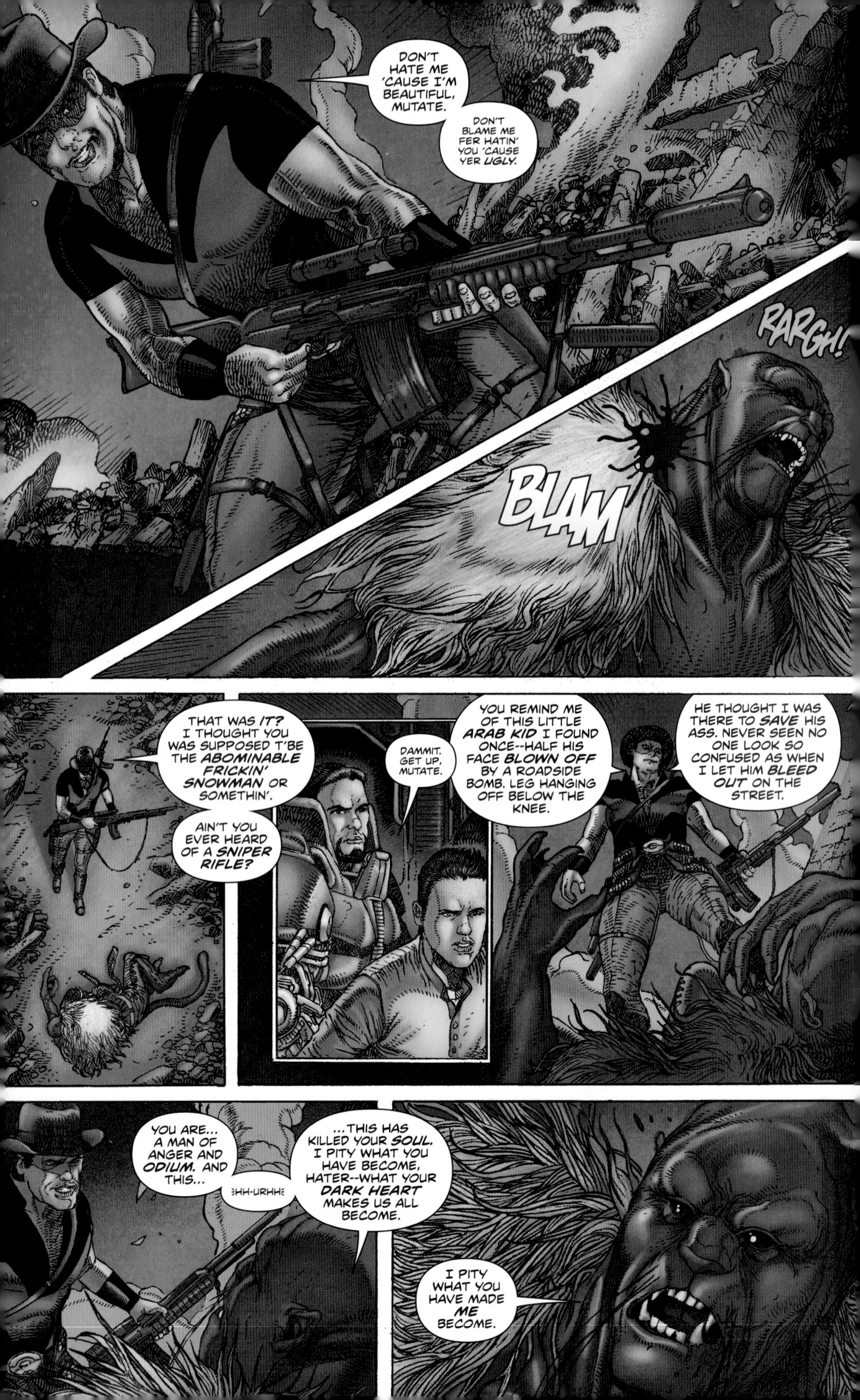
DON'T HATE ME 'CAUSE I'M BEAUTIFUL, MUTATE.
DON'T BLAME ME FER HATIN' YOU 'CAUSE YER UGLY.
RARGH!
BLAM
THAT WAS IT? I THOUGHT YOU WAS SUPPOSED T'BE THE ABOMINABLE FRICKIN' SNOWMAN OR SOMETHIN'.
AIN'T YOU EVER HEARD OF A SNIPER RIFLE?
DAMMIT. GET UP, MUTATE.
YOU REMIND ME OF THIS LITTLE ARAB KID I FOUND ONCE--HALF HIS FACE BLOWN OFF BY A ROADSIDE BOMB. LEG HANGING OFF BELOW THE KNEE.
HE THOUGHT I WAS THERE TO SAVE HIS ASS. NEVER SEEN NO ONE LOOK SO CONFUSED AS WHEN I LET HIM BLEED OUT ON THE STREET.
YOU ARE... A MAN OF ANGER AND ODIUM. AND THIS...
...THIS HAS KILLED YOUR SOUL. I PITY WHAT YOU HAVE BECOME, HATER--WHAT YOUR DARK HEART MAKES US ALL BECOME.
I PITY WHAT YOU HAVE MADE ME BECOME.

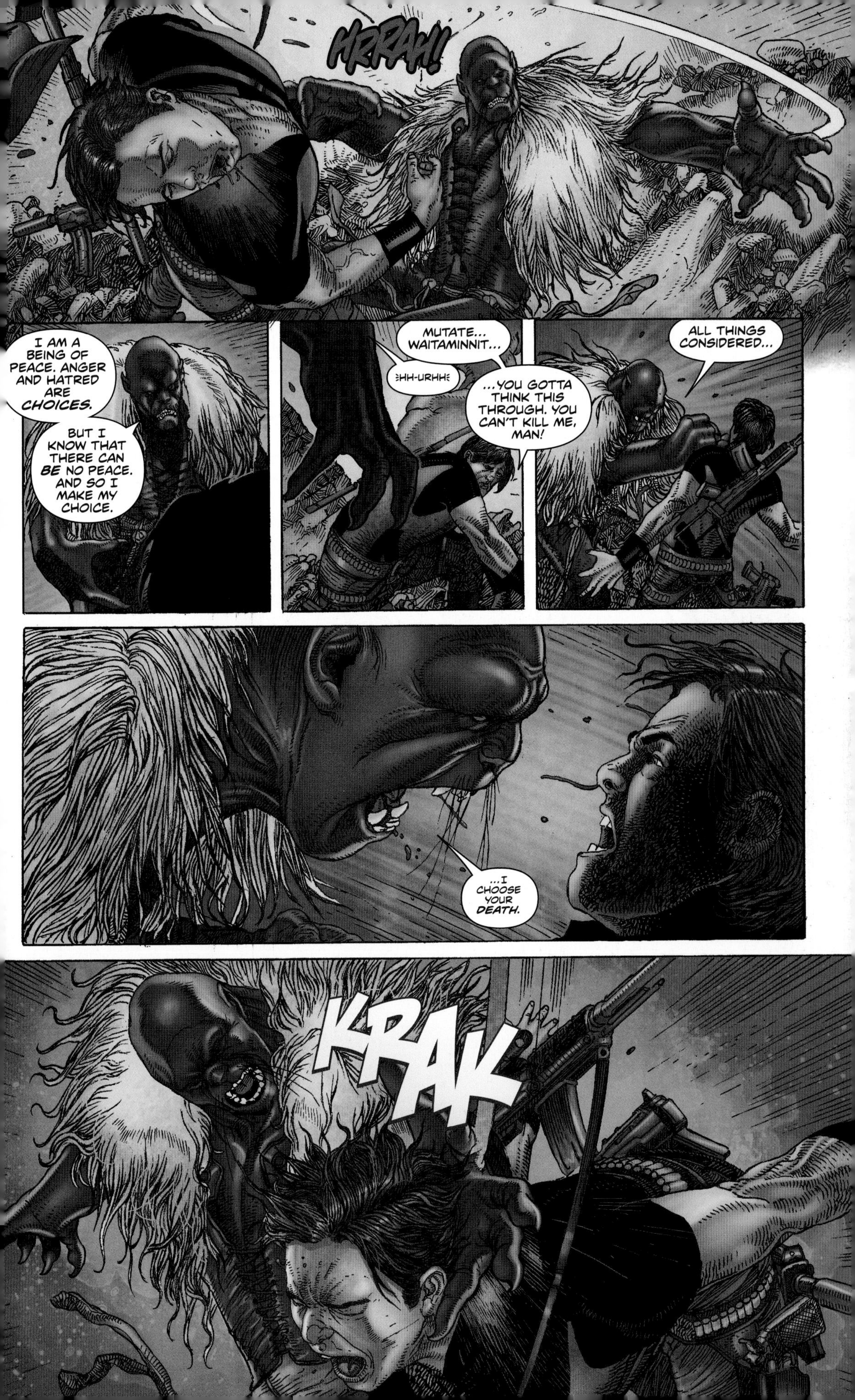
HRRAH!
I AM A BEING OF PEACE. ANGER AND HATRED ARE CHOICES.
BUT I KNOW THAT THERE CAN BE NO PEACE. AND SO I MAKE MY CHOICE.
MUTATE... WAITAMINNIT...
HH-URHH
...YOU GOTTA THINK THIS THROUGH. YOU CAN'T KILL ME, MAN!
ALL THINGS CONSIDERED...
...I CHOOSE YOUR DEATH.
KRAK

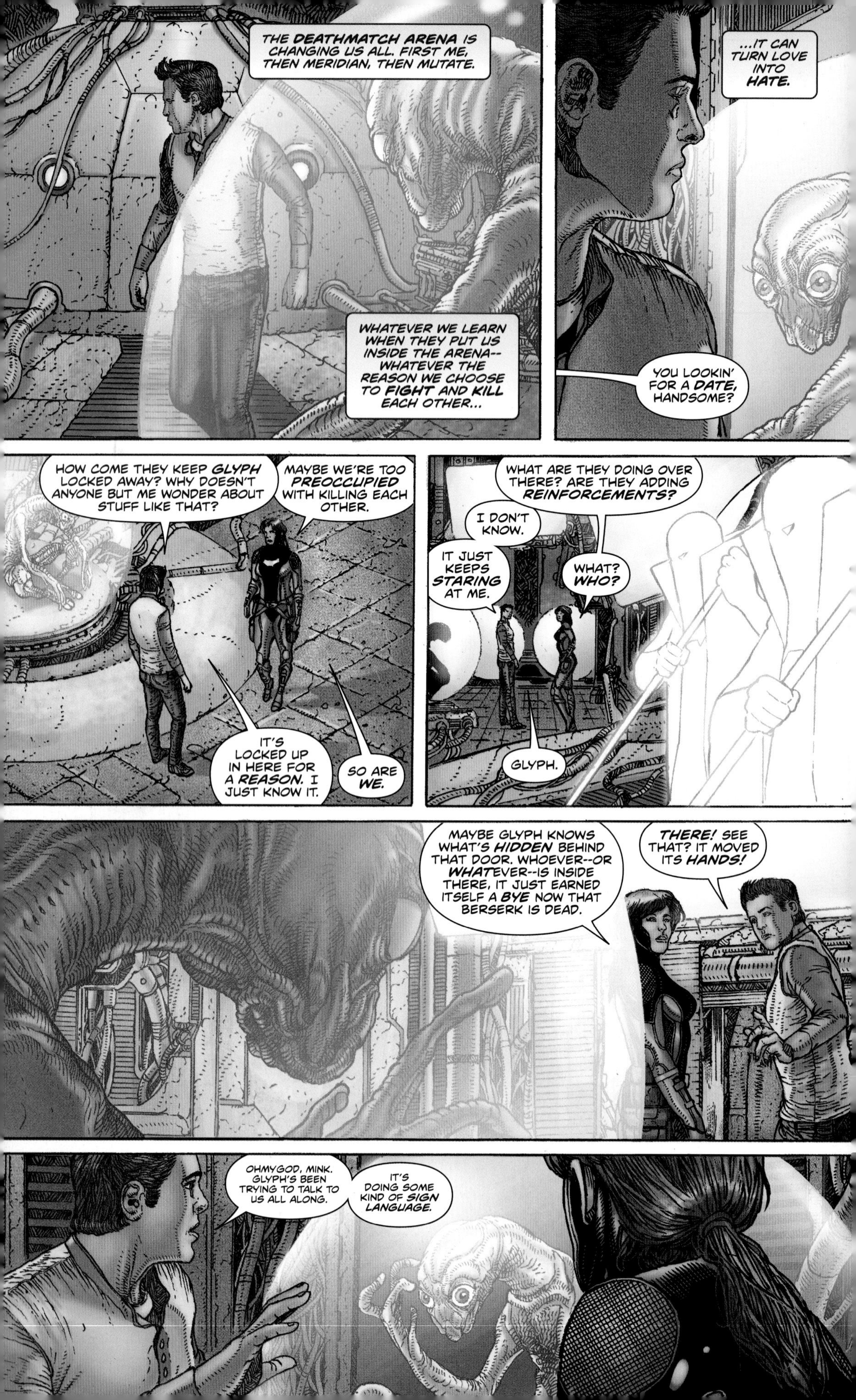
THE DEATHMATCH ARENA IS CHANGING US ALL. FIRST ME, THEN MERIDIAN, THEN MUTATE.
WHATEVER WE LEARN WHEN THEY PUT US INSIDE THE ARENA--WHATEVER THE REASON WE CHOOSE TO FIGHT AND KILL EACH OTHER...
...IT CAN TURN LOVE INTO HATE.
YOU LOOKIN' FOR A DATE, HANDSOME?
HOW COME THEY KEEP GLYPH LOCKED AWAY? WHY DOESN'T ANYONE BUT ME WONDER ABOUT STUFF LIKE THAT?
MAYBE WE'RE TOO PREOCCUPIED WITH KILLING EACH OTHER.
IT'S LOCKED UP IN HERE FOR A REASON. I JUST KNOW IT.
SO ARE WE.
WHAT ARE THEY DOING OVER THERE? ARE THEY ADDING REINFORCEMENTS?
I DON'T KNOW.
IT JUST KEEPS STARING AT ME.
WHAT? WHO?
GLYPH.
MAYBE GLYPH KNOWS WHAT'S HIDDEN BEHIND THAT DOOR. WHOEVER--OR WHATEVER--IS INSIDE THERE, IT JUST EARNED ITSELF A BYE NOW THAT BERSERK IS DEAD.
THERE! SEE THAT? IT MOVED ITS HANDS!
OHMYGOD, MINK. GLYPH'S BEEN TRYING TO TALK TO US ALL ALONG.
IT'S DOING SOME KIND OF SIGN LANGUAGE.

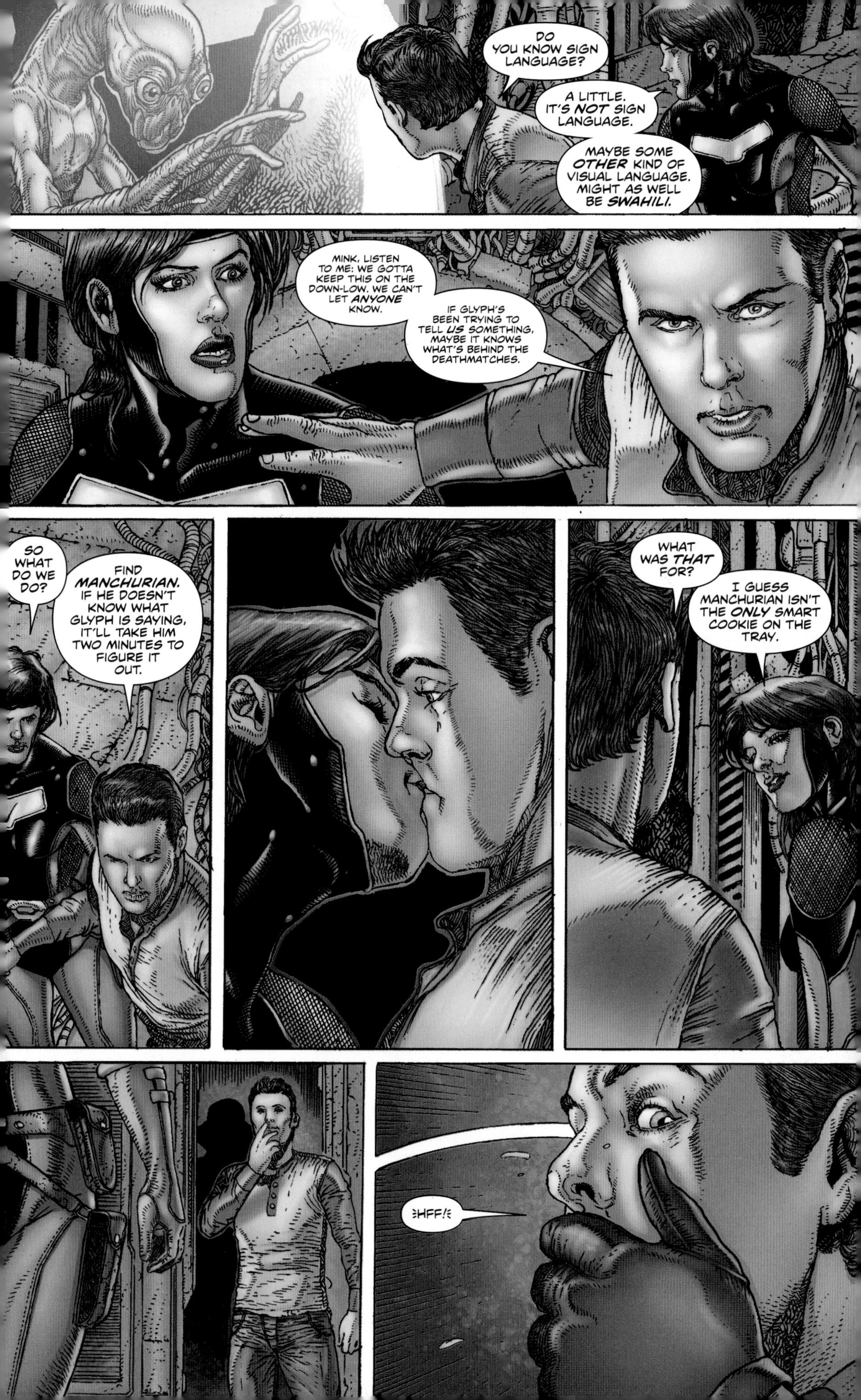
DO YOU KNOW SIGN LANGUAGE?
A LITTLE. IT'S NOT SIGN LANGUAGE.
MAYBE SOME OTHER KIND OF VISUAL LANGUAGE. MIGHT AS WELL BE SWAHILI.
MINK, LISTEN TO ME: WE GOTTA KEEP THIS ON THE DOWN-LOW. WE CAN'T LET ANYONE KNOW.
IF GLYPH'S BEEN TRYING TO TELL US SOMETHING, MAYBE IT KNOWS WHAT'S BEHIND THE DEATHMATCHES.
SO WHAT DO WE DO?
FIND MANCHURIAN. IF HE DOESN'T KNOW WHAT GLYPH IS SAYING, IT'LL TAKE HIM TWO MINUTES TO FIGURE IT OUT.
WHAT WAS THAT FOR?
I GUESS MANCHURIAN ISN'T THE ONLY SMART COOKIE ON THE TRAY.
HFF!

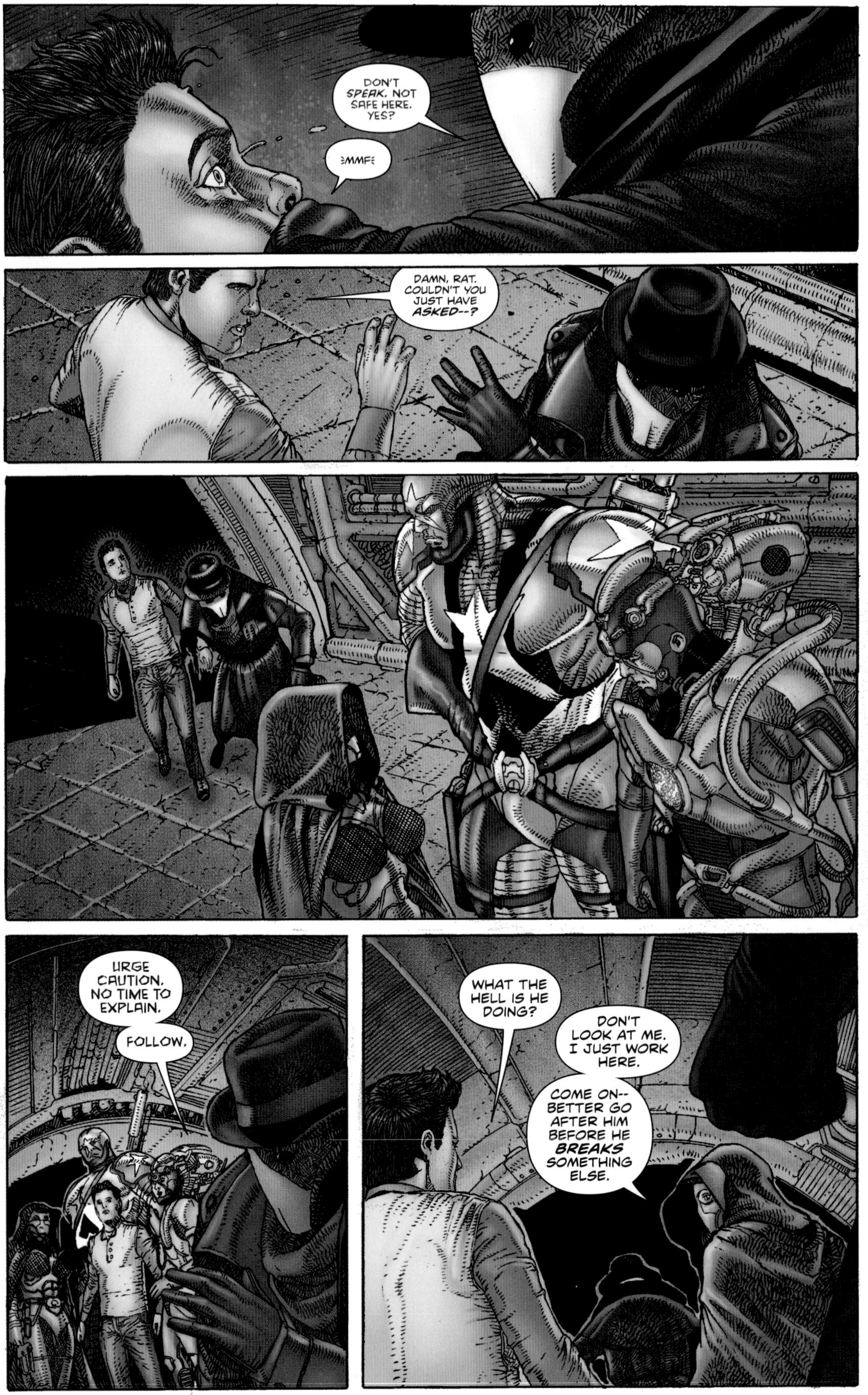
DON'T SPEAK. NOT SAFE HERE. YES?
≷MMF≶
DAMN, RAT. COULDN'T YOU JUST HAVE ASKED--?
URGE CAUTION. NO TIME TO EXPLAIN.
FOLLOW.
WHAT THE HELL IS HE DOING?
DON'T LOOK AT ME. I JUST WORK HERE.
COME ON-- BETTER GO AFTER HIM BEFORE HE BREAKS SOMETHING ELSE.

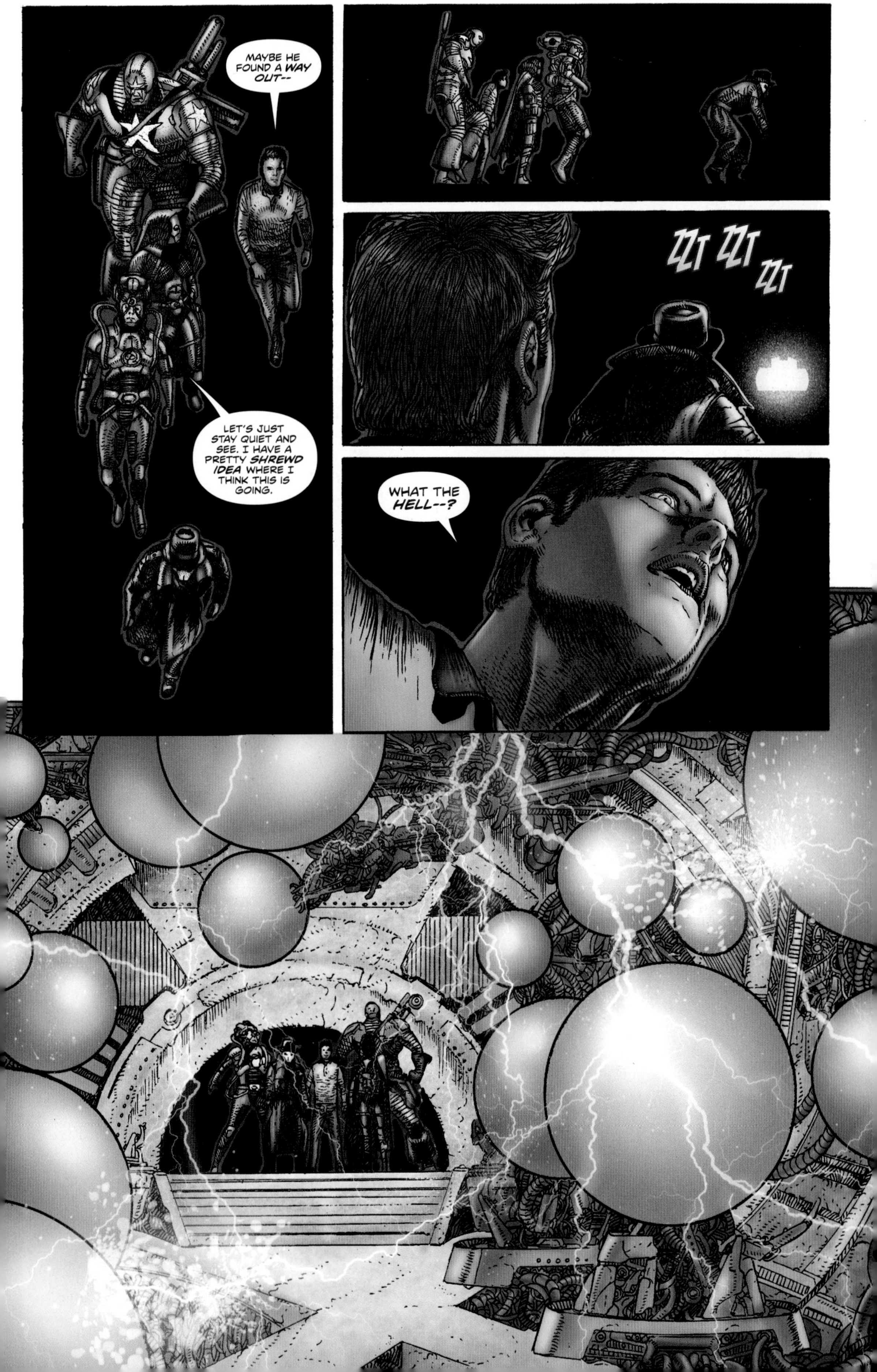
MAYBE HE FOUND A WAY OUT--
LET'S JUST STAY QUIET AND SEE. I HAVE A PRETTY SHREWD IDEA WHERE I THINK THIS IS GOING.
ZZT ZZT ZZT
WHAT THE HELL--?

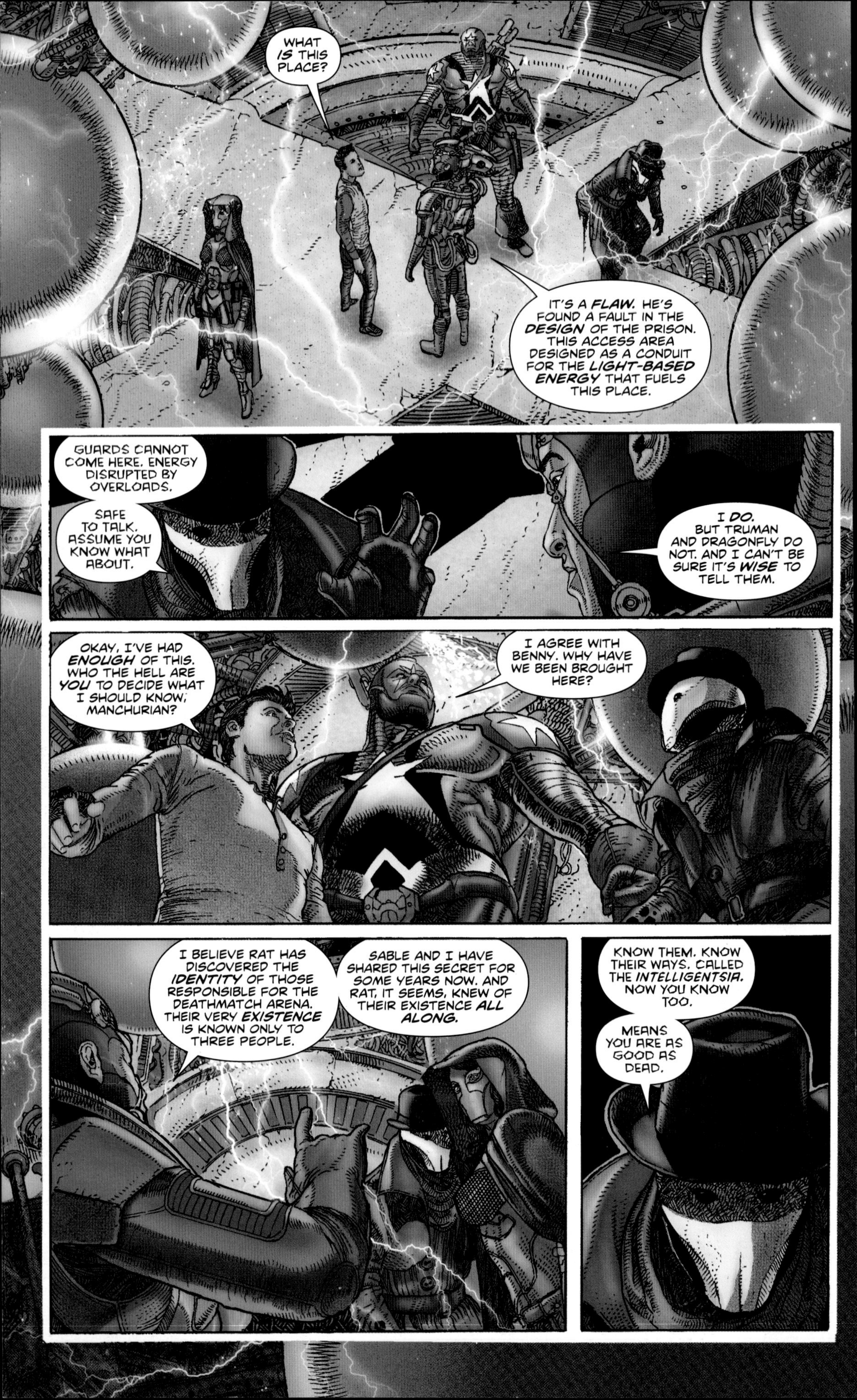
WHAT *IS* THIS PLACE?
IT'S A ***FLAW.*** HE'S FOUND A FAULT IN THE ***DESIGN*** OF THE PRISON. THIS ACCESS AREA DESIGNED AS A CONDUIT FOR THE ***LIGHT-BASED ENERGY*** THAT FUELS THIS PLACE.
GUARDS CANNOT COME HERE. ENERGY DISRUPTED BY OVERLOADS.
SAFE TO TALK. ASSUME YOU KNOW WHAT ABOUT.
I ***DO.*** BUT TRUMAN AND DRAGONFLY DO NOT. AND I CAN'T BE SURE IT'S ***WISE*** TO TELL THEM.
OKAY, I'VE HAD ***ENOUGH*** OF THIS. WHO THE HELL ARE ***YOU*** TO DECIDE WHAT I SHOULD KNOW, MANCHURIAN?
I AGREE WITH BENNY. WHY HAVE WE BEEN BROUGHT HERE?
I BELIEVE RAT HAS DISCOVERED THE ***IDENTITY*** OF THOSE RESPONSIBLE FOR THE DEATHMATCH ARENA. THEIR VERY ***EXISTENCE*** IS KNOWN ONLY TO THREE PEOPLE.
SABLE AND I HAVE SHARED THIS SECRET FOR SOME YEARS NOW. AND RAT, IT SEEMS, KNEW OF THEIR EXISTENCE ***ALL ALONG.***
KNOW THEM. KNOW THEIR WAYS. CALLED THE ***INTELLIGENTSIA.*** NOW YOU KNOW TOO.
MEANS YOU ARE AS GOOD AS DEAD.

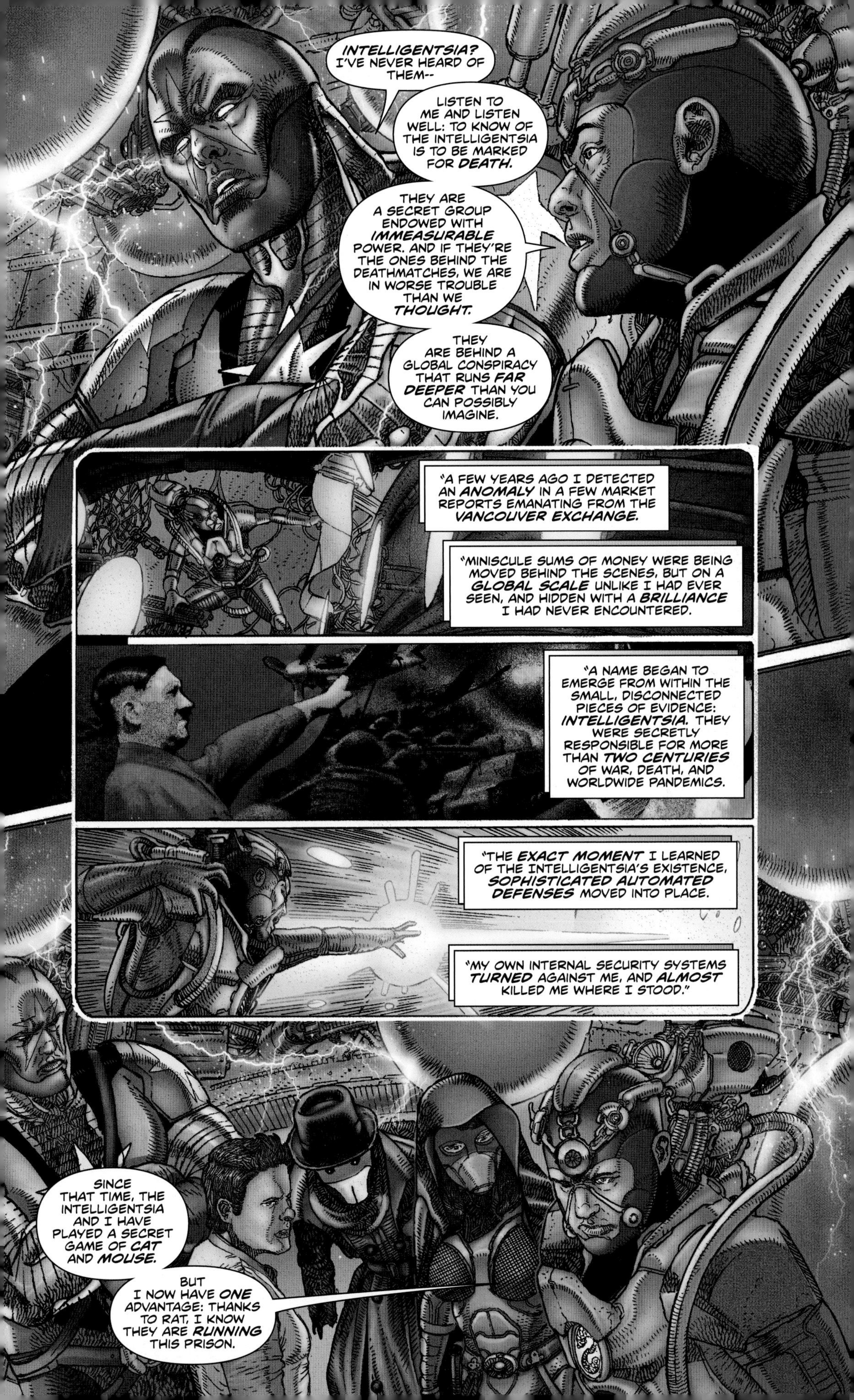
INTELLIGENTSIA? I'VE NEVER HEARD OF THEM--
LISTEN TO ME AND LISTEN WELL: TO KNOW OF THE INTELLIGENTSIA IS TO BE MARKED FOR DEATH.
THEY ARE A SECRET GROUP ENDOWED WITH IMMEASURABLE POWER. AND IF THEY'RE THE ONES BEHIND THE DEATHMATCHES, WE ARE IN WORSE TROUBLE THAN WE THOUGHT.
THEY ARE BEHIND A GLOBAL CONSPIRACY THAT RUNS FAR DEEPER THAN YOU CAN POSSIBLY IMAGINE.
"A FEW YEARS AGO I DETECTED AN ANOMALY IN A FEW MARKET REPORTS EMANATING FROM THE VANCOUVER EXCHANGE.
"MINISCULE SUMS OF MONEY WERE BEING MOVED BEHIND THE SCENES, BUT ON A GLOBAL SCALE UNLIKE I HAD EVER SEEN, AND HIDDEN WITH A BRILLIANCE I HAD NEVER ENCOUNTERED.
"A NAME BEGAN TO EMERGE FROM WITHIN THE SMALL, DISCONNECTED PIECES OF EVIDENCE: INTELLIGENTSIA. THEY WERE SECRETLY RESPONSIBLE FOR MORE THAN TWO CENTURIES OF WAR, DEATH, AND WORLDWIDE PANDEMICS.
"THE EXACT MOMENT I LEARNED OF THE INTELLIGENTSIA'S EXISTENCE, SOPHISTICATED AUTOMATED DEFENSES MOVED INTO PLACE.
"MY OWN INTERNAL SECURITY SYSTEMS TURNED AGAINST ME, AND ALMOST KILLED ME WHERE I STOOD."
SINCE THAT TIME, THE INTELLIGENTSIA AND I HAVE PLAYED A SECRET GAME OF CAT AND MOUSE.
BUT I NOW HAVE ONE ADVANTAGE: THANKS TO RAT, I KNOW THEY ARE RUNNING THIS PRISON.

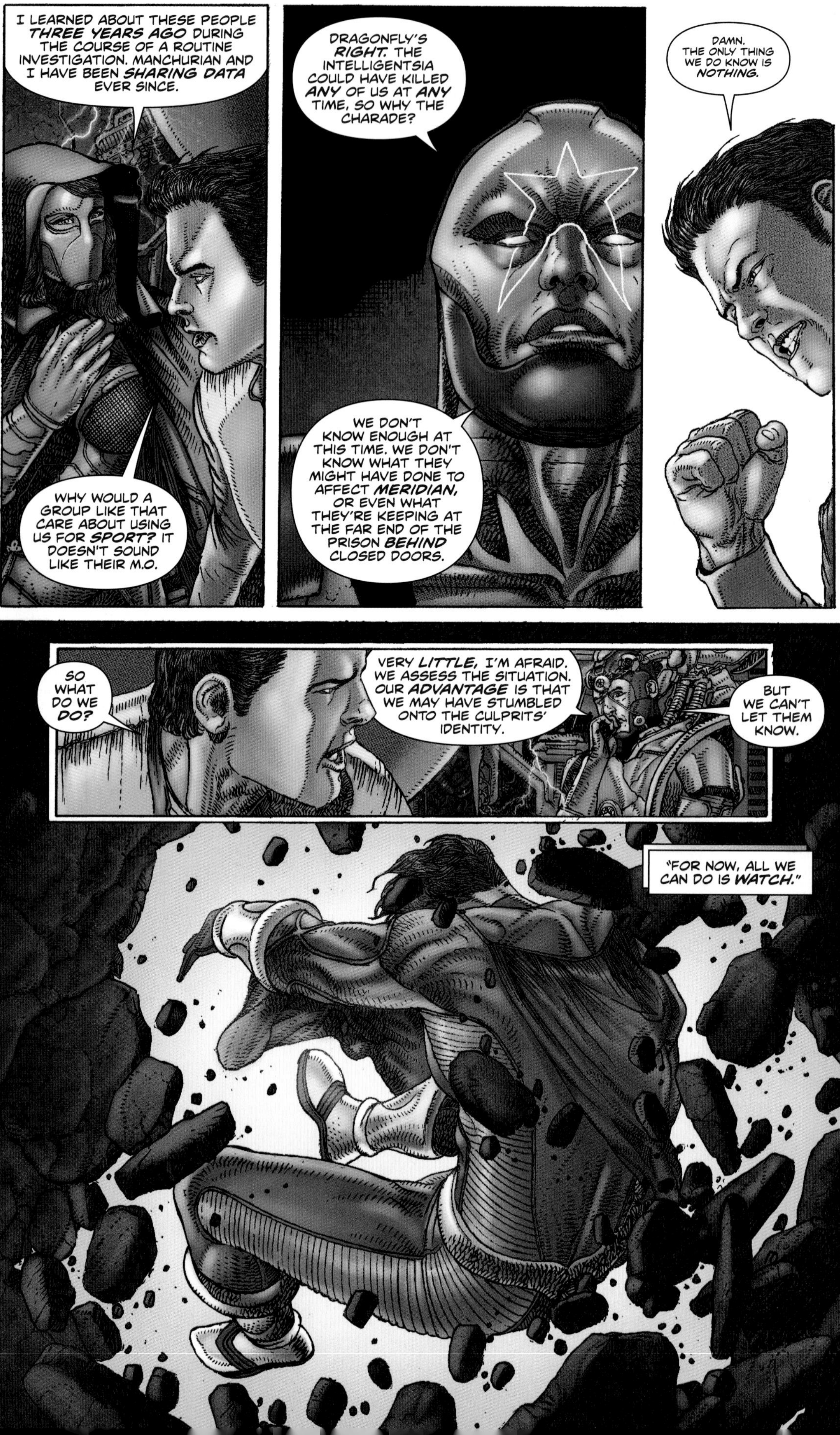
I LEARNED ABOUT THESE PEOPLE THREE YEARS AGO DURING THE COURSE OF A ROUTINE INVESTIGATION. MANCHURIAN AND I HAVE BEEN SHARING DATA EVER SINCE.
WHY WOULD A GROUP LIKE THAT CARE ABOUT USING US FOR SPORT? IT DOESN'T SOUND LIKE THEIR M.O.
DRAGONFLY'S RIGHT. THE INTELLIGENTSIA COULD HAVE KILLED ANY OF US AT ANY TIME, SO WHY THE CHARADE?
WE DON'T KNOW ENOUGH AT THIS TIME. WE DON'T KNOW WHAT THEY MIGHT HAVE DONE TO AFFECT MERIDIAN, OR EVEN WHAT THEY'RE KEEPING AT THE FAR END OF THE PRISON BEHIND CLOSED DOORS.
DAMN. THE ONLY THING WE DO KNOW IS NOTHING.
SO WHAT DO WE DO?
VERY LITTLE, I'M AFRAID. WE ASSESS THE SITUATION. OUR ADVANTAGE IS THAT WE MAY HAVE STUMBLED ONTO THE CULPRITS' IDENTITY.
BUT WE CAN'T LET THEM KNOW.
"FOR NOW, ALL WE CAN DO IS WATCH."

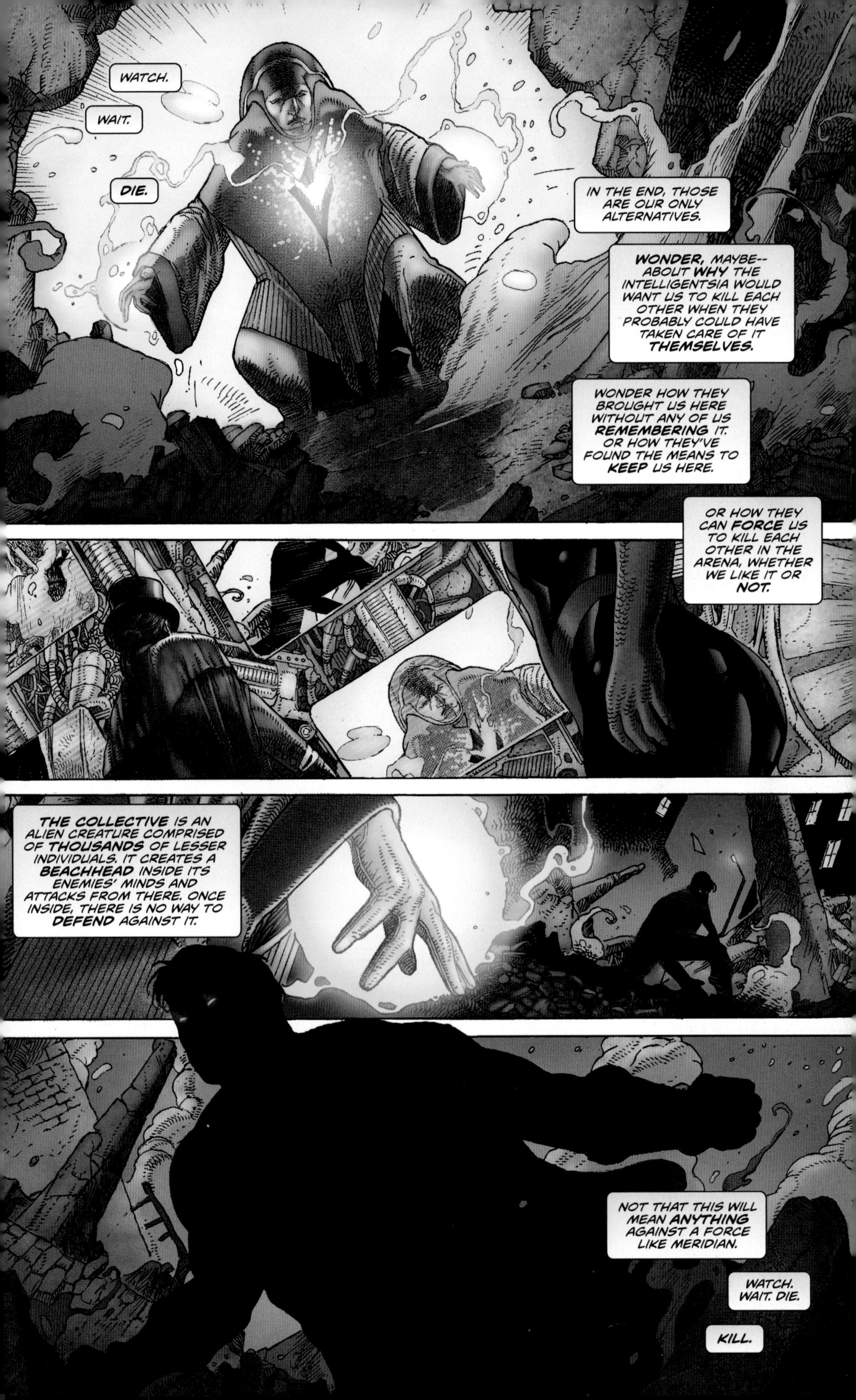
WATCH.
WAIT.
DIE.
IN THE END, THOSE ARE OUR ONLY ALTERNATIVES.
WONDER, MAYBE-- ABOUT WHY THE INTELLIGENTSIA WOULD WANT US TO KILL EACH OTHER WHEN THEY PROBABLY COULD HAVE TAKEN CARE OF IT THEMSELVES.
WONDER HOW THEY BROUGHT US HERE WITHOUT ANY OF US REMEMBERING IT. OR HOW THEY'VE FOUND THE MEANS TO KEEP US HERE.
OR HOW THEY CAN FORCE US TO KILL EACH OTHER IN THE ARENA, WHETHER WE LIKE IT OR NOT.
THE COLLECTIVE IS AN ALIEN CREATURE COMPRISED OF THOUSANDS OF LESSER INDIVIDUALS. IT CREATES A BEACHHEAD INSIDE ITS ENEMIES' MINDS AND ATTACKS FROM THERE. ONCE INSIDE, THERE IS NO WAY TO DEFEND AGAINST IT.
NOT THAT THIS WILL MEAN ANYTHING AGAINST A FORCE LIKE MERIDIAN.
WATCH. WAIT. DIE.
KILL.

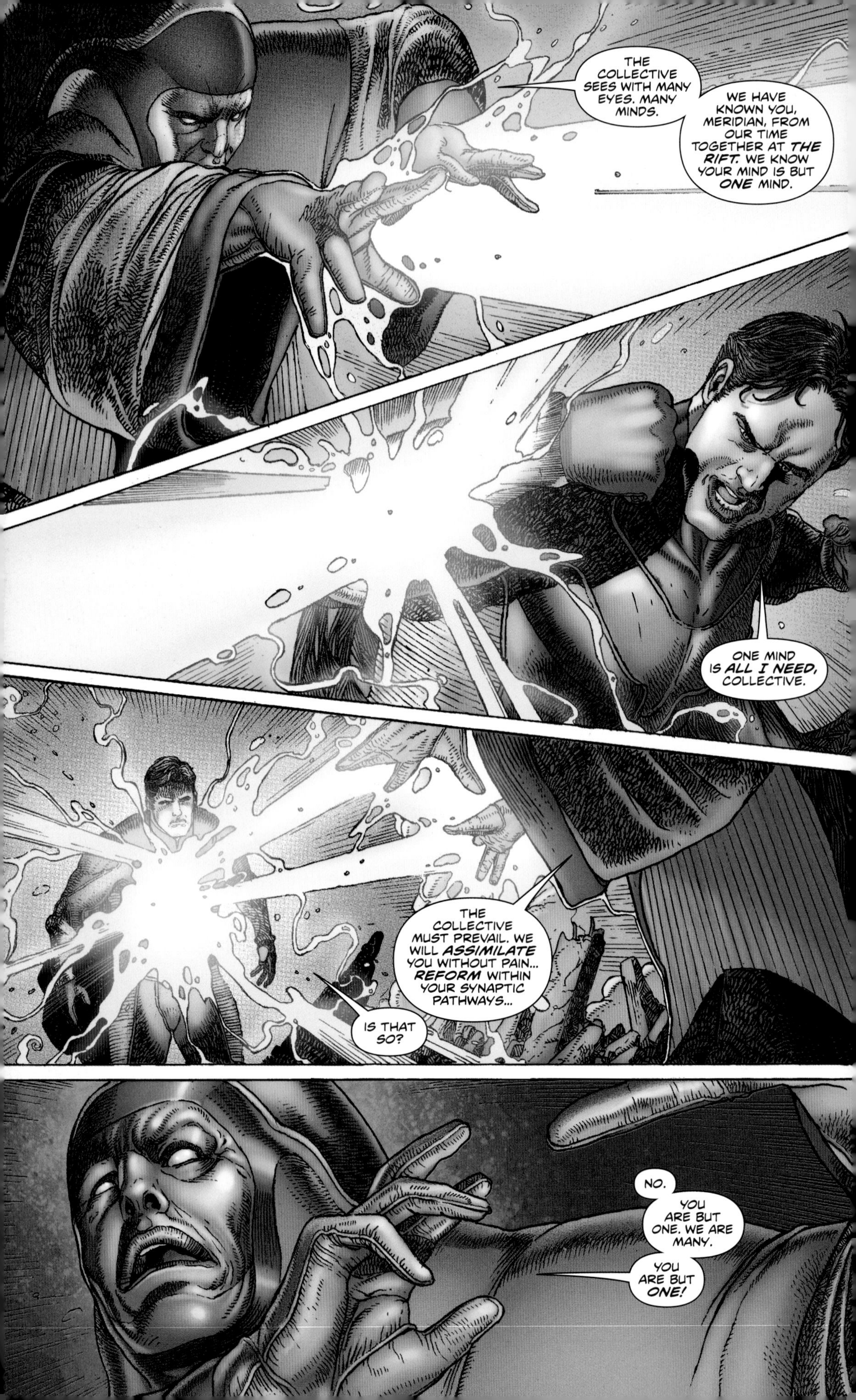
THE COLLECTIVE SEES WITH MANY EYES. MANY MINDS.
WE HAVE KNOWN YOU, MERIDIAN, FROM OUR TIME TOGETHER AT THE RIFT. WE KNOW YOUR MIND IS BUT ONE MIND.
ONE MIND IS ALL I NEED, COLLECTIVE.
THE COLLECTIVE MUST PREVAIL. WE WILL ASSIMILATE YOU WITHOUT PAIN... REFORM WITHIN YOUR SYNAPTIC PATHWAYS...
IS THAT SO?
NO.
YOU ARE BUT ONE. WE ARE MANY.
YOU ARE BUT ONE!

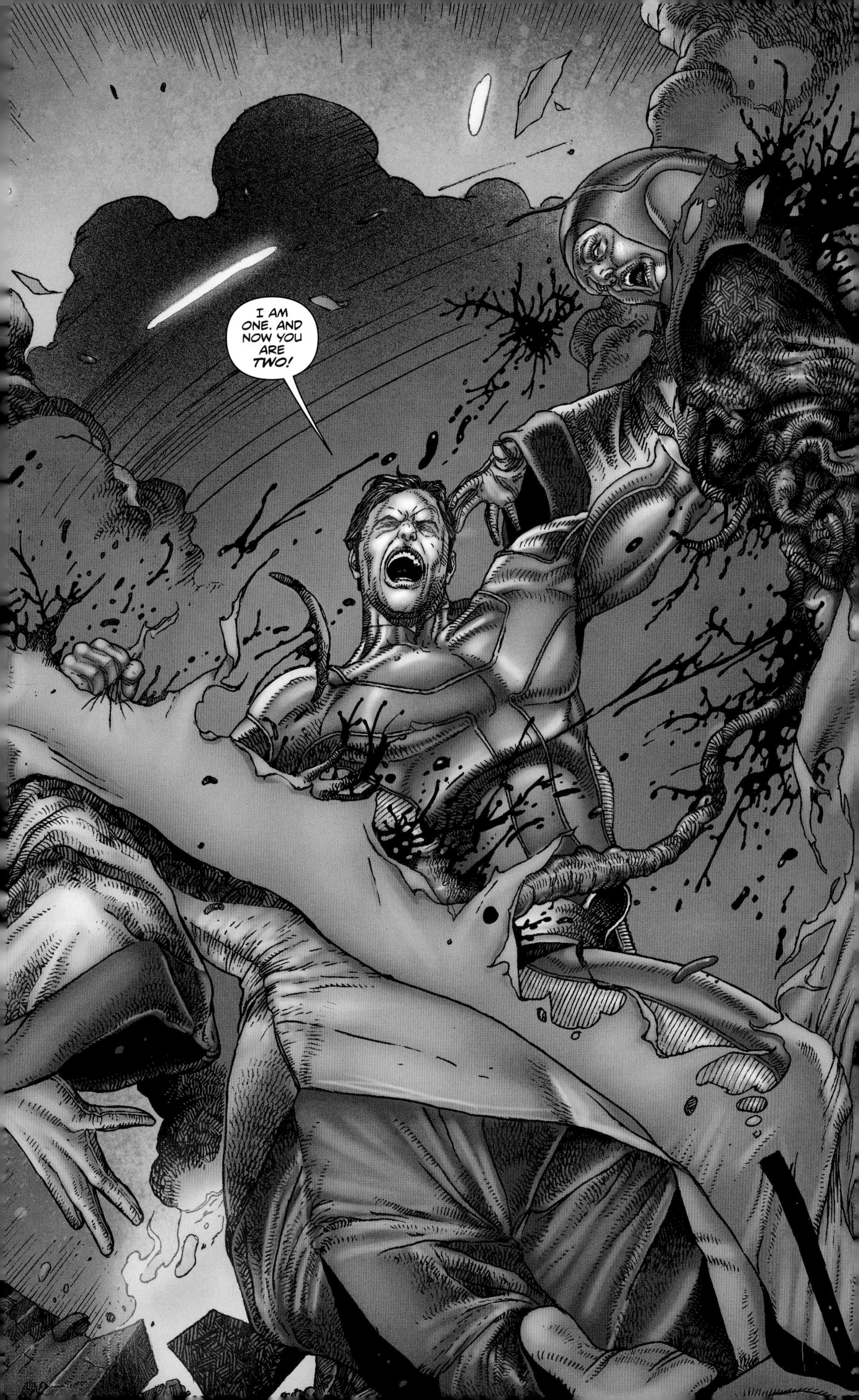
I AM ONE. AND NOW YOU ARE *TWO!*

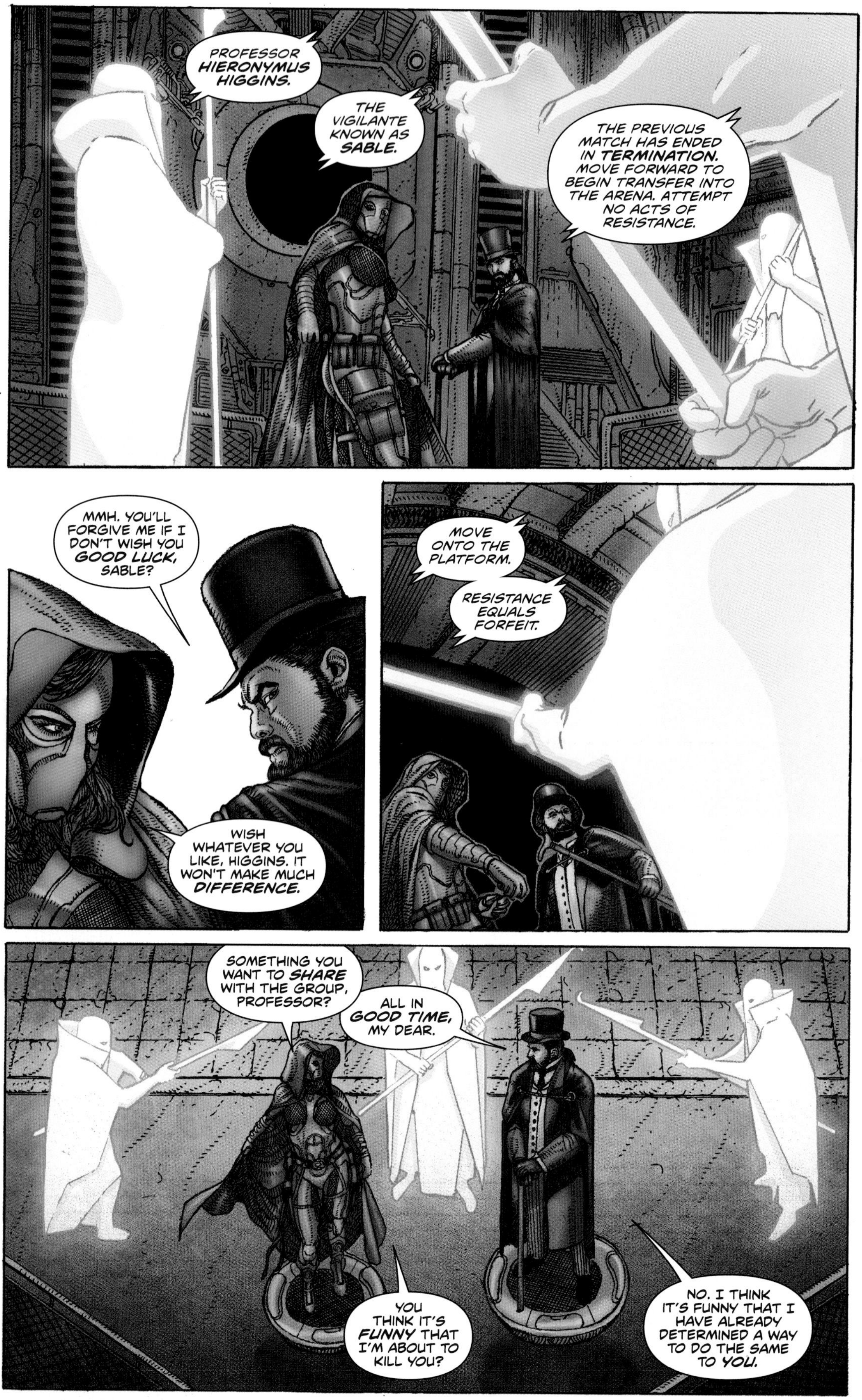
PROFESSOR HIERONYMUS HIGGINS.
THE VIGILANTE KNOWN AS SABLE.
THE PREVIOUS MATCH HAS ENDED IN TERMINATION. MOVE FORWARD TO BEGIN TRANSFER INTO THE ARENA. ATTEMPT NO ACTS OF RESISTANCE.
MMH. YOU'LL FORGIVE ME IF I DON'T WISH YOU GOOD LUCK, SABLE?
WISH WHATEVER YOU LIKE, HIGGINS. IT WON'T MAKE MUCH DIFFERENCE.
MOVE ONTO THE PLATFORM.
RESISTANCE EQUALS FORFEIT.
SOMETHING YOU WANT TO SHARE WITH THE GROUP, PROFESSOR?
ALL IN GOOD TIME, MY DEAR.
YOU THINK IT'S FUNNY THAT I'M ABOUT TO KILL YOU?
NO. I THINK IT'S FUNNY THAT I HAVE ALREADY DETERMINED A WAY TO DO THE SAME TO YOU.

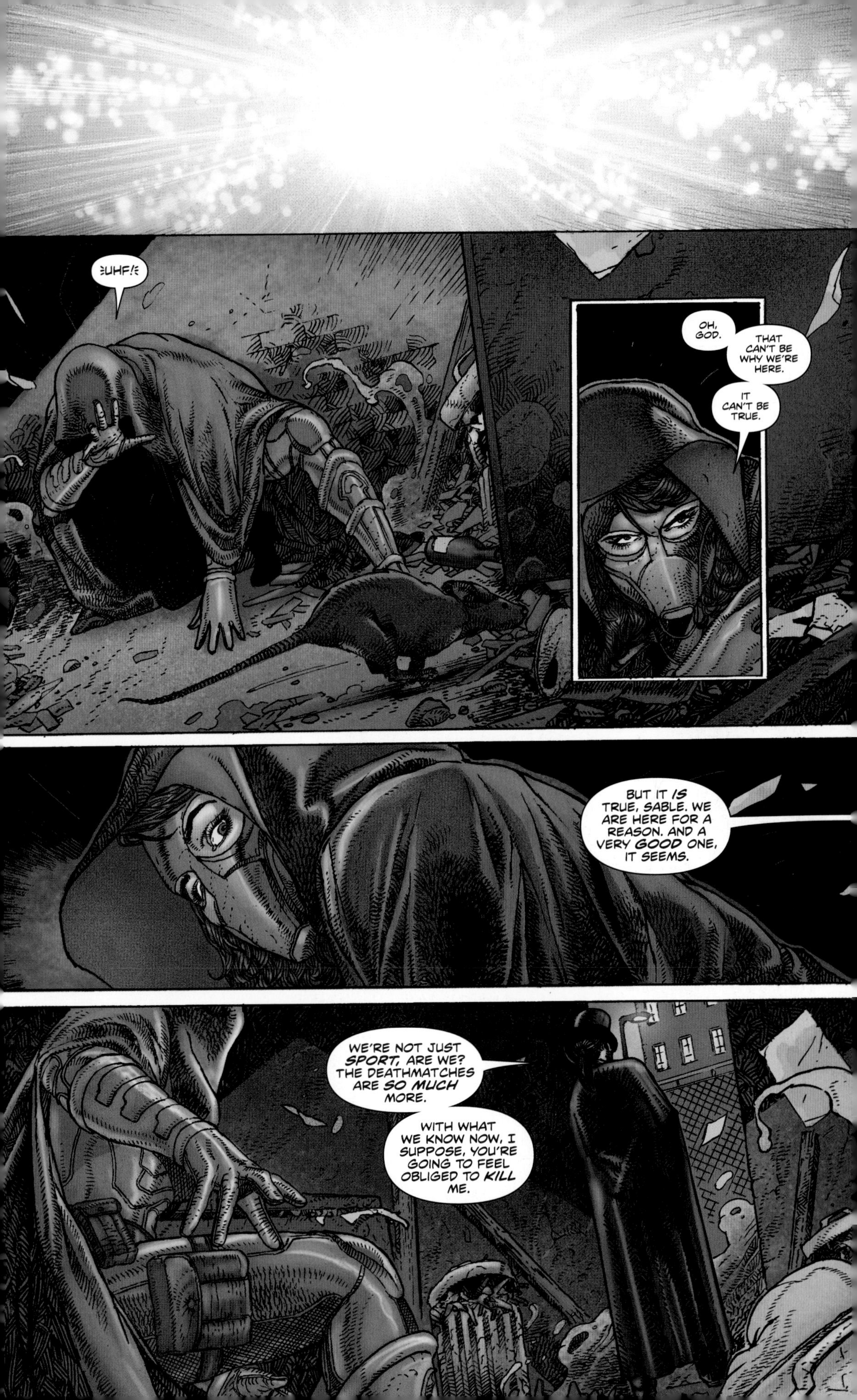

UHF!
OH, GOD.
THAT CAN'T BE WHY WE'RE HERE.
IT CAN'T BE TRUE.
BUT IT IS TRUE, SABLE. WE ARE HERE FOR A REASON. AND A VERY GOOD ONE, IT SEEMS.
WE'RE NOT JUST SPORT, ARE WE? THE DEATHMATCHES ARE SO MUCH MORE.
WITH WHAT WE KNOW NOW, I SUPPOSE, YOU'RE GOING TO FEEL OBLIGED TO KILL ME.

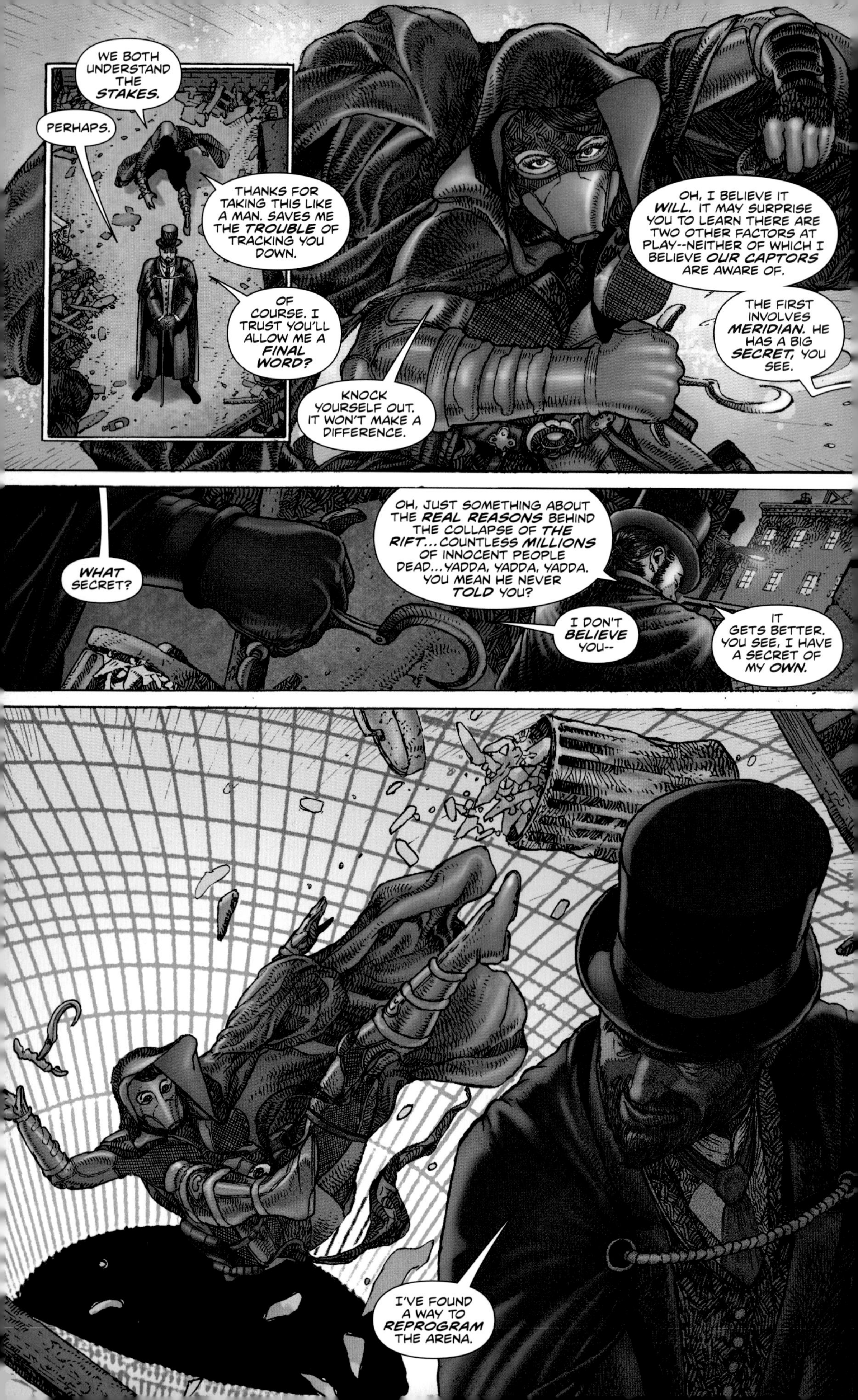
WE BOTH UNDERSTAND THE STAKES.
PERHAPS.
THANKS FOR TAKING THIS LIKE A MAN. SAVES ME THE TROUBLE OF TRACKING YOU DOWN.
OF COURSE. I TRUST YOU'LL ALLOW ME A FINAL WORD?
KNOCK YOURSELF OUT. IT WON'T MAKE A DIFFERENCE.
OH, I BELIEVE IT WILL. IT MAY SURPRISE YOU TO LEARN THERE ARE TWO OTHER FACTORS AT PLAY--NEITHER OF WHICH I BELIEVE OUR CAPTORS ARE AWARE OF.
THE FIRST INVOLVES MERIDIAN. HE HAS A BIG SECRET, YOU SEE.
WHAT SECRET?
OH, JUST SOMETHING ABOUT THE REAL REASONS BEHIND THE COLLAPSE OF THE RIFT... COUNTLESS MILLIONS OF INNOCENT PEOPLE DEAD... YADDA, YADDA, YADDA. YOU MEAN HE NEVER TOLD YOU?
I DON'T BELIEVE YOU--
IT GETS BETTER. YOU SEE, I HAVE A SECRET OF MY OWN.
I'VE FOUND A WAY TO REPROGRAM THE ARENA.

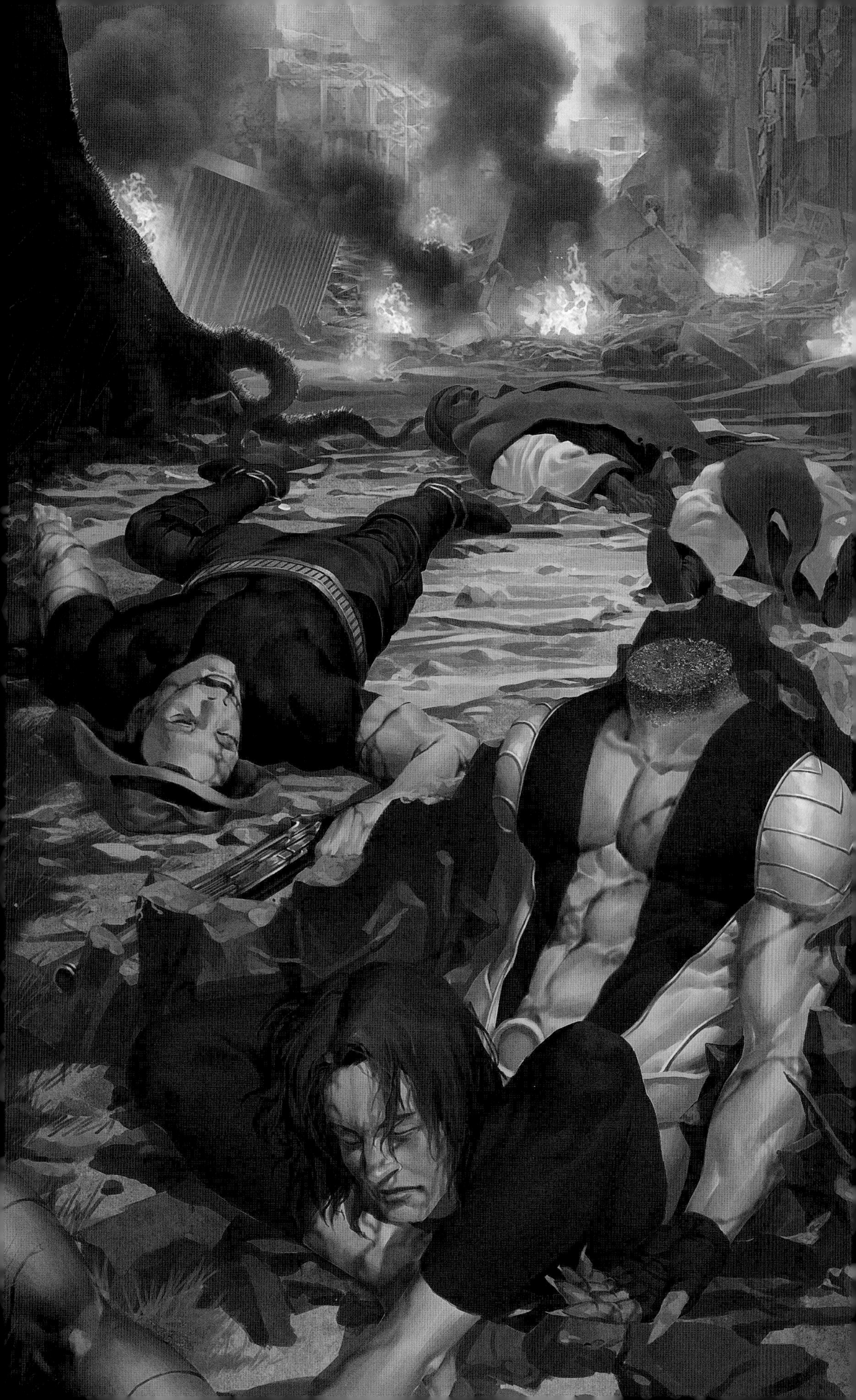

CHAPTER **FOUR**

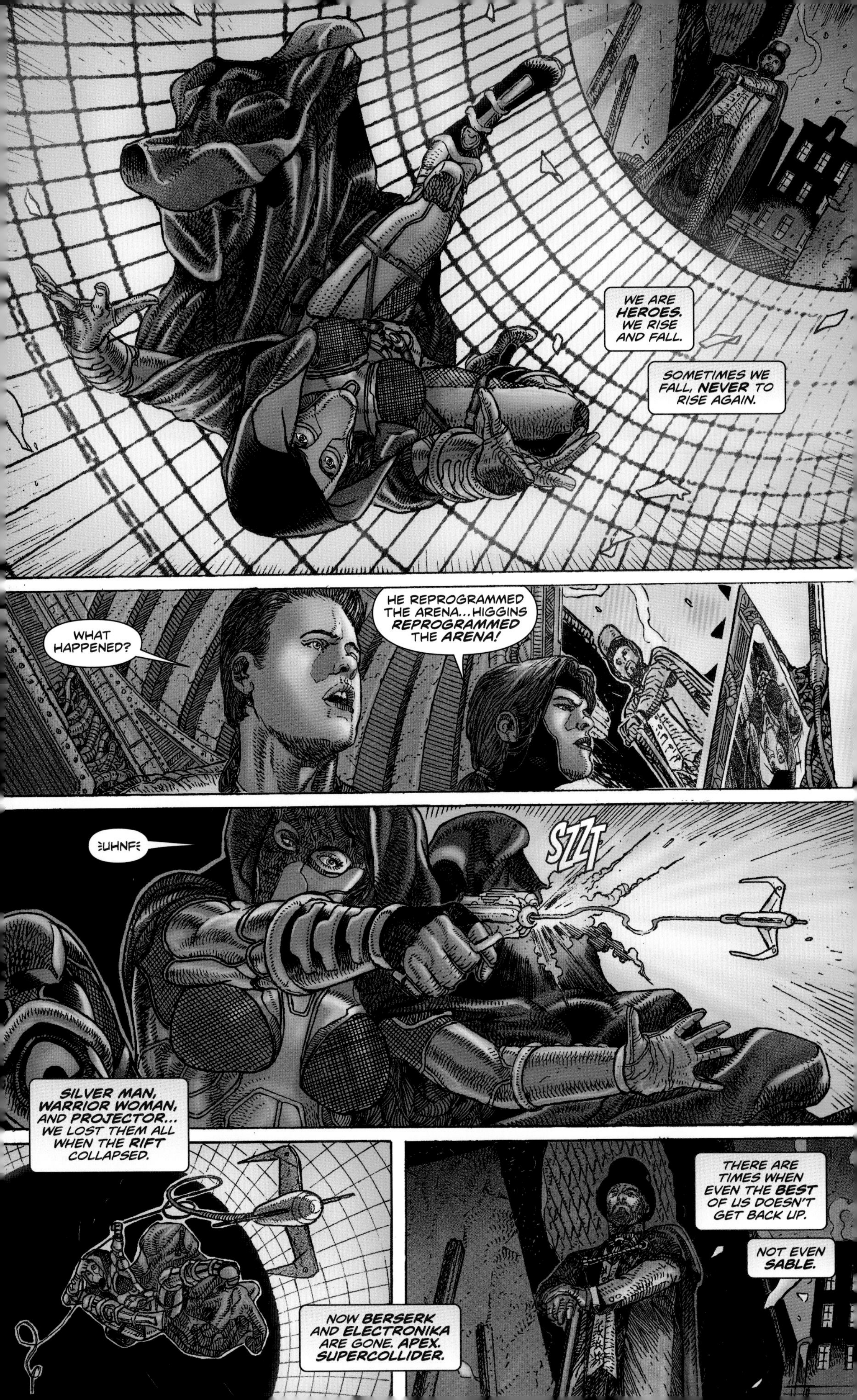
WE ARE HEROES. WE RISE AND FALL.
SOMETIMES WE FALL, NEVER TO RISE AGAIN.
WHAT HAPPENED?
HE REPROGRAMMED THE ARENA... HIGGINS REPROGRAMMED THE ARENA!
UHNF
SZZT
SILVER MAN, WARRIOR WOMAN, AND PROJECTOR... WE LOST THEM ALL WHEN THE RIFT COLLAPSED.
NOW BERSERK AND ELECTRONIKA ARE GONE. APEX. SUPERCOLLIDER.
THERE ARE TIMES WHEN EVEN THE BEST OF US DOESN'T GET BACK UP.
NOT EVEN SABLE.

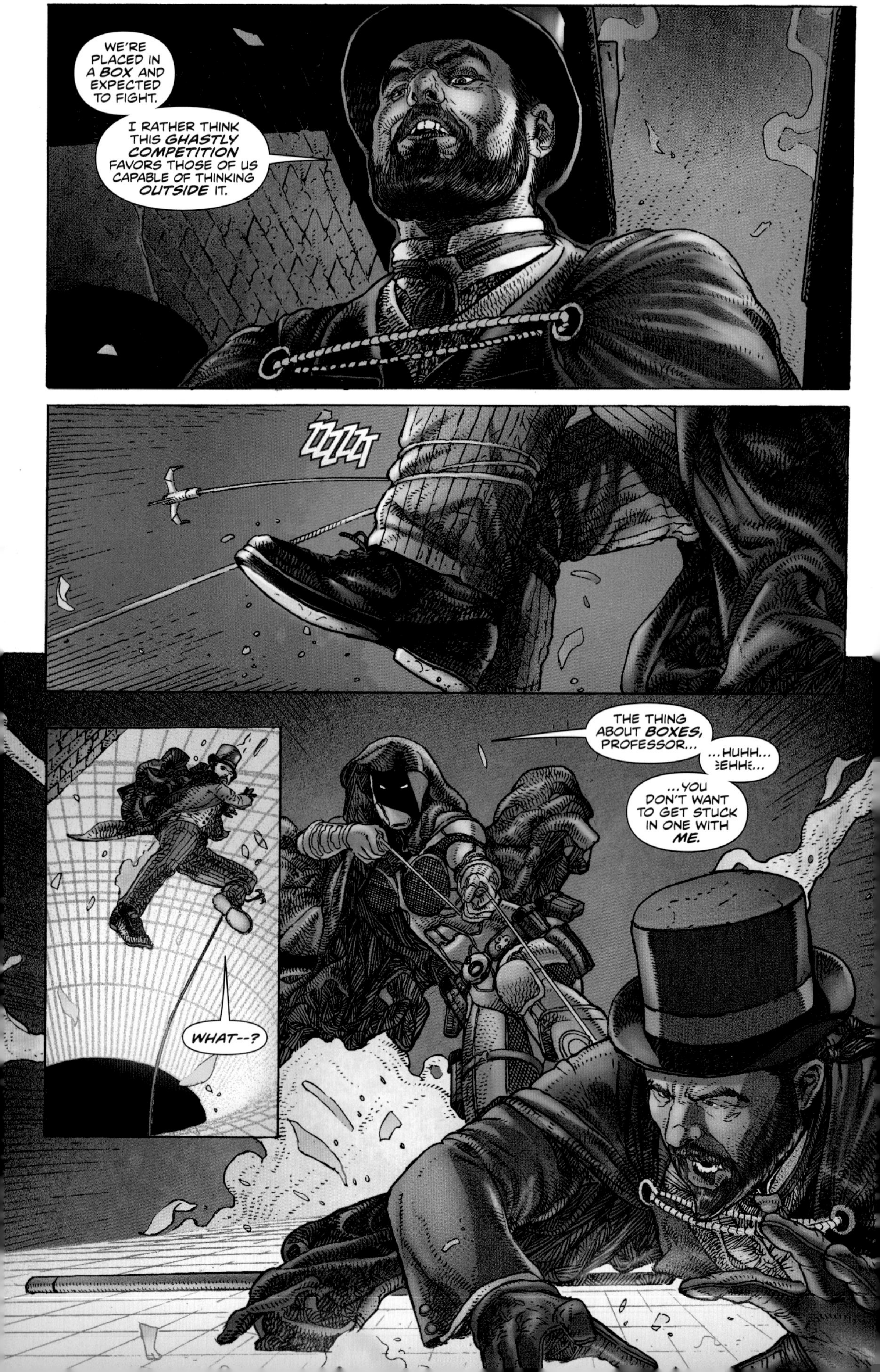
WE'RE PLACED IN A BOX AND EXPECTED TO FIGHT.
I RATHER THINK THIS GHASTLY COMPETITION FAVORS THOSE OF US CAPABLE OF THINKING OUTSIDE IT.
ZZZZT
WHAT--?
THE THING ABOUT BOXES, PROFESSOR...
...HUHH... EHHH...
...YOU DON'T WANT TO GET STUCK IN ONE WITH ME.

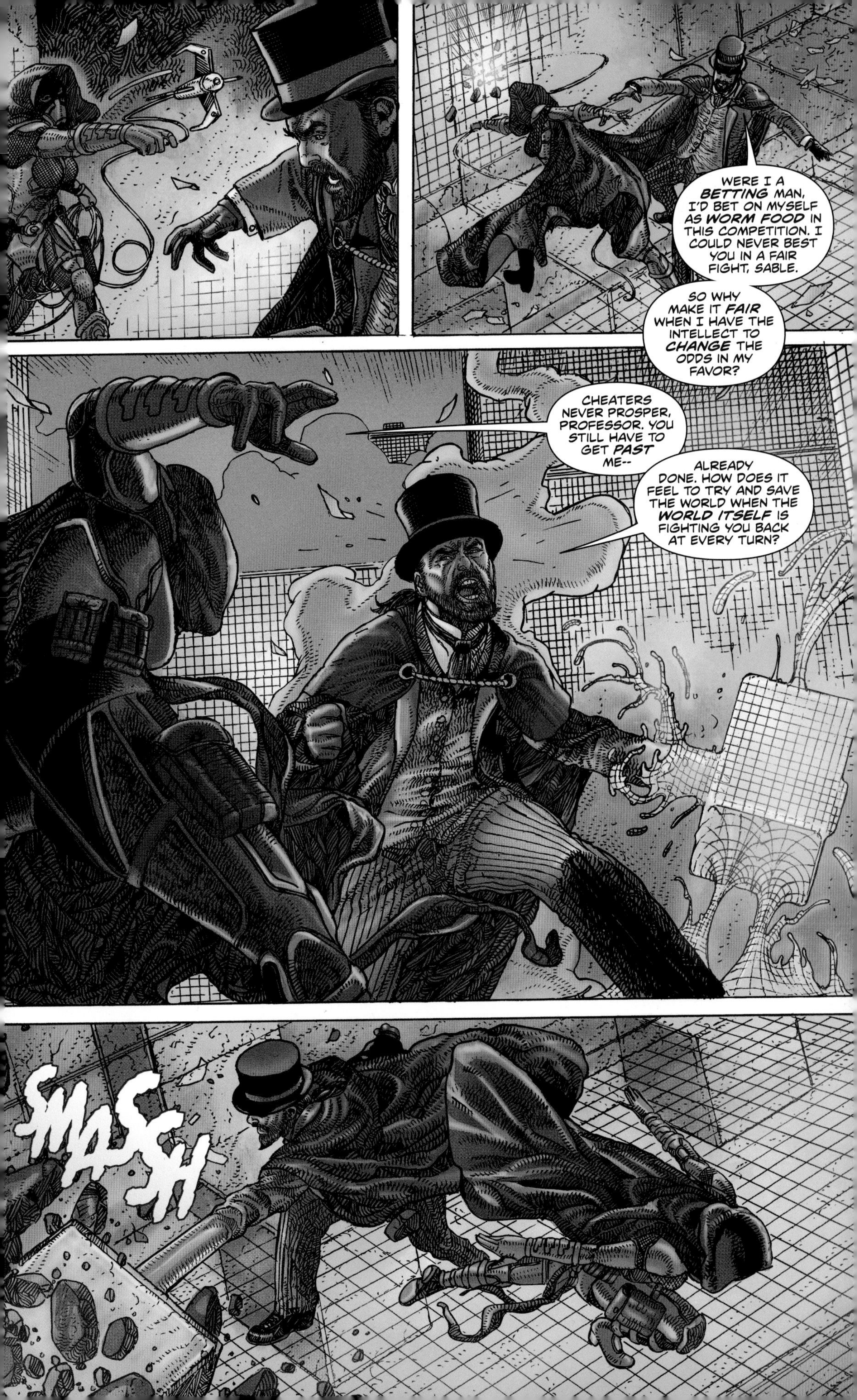
WERE I A BETTING MAN, I'D BET ON MYSELF AS WORM FOOD IN THIS COMPETITION. I COULD NEVER BEST YOU IN A FAIR FIGHT, SABLE.
SO WHY MAKE IT FAIR WHEN I HAVE THE INTELLECT TO CHANGE THE ODDS IN MY FAVOR?
CHEATERS NEVER PROSPER, PROFESSOR. YOU STILL HAVE TO GET PAST ME--
ALREADY DONE. HOW DOES IT FEEL TO TRY AND SAVE THE WORLD WHEN THE WORLD ITSELF IS FIGHTING YOU BACK AT EVERY TURN?
SMASH

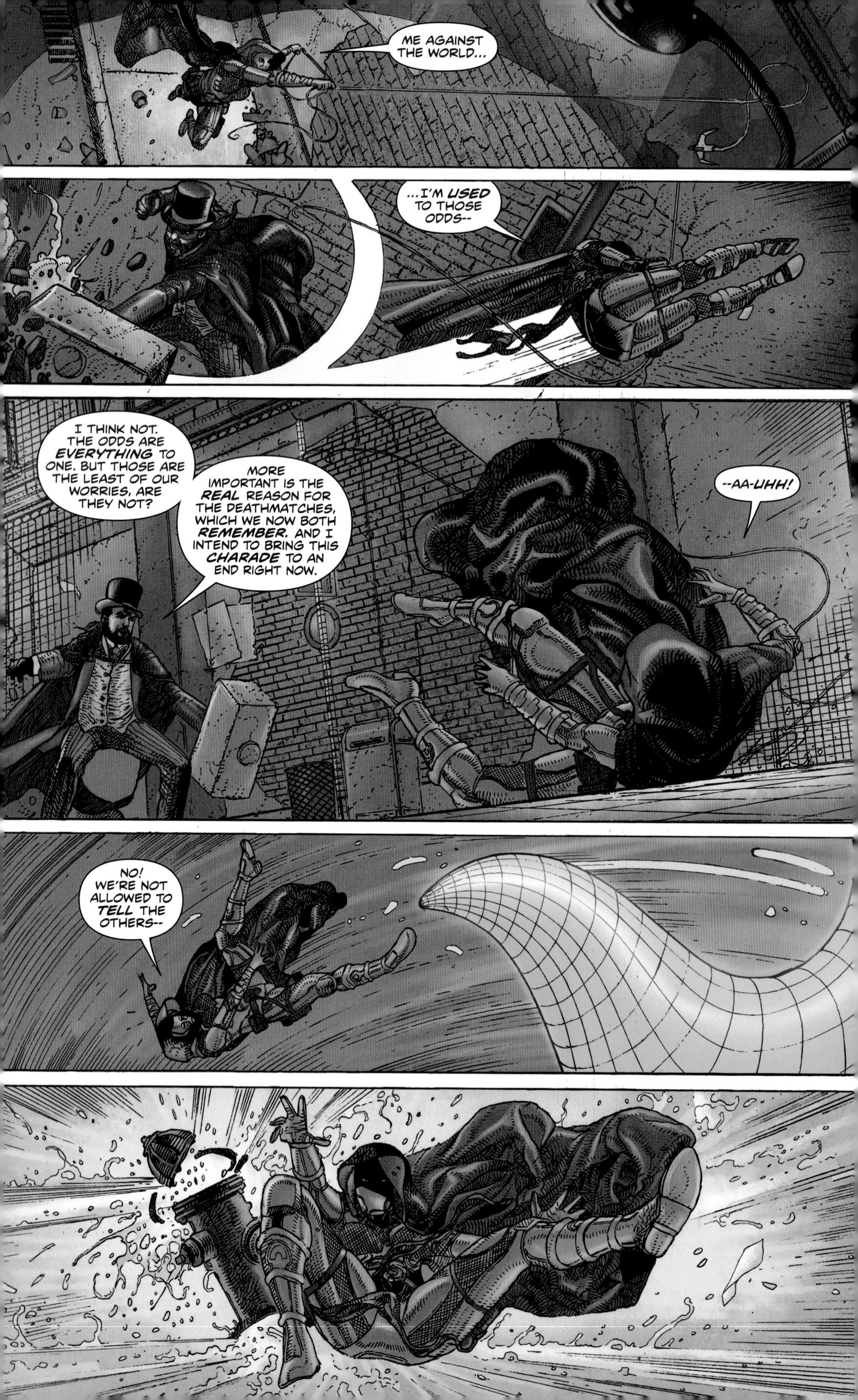
ME AGAINST THE WORLD...
...I'M USED TO THOSE ODDS--
I THINK NOT. THE ODDS ARE EVERYTHING TO ONE. BUT THOSE ARE THE LEAST OF OUR WORRIES, ARE THEY NOT?
MORE IMPORTANT IS THE REAL REASON FOR THE DEATHMATCHES, WHICH WE NOW BOTH REMEMBER. AND I INTEND TO BRING THIS CHARADE TO AN END RIGHT NOW.
--AA-UHH!
NO! WE'RE NOT ALLOWED TO TELL THE OTHERS--

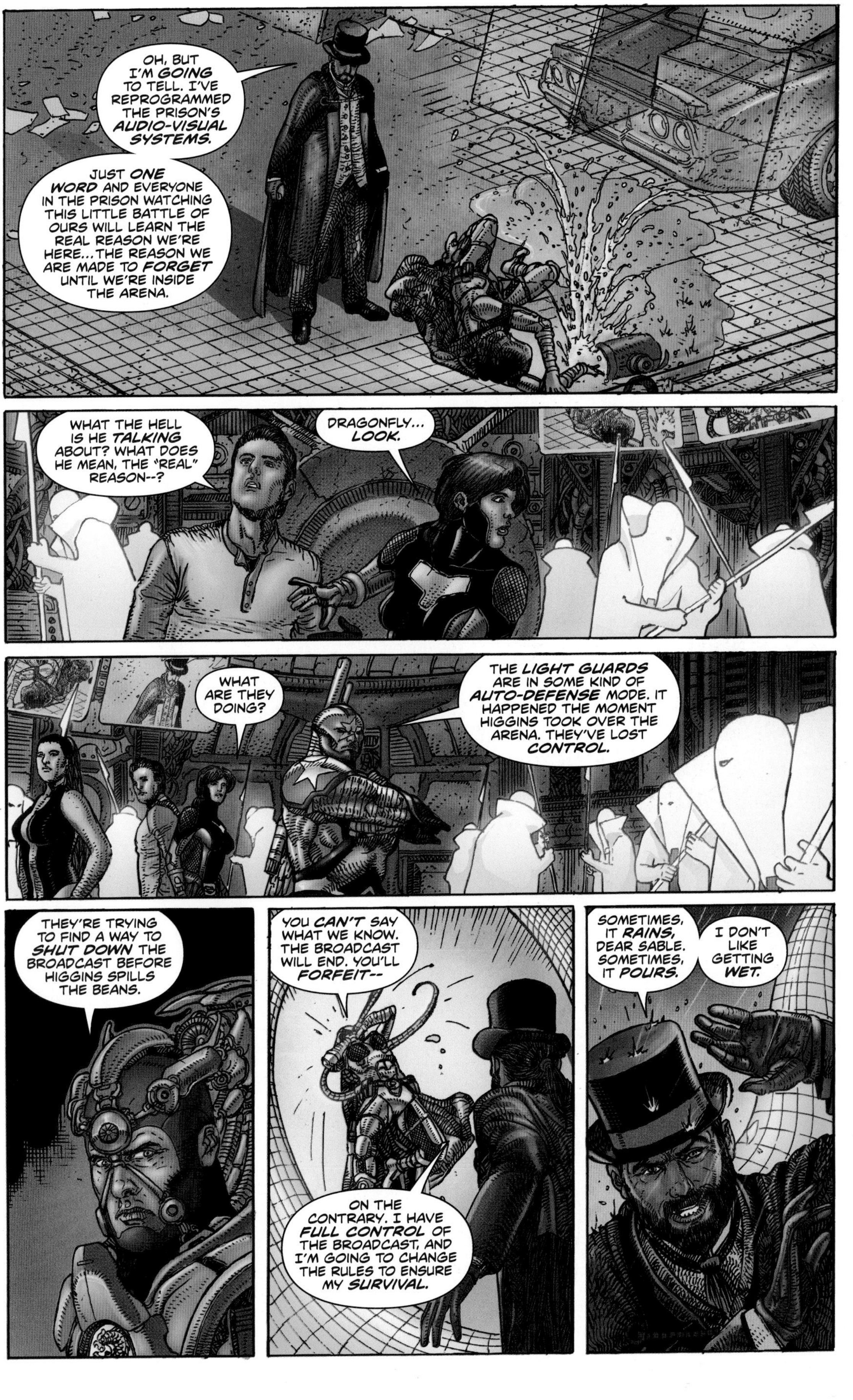
OH, BUT I'M GOING TO TELL. I'VE REPROGRAMMED THE PRISON'S AUDIO-VISUAL SYSTEMS.
JUST ONE WORD AND EVERYONE IN THE PRISON WATCHING THIS LITTLE BATTLE OF OURS WILL LEARN THE REAL REASON WE'RE HERE... THE REASON WE ARE MADE TO FORGET UNTIL WE'RE INSIDE THE ARENA.
WHAT THE HELL IS HE TALKING ABOUT? WHAT DOES HE MEAN, THE "REAL" REASON--?
DRAGONFLY... LOOK.
WHAT ARE THEY DOING?
THE LIGHT GUARDS ARE IN SOME KIND OF AUTO-DEFENSE MODE. IT HAPPENED THE MOMENT HIGGINS TOOK OVER THE ARENA. THEY'VE LOST CONTROL.
THEY'RE TRYING TO FIND A WAY TO SHUT DOWN THE BROADCAST BEFORE HIGGINS SPILLS THE BEANS.
YOU CAN'T SAY WHAT WE KNOW. THE BROADCAST WILL END. YOU'LL FORFEIT--
ON THE CONTRARY. I HAVE FULL CONTROL OF THE BROADCAST, AND I'M GOING TO CHANGE THE RULES TO ENSURE MY SURVIVAL.
SOMETIMES, IT RAINS, DEAR SABLE. SOMETIMES, IT POURS.
I DON'T LIKE GETTING WET.

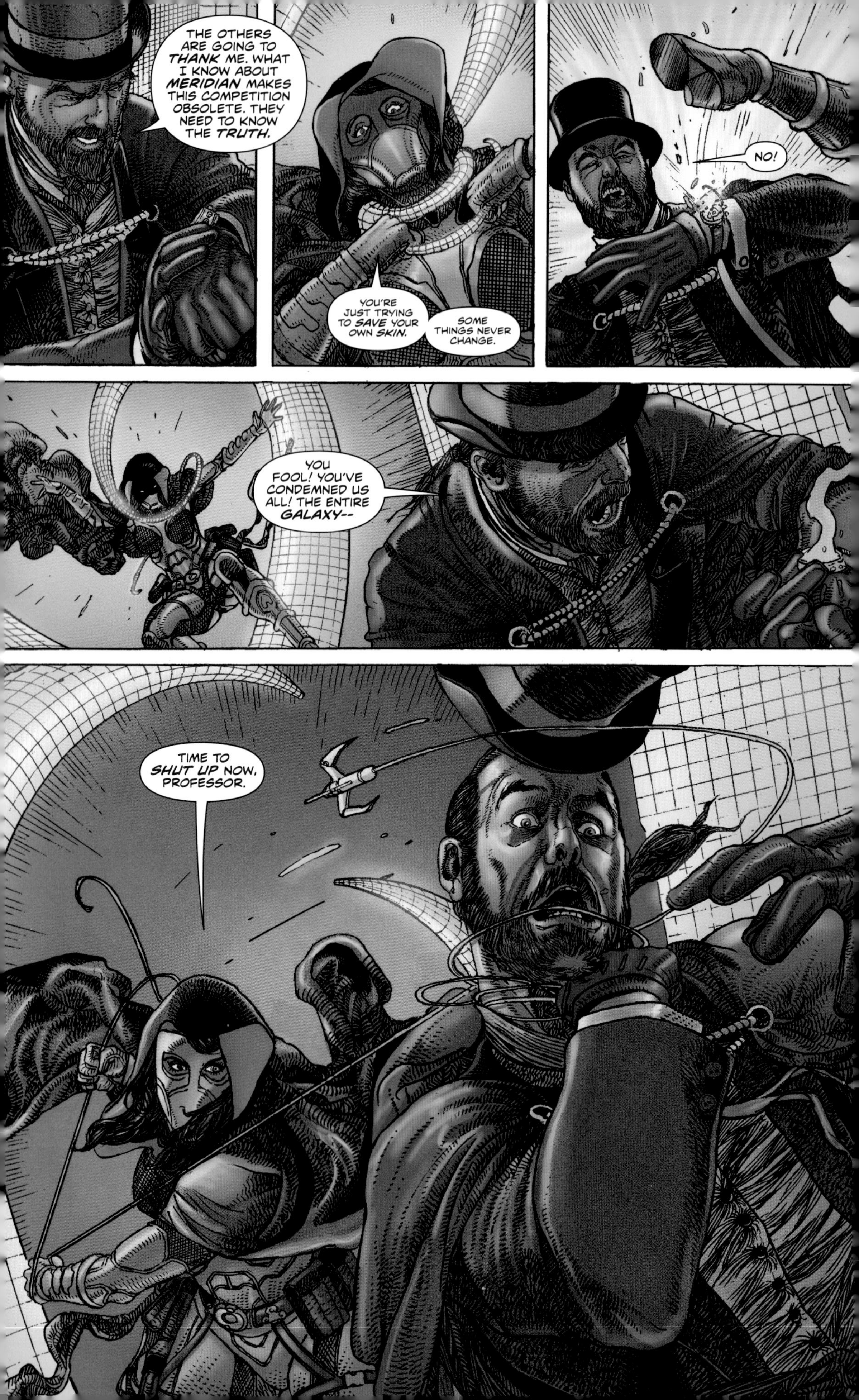
THE OTHERS ARE GOING TO THANK ME. WHAT I KNOW ABOUT MERIDIAN MAKES THIS COMPETITION OBSOLETE. THEY NEED TO KNOW THE TRUTH.
YOU'RE JUST TRYING TO SAVE YOUR OWN SKIN.
SOME THINGS NEVER CHANGE.
NO!
YOU FOOL! YOU'VE CONDEMNED US ALL! THE ENTIRE GALAXY--
TIME TO SHUT UP NOW, PROFESSOR.

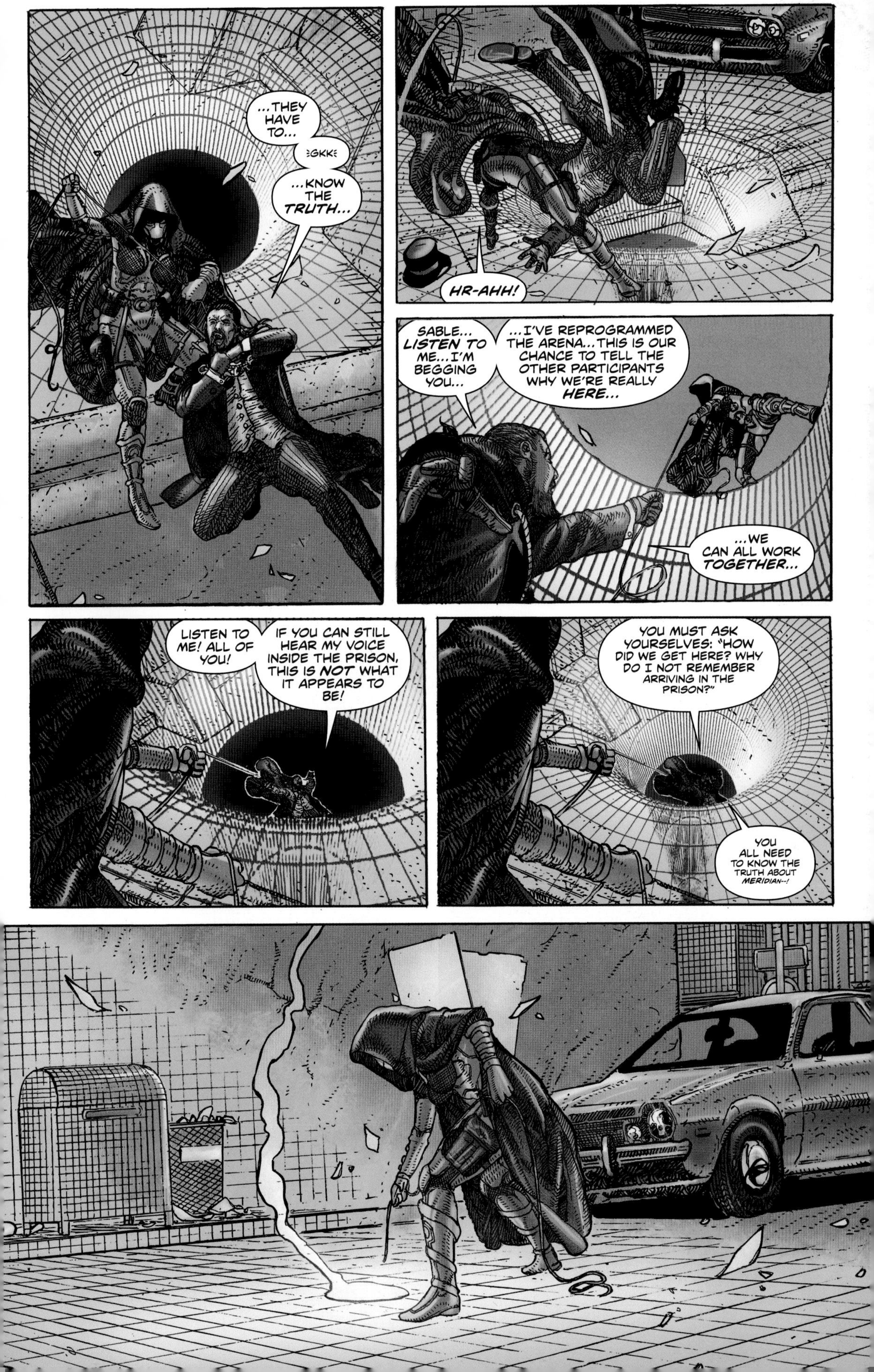
...THEY HAVE TO...
GKK
...KNOW THE TRUTH...
HR-AHH!
SABLE... LISTEN TO ME...I'M BEGGING YOU...
...I'VE REPROGRAMMED THE ARENA...THIS IS OUR CHANCE TO TELL THE OTHER PARTICIPANTS WHY WE'RE REALLY HERE...
...WE CAN ALL WORK TOGETHER...
LISTEN TO ME! ALL OF YOU!
IF YOU CAN STILL HEAR MY VOICE INSIDE THE PRISON, THIS IS NOT WHAT IT APPEARS TO BE!
YOU MUST ASK YOURSELVES: "HOW DID WE GET HERE? WHY DO I NOT REMEMBER ARRIVING IN THE PRISON?"
YOU ALL NEED TO KNOW THE TRUTH ABOUT MERIDIAN--!

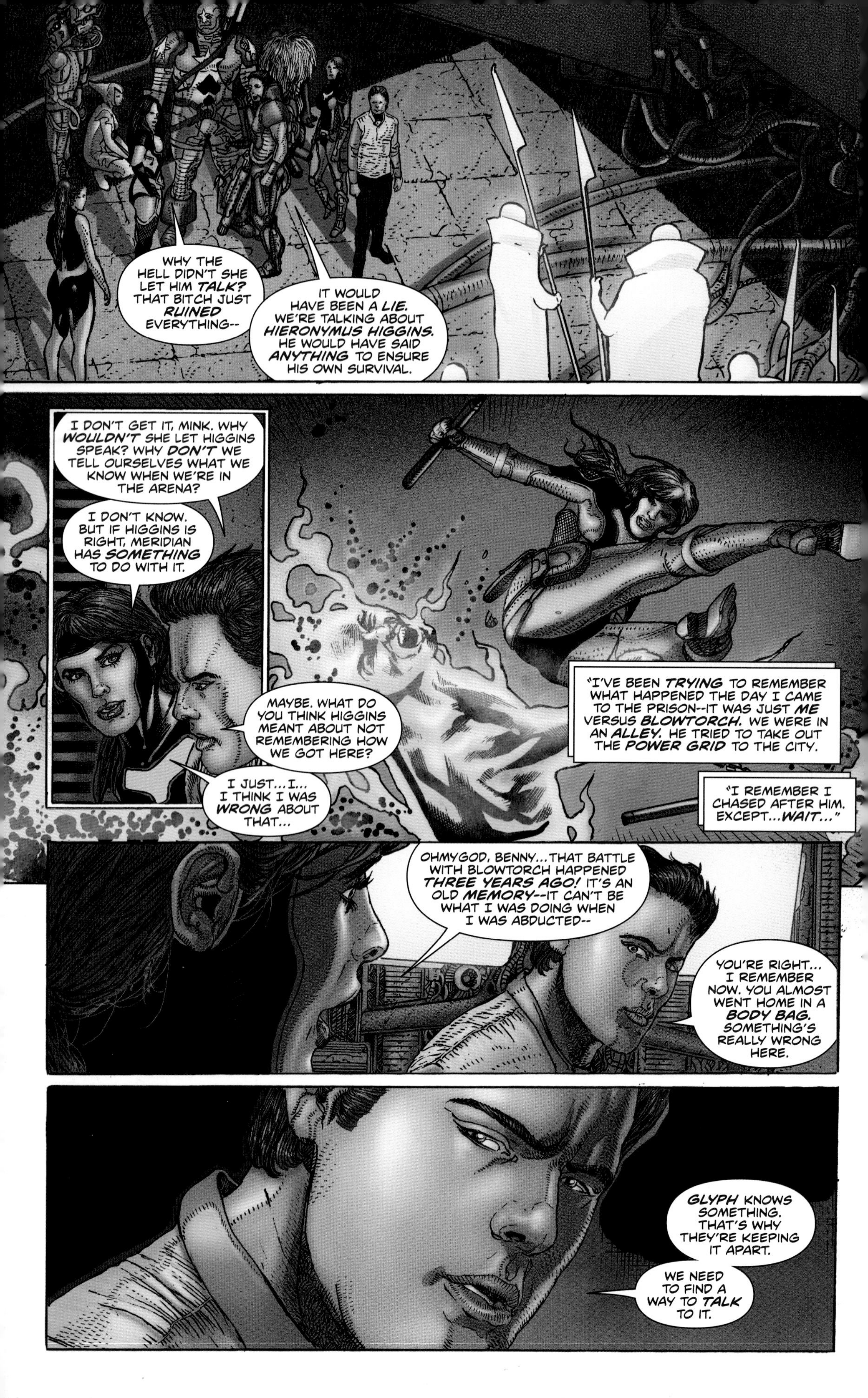
WHY THE HELL DIDN'T SHE LET HIM TALK? THAT BITCH JUST RUINED EVERYTHING--
IT WOULD HAVE BEEN A LIE. WE'RE TALKING ABOUT HIERONYMUS HIGGINS. HE WOULD HAVE SAID ANYTHING TO ENSURE HIS OWN SURVIVAL.
I DON'T GET IT, MINK. WHY WOULDN'T SHE LET HIGGINS SPEAK? WHY DON'T WE TELL OURSELVES WHAT WE KNOW WHEN WE'RE IN THE ARENA?
I DON'T KNOW. BUT IF HIGGINS IS RIGHT, MERIDIAN HAS SOMETHING TO DO WITH IT.
MAYBE. WHAT DO YOU THINK HIGGINS MEANT ABOUT NOT REMEMBERING HOW WE GOT HERE?
I JUST... I... I THINK I WAS WRONG ABOUT THAT...
"I'VE BEEN TRYING TO REMEMBER WHAT HAPPENED THE DAY I CAME TO THE PRISON--IT WAS JUST ME VERSUS BLOWTORCH. WE WERE IN AN ALLEY. HE TRIED TO TAKE OUT THE POWER GRID TO THE CITY.
"I REMEMBER I CHASED AFTER HIM. EXCEPT...WAIT..."
OHMYGOD, BENNY...THAT BATTLE WITH BLOWTORCH HAPPENED THREE YEARS AGO! IT'S AN OLD MEMORY--IT CAN'T BE WHAT I WAS DOING WHEN I WAS ABDUCTED--
YOU'RE RIGHT... I REMEMBER NOW. YOU ALMOST WENT HOME IN A BODY BAG. SOMETHING'S REALLY WRONG HERE.
GLYPH KNOWS SOMETHING. THAT'S WHY THEY'RE KEEPING IT APART.
WE NEED TO FIND A WAY TO TALK TO IT.

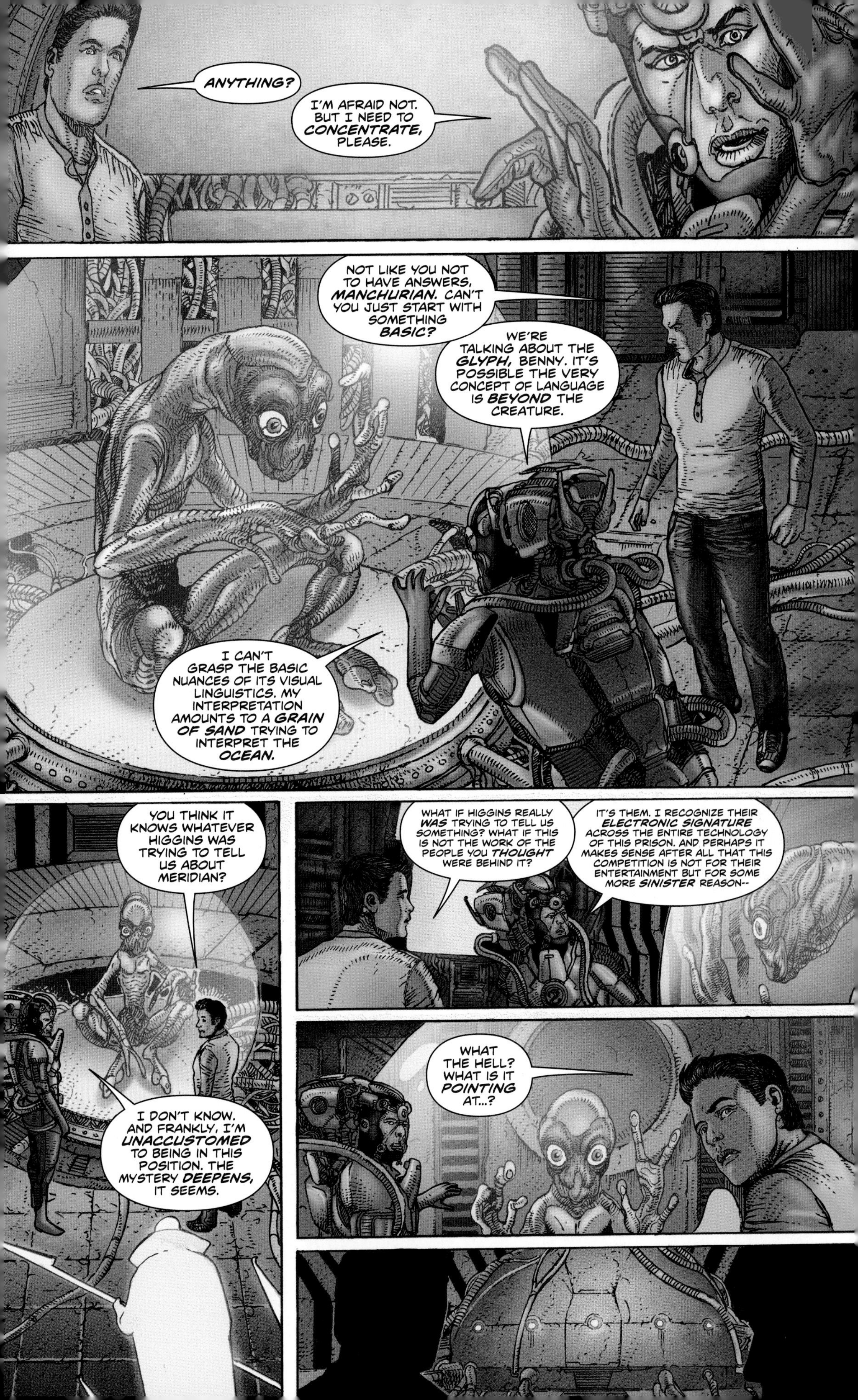

ANYTHING?
I'M AFRAID NOT. BUT I NEED TO CONCENTRATE, PLEASE.
NOT LIKE YOU NOT TO HAVE ANSWERS, MANCHURIAN. CAN'T YOU JUST START WITH SOMETHING BASIC?
WE'RE TALKING ABOUT THE GLYPH, BENNY. IT'S POSSIBLE THE VERY CONCEPT OF LANGUAGE IS BEYOND THE CREATURE.
I CAN'T GRASP THE BASIC NUANCES OF ITS VISUAL LINGUISTICS. MY INTERPRETATION AMOUNTS TO A GRAIN OF SAND TRYING TO INTERPRET THE OCEAN.
YOU THINK IT KNOWS WHATEVER HIGGINS WAS TRYING TO TELL US ABOUT MERIDIAN?
I DON'T KNOW. AND FRANKLY, I'M UNACCUSTOMED TO BEING IN THIS POSITION. THE MYSTERY DEEPENS, IT SEEMS.
WHAT IF HIGGINS REALLY WAS TRYING TO TELL US SOMETHING? WHAT IF THIS IS NOT THE WORK OF THE PEOPLE YOU THOUGHT WERE BEHIND IT?
IT'S THEM. I RECOGNIZE THEIR ELECTRONIC SIGNATURE ACROSS THE ENTIRE TECHNOLOGY OF THIS PRISON. AND PERHAPS IT MAKES SENSE AFTER ALL THAT THIS COMPETITION IS NOT FOR THEIR ENTERTAINMENT BUT FOR SOME MORE SINISTER REASON--
WHAT THE HELL? WHAT IS IT POINTING AT...?

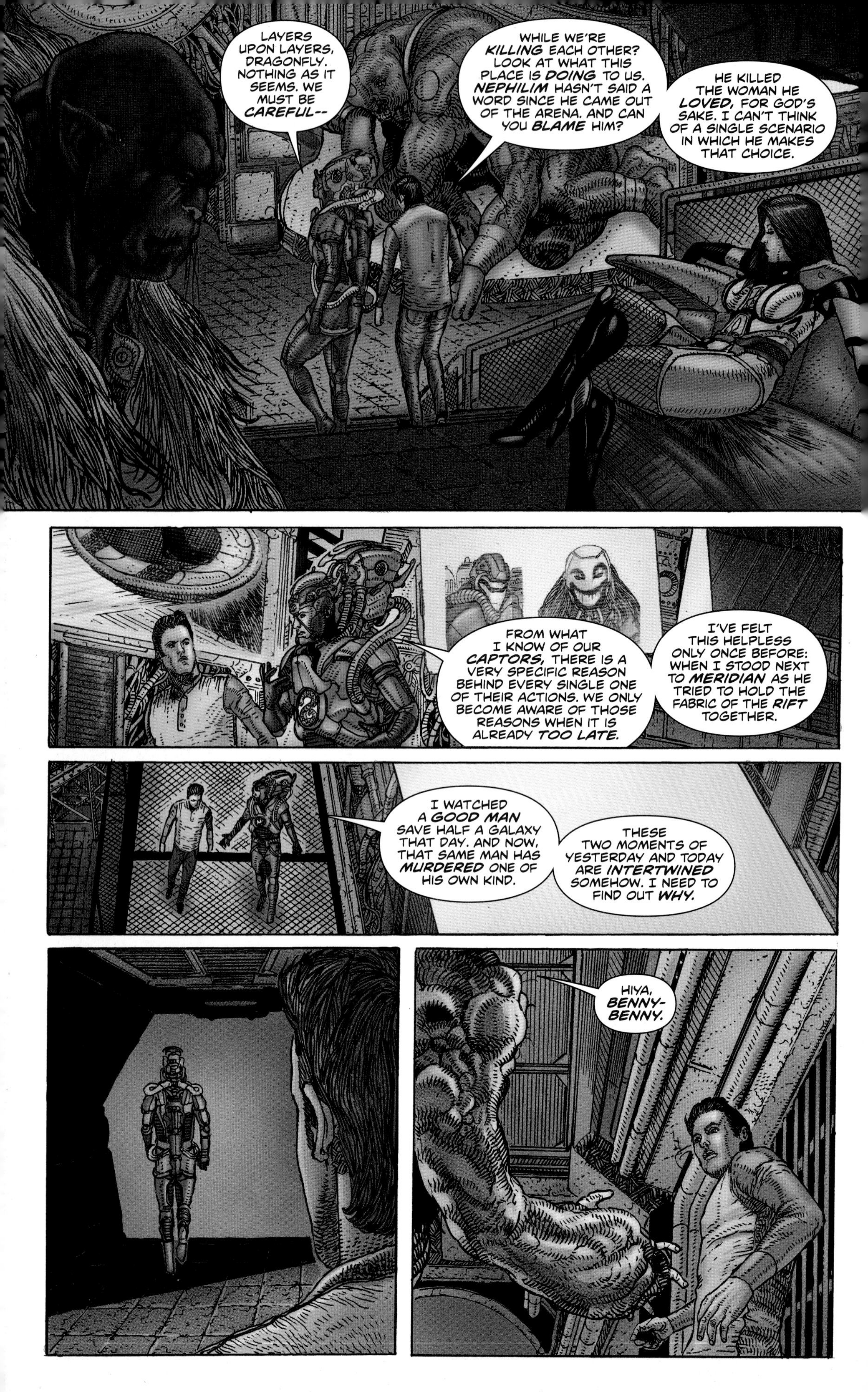
LAYERS UPON LAYERS, DRAGONFLY. NOTHING AS IT SEEMS. WE MUST BE CAREFUL--
WHILE WE'RE KILLING EACH OTHER? LOOK AT WHAT THIS PLACE IS DOING TO US. NEPHILIM HASN'T SAID A WORD SINCE HE CAME OUT OF THE ARENA. AND CAN YOU BLAME HIM?
HE KILLED THE WOMAN HE LOVED, FOR GOD'S SAKE. I CAN'T THINK OF A SINGLE SCENARIO IN WHICH HE MAKES THAT CHOICE.
FROM WHAT I KNOW OF OUR CAPTORS, THERE IS A VERY SPECIFIC REASON BEHIND EVERY SINGLE ONE OF THEIR ACTIONS. WE ONLY BECOME AWARE OF THOSE REASONS WHEN IT IS ALREADY TOO LATE.
I'VE FELT THIS HELPLESS ONLY ONCE BEFORE: WHEN I STOOD NEXT TO MERIDIAN AS HE TRIED TO HOLD THE FABRIC OF THE RIFT TOGETHER.
I WATCHED A GOOD MAN SAVE HALF A GALAXY THAT DAY. AND NOW, THAT SAME MAN HAS MURDERED ONE OF HIS OWN KIND.
THESE TWO MOMENTS OF YESTERDAY AND TODAY ARE INTERTWINED SOMEHOW. I NEED TO FIND OUT WHY.
HIYA, BENNY-BENNY.

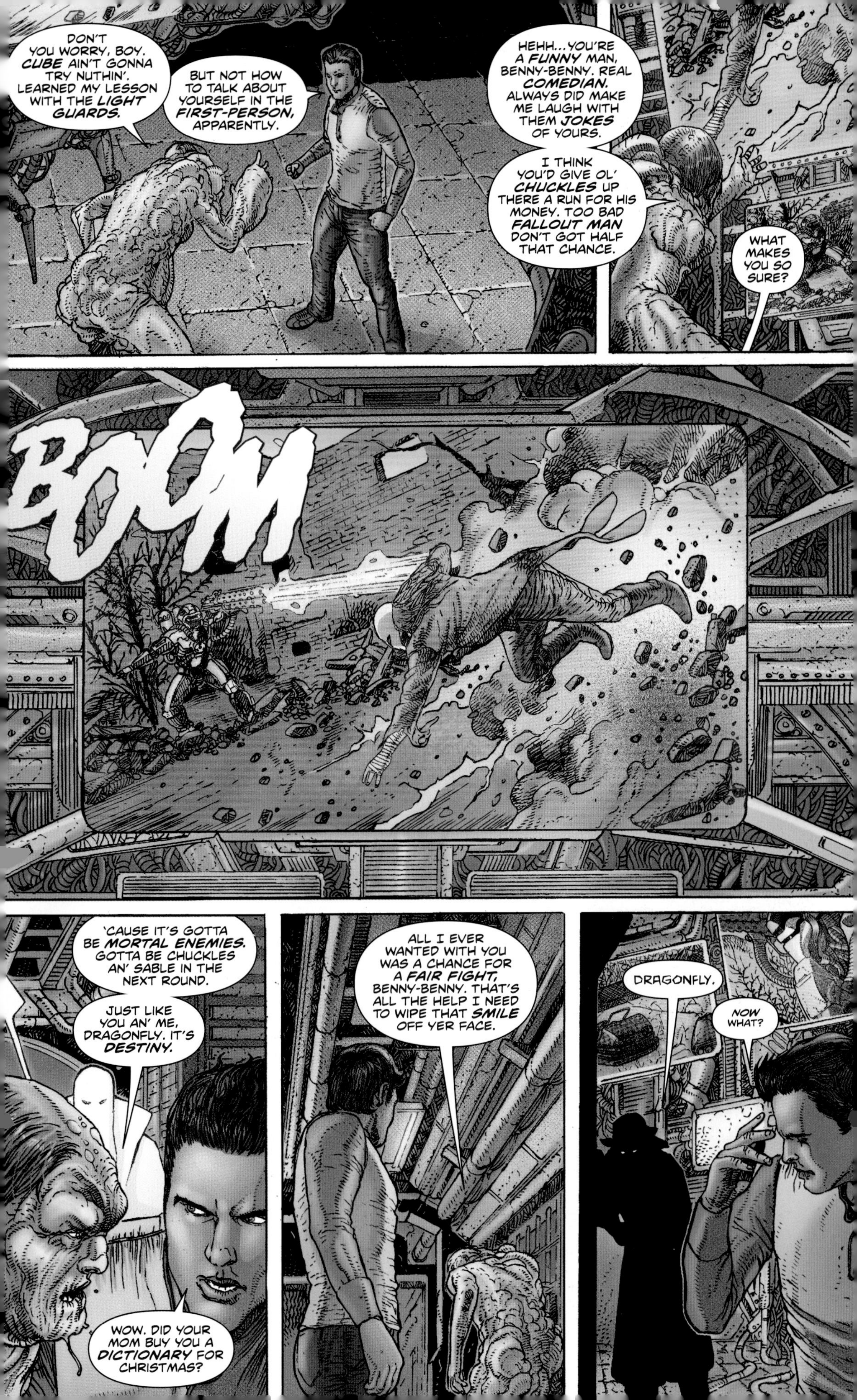
DON'T YOU WORRY, BOY. CUBE AIN'T GONNA TRY NUTHIN'. LEARNED MY LESSON WITH THE LIGHT GUARDS.
BUT NOT HOW TO TALK ABOUT YOURSELF IN THE FIRST-PERSON, APPARENTLY.
HEHH...YOU'RE A FUNNY MAN, BENNY-BENNY. REAL COMEDIAN. ALWAYS DID MAKE ME LAUGH WITH THEM JOKES OF YOURS.
I THINK YOU'D GIVE OL' CHUCKLES UP THERE A RUN FOR HIS MONEY. TOO BAD FALLOUT MAN DON'T GOT HALF THAT CHANCE.
WHAT MAKES YOU SO SURE?
BOOM
'CAUSE IT'S GOTTA BE MORTAL ENEMIES. GOTTA BE CHUCKLES AN' SABLE IN THE NEXT ROUND.
JUST LIKE YOU AN' ME, DRAGONFLY. IT'S DESTINY.
WOW. DID YOUR MOM BUY YOU A DICTIONARY FOR CHRISTMAS?
ALL I EVER WANTED WITH YOU WAS A CHANCE FOR A FAIR FIGHT, BENNY-BENNY. THAT'S ALL THE HELP I NEED TO WIPE THAT SMILE OFF YER FACE.
DRAGONFLY.
NOW WHAT?

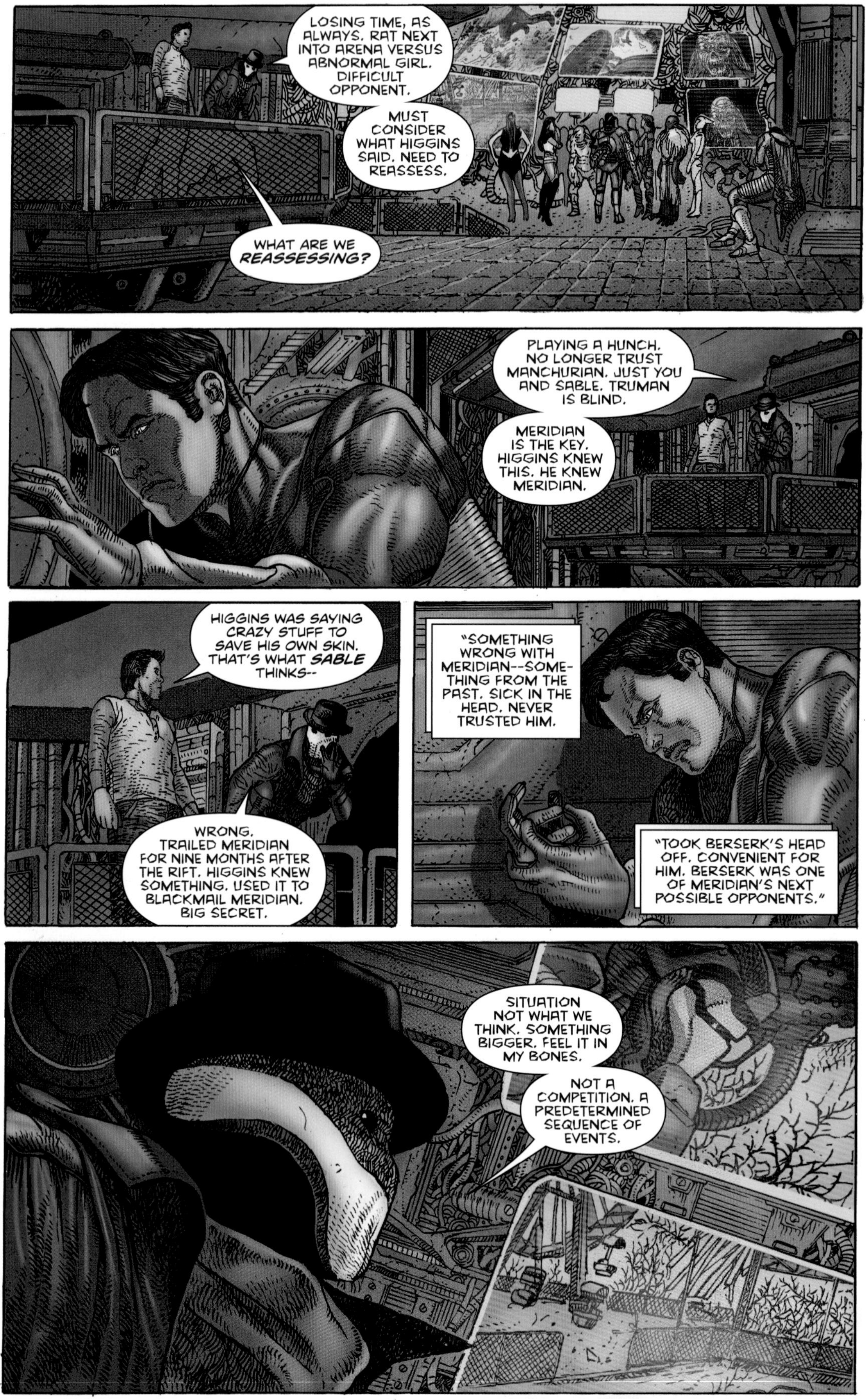

LOSING TIME, AS ALWAYS. RAT NEXT INTO ARENA VERSUS ABNORMAL GIRL. DIFFICULT OPPONENT.
MUST CONSIDER WHAT HIGGINS SAID. NEED TO REASSESS.
WHAT ARE WE REASSESSING?
PLAYING A HUNCH. NO LONGER TRUST MANCHURIAN. JUST YOU AND SABLE. TRUMAN IS BLIND.
MERIDIAN IS THE KEY. HIGGINS KNEW THIS. HE KNEW MERIDIAN.
HIGGINS WAS SAYING CRAZY STUFF TO SAVE HIS OWN SKIN. THAT'S WHAT SABLE THINKS--
WRONG. TRAILED MERIDIAN FOR NINE MONTHS AFTER THE RIFT. HIGGINS KNEW SOMETHING. USED IT TO BLACKMAIL MERIDIAN. BIG SECRET.
"SOMETHING WRONG WITH MERIDIAN--SOMETHING FROM THE PAST. SICK IN THE HEAD. NEVER TRUSTED HIM.
"TOOK BERSERK'S HEAD OFF. CONVENIENT FOR HIM. BERSERK WAS ONE OF MERIDIAN'S NEXT POSSIBLE OPPONENTS."
SITUATION NOT WHAT WE THINK. SOMETHING BIGGER. FEEL IT IN MY BONES.
NOT A COMPETITION. A PREDETERMINED SEQUENCE OF EVENTS.

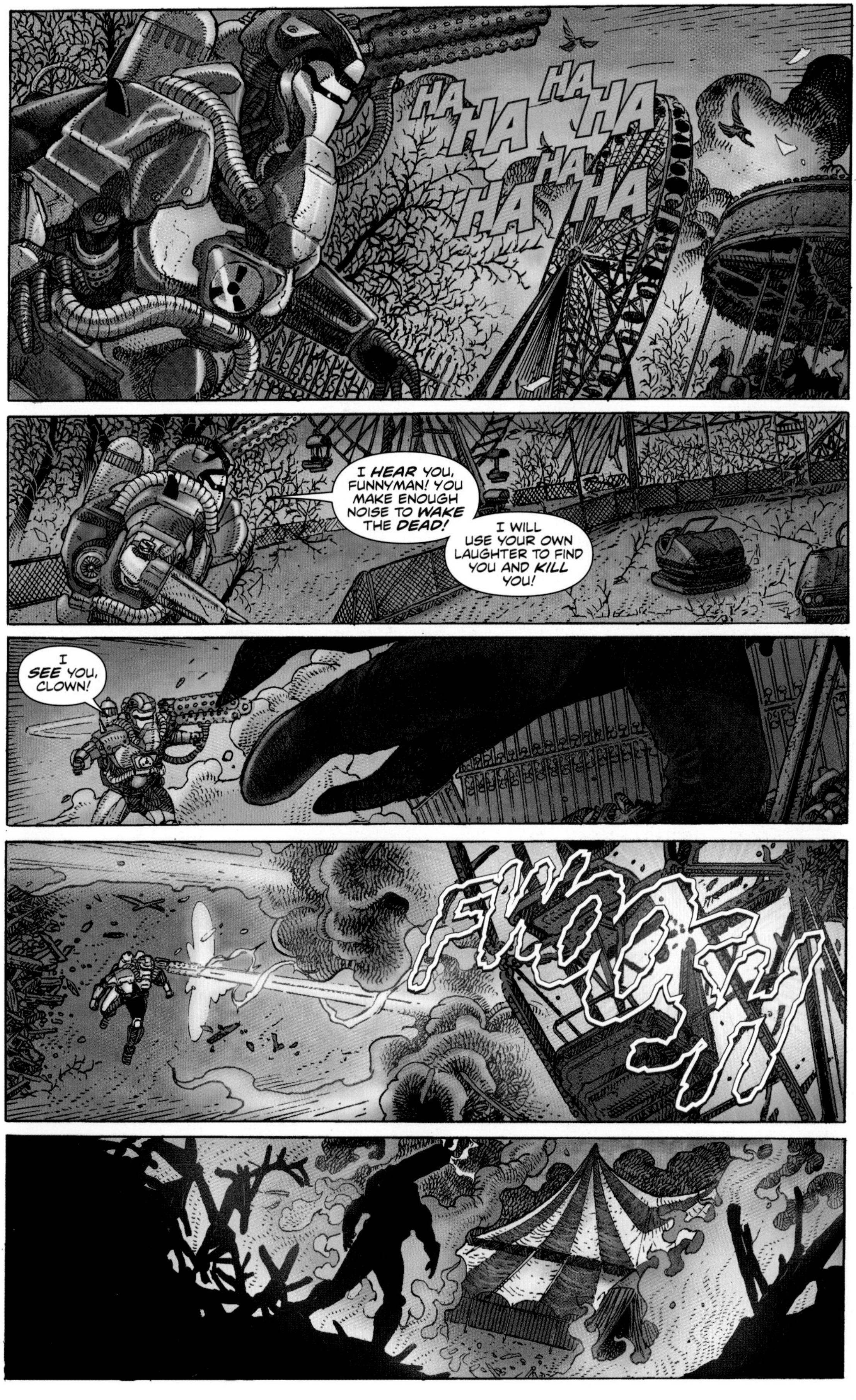
HA HA HA HA HA HA HA HA
I HEAR YOU, FUNNYMAN! YOU MAKE ENOUGH NOISE TO WAKE THE DEAD!
I WILL USE YOUR OWN LAUGHTER TO FIND YOU AND KILL YOU!
I SEE YOU, CLOWN!

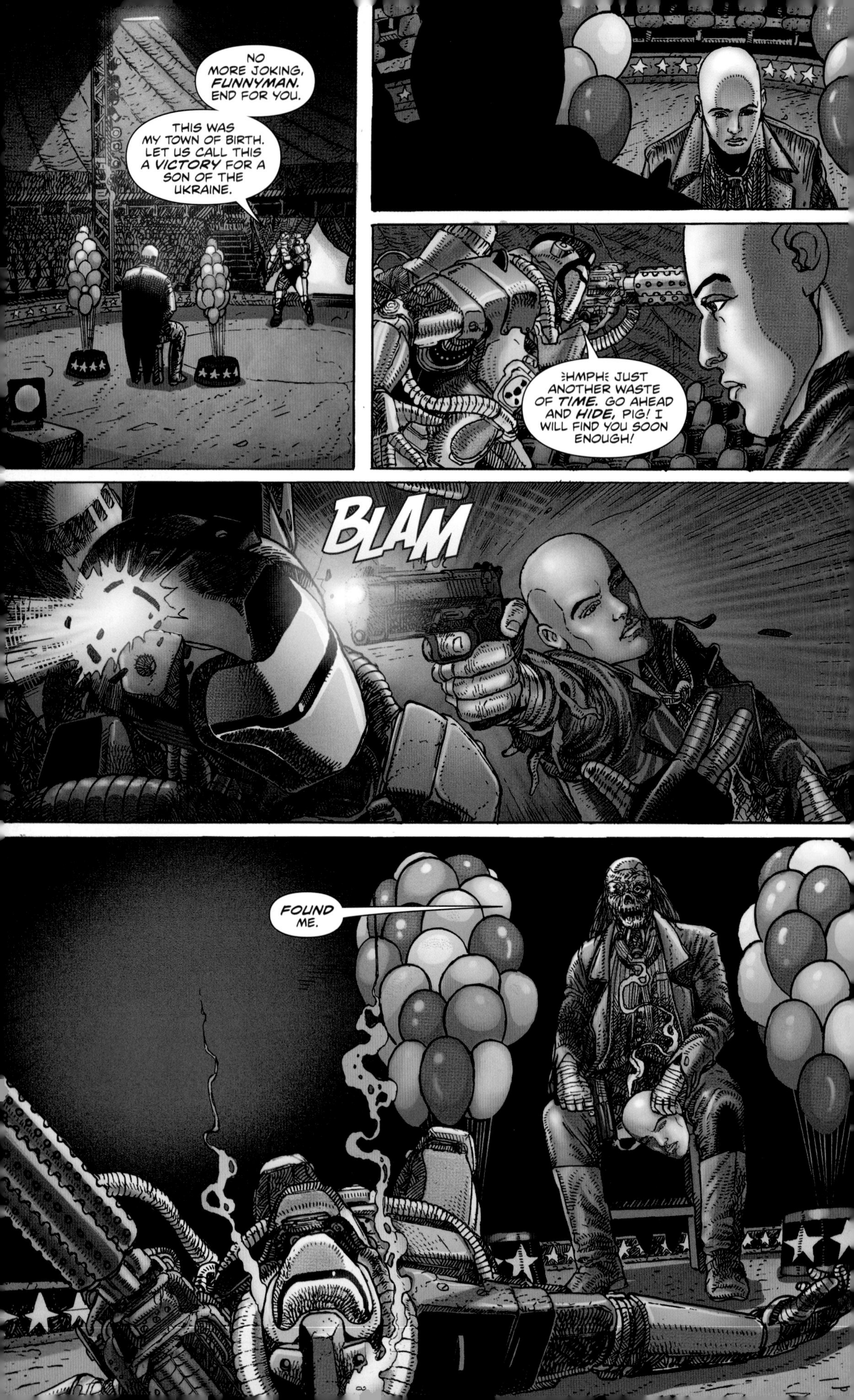
NO MORE JOKING, FUNNYMAN. END FOR YOU.
THIS WAS MY TOWN OF BIRTH. LET US CALL THIS A VICTORY FOR A SON OF THE UKRAINE.
HMPH JUST ANOTHER WASTE OF TIME. GO AHEAD AND HIDE, PIG! I WILL FIND YOU SOON ENOUGH!
BLAM
FOUND ME.

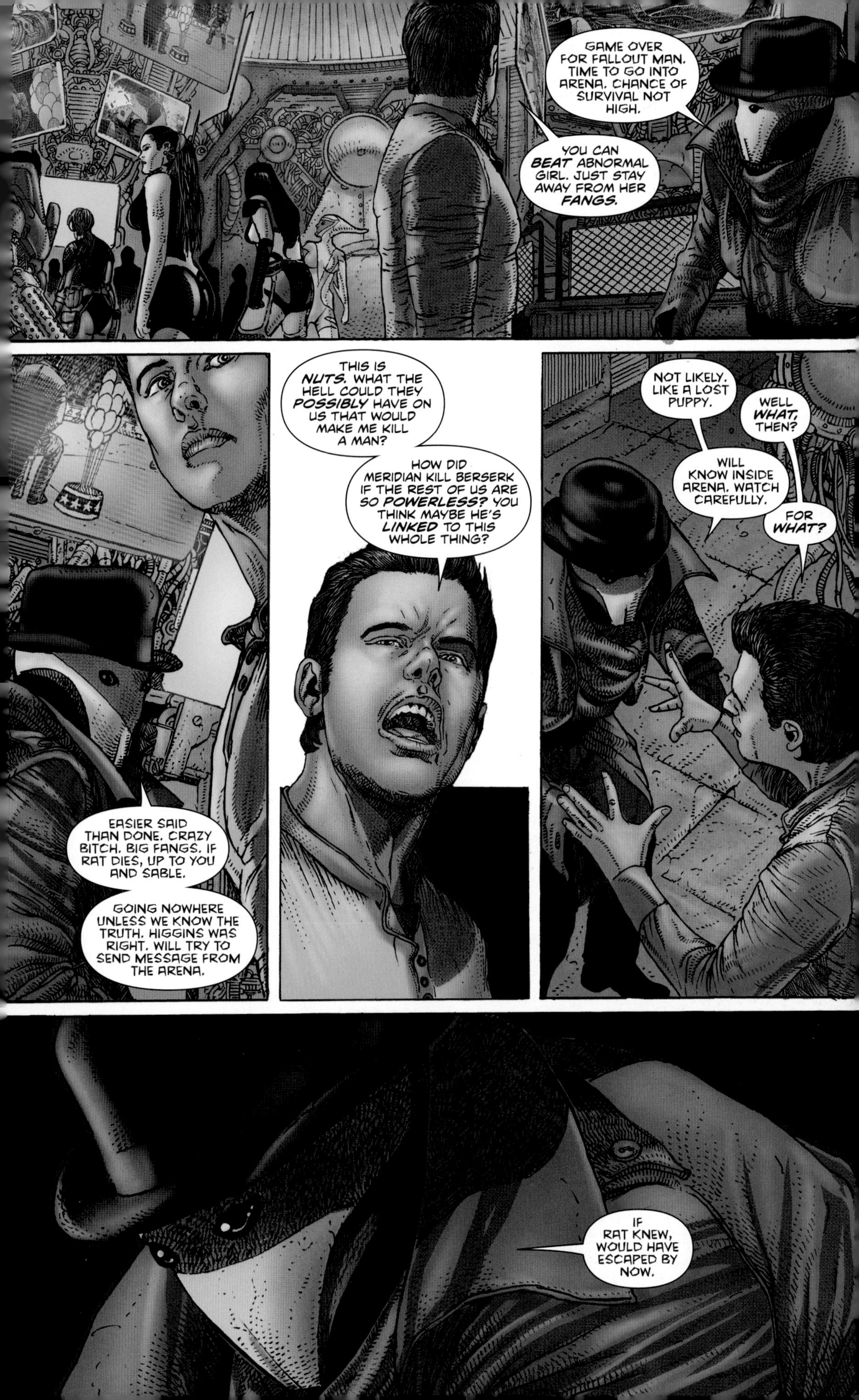
GAME OVER FOR FALLOUT MAN. TIME TO GO INTO ARENA. CHANCE OF SURVIVAL NOT HIGH.
YOU CAN BEAT ABNORMAL GIRL. JUST STAY AWAY FROM HER FANGS.
EASIER SAID THAN DONE. CRAZY BITCH. BIG FANGS. IF RAT DIES, UP TO YOU AND SABLE.
GOING NOWHERE UNLESS WE KNOW THE TRUTH. HIGGINS WAS RIGHT. WILL TRY TO SEND MESSAGE FROM THE ARENA.
THIS IS NUTS. WHAT THE HELL COULD THEY POSSIBLY HAVE ON US THAT WOULD MAKE ME KILL A MAN?
HOW DID MERIDIAN KILL BERSERK IF THE REST OF US ARE SO POWERLESS? YOU THINK MAYBE HE'S LINKED TO THIS WHOLE THING?
NOT LIKELY. LIKE A LOST PUPPY.
WELL WHAT, THEN?
WILL KNOW INSIDE ARENA. WATCH CAREFULLY.
FOR WHAT?
IF RAT KNEW, WOULD HAVE ESCAPED BY NOW.

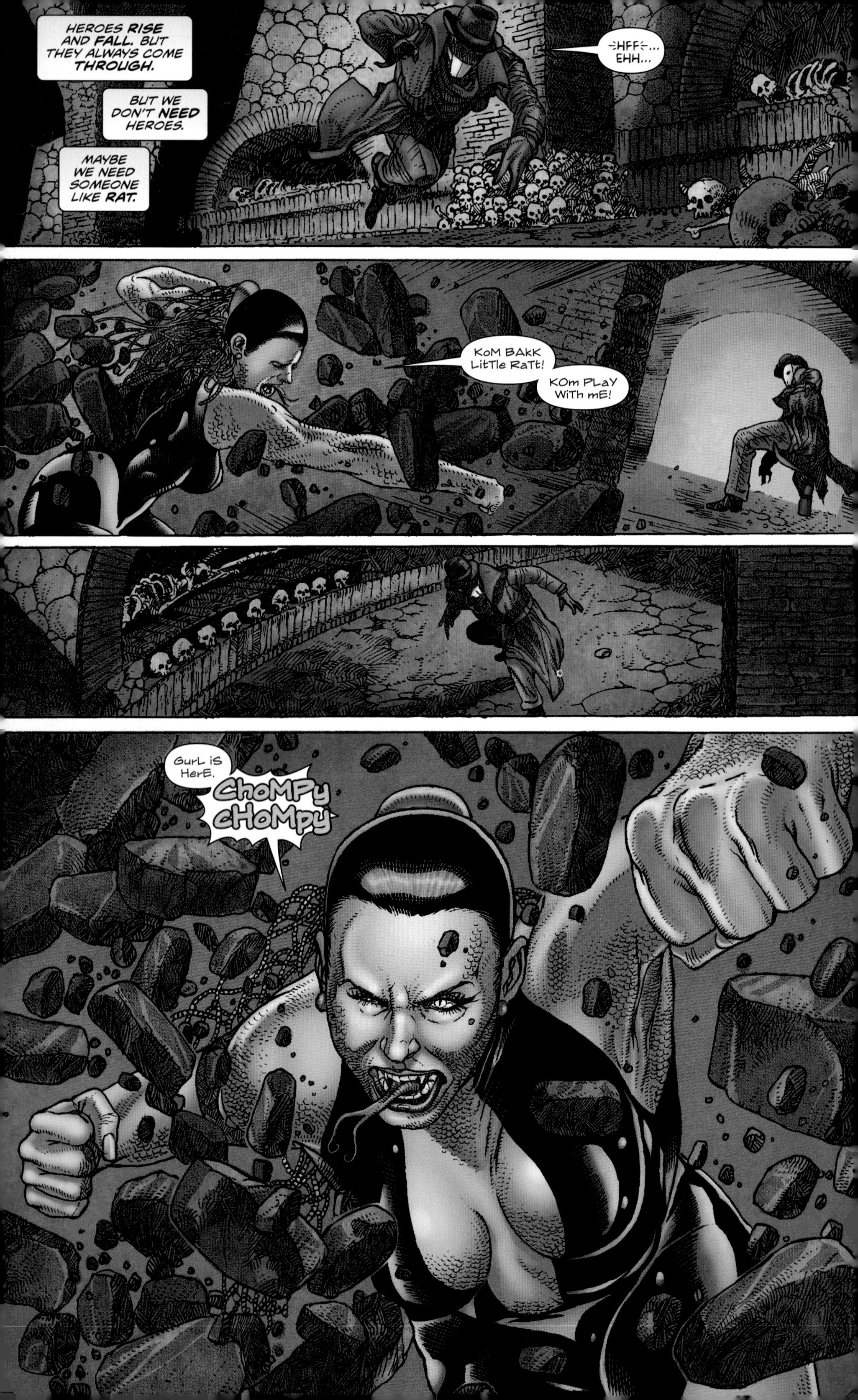
HEROES RISE AND FALL. BUT THEY ALWAYS COME THROUGH.
BUT WE DON'T NEED HEROES.
MAYBE WE NEED SOMEONE LIKE RAT.
HFF...
EHH...
KoM BAkK LitTle RaTt!
KOm PLaY WiTh mE!
GurL iS HerE.
ChoMPy cHoMpy

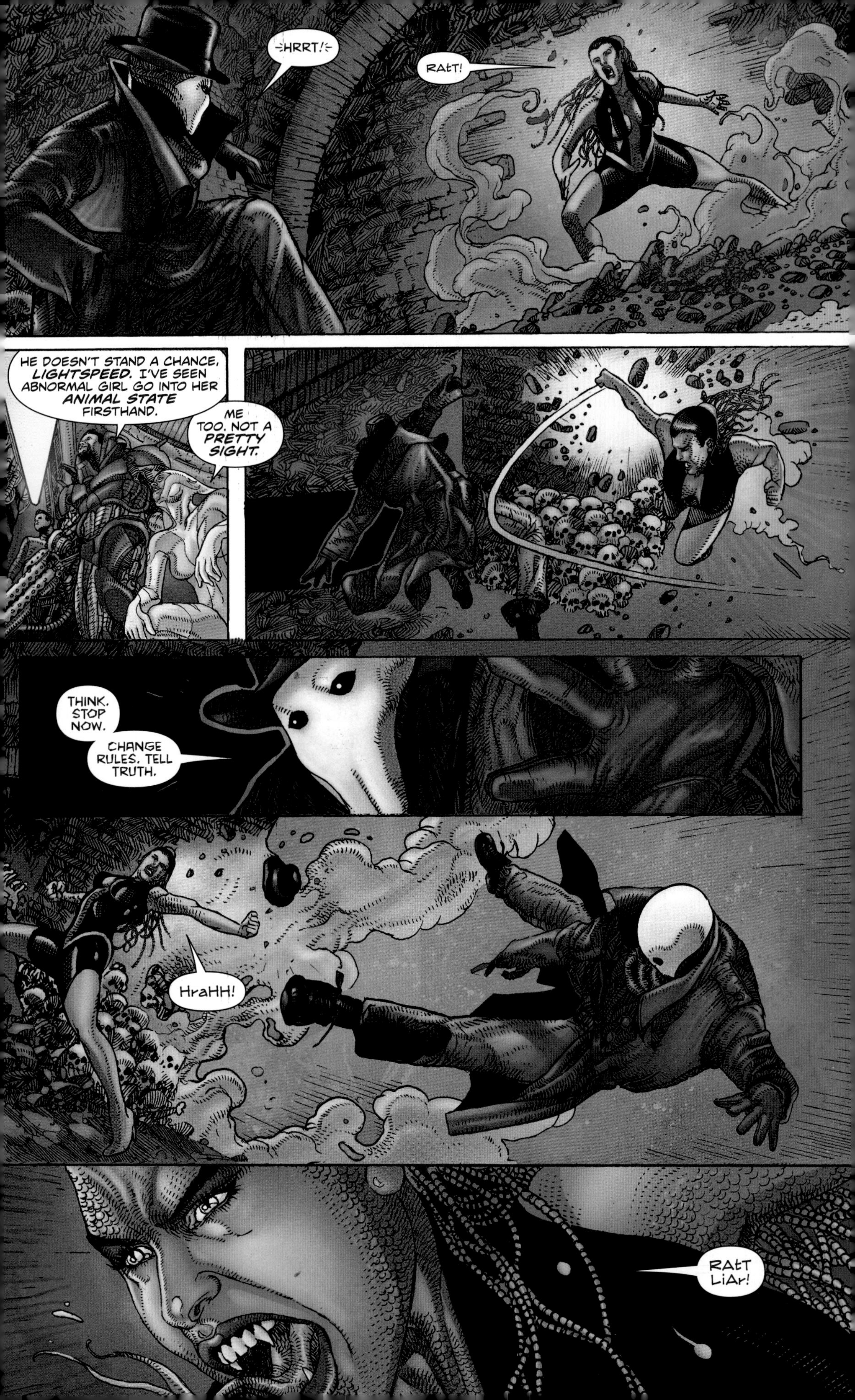

HRRT!
RAtT!
HE DOESN'T STAND A CHANCE, LIGHTSPEED. I'VE SEEN ABNORMAL GIRL GO INTO HER ANIMAL STATE FIRSTHAND.
ME TOO. NOT A PRETTY SIGHT.
THINK. STOP NOW.
CHANGE RULES. TELL TRUTH.
HraHH!
RAtT LiAr!

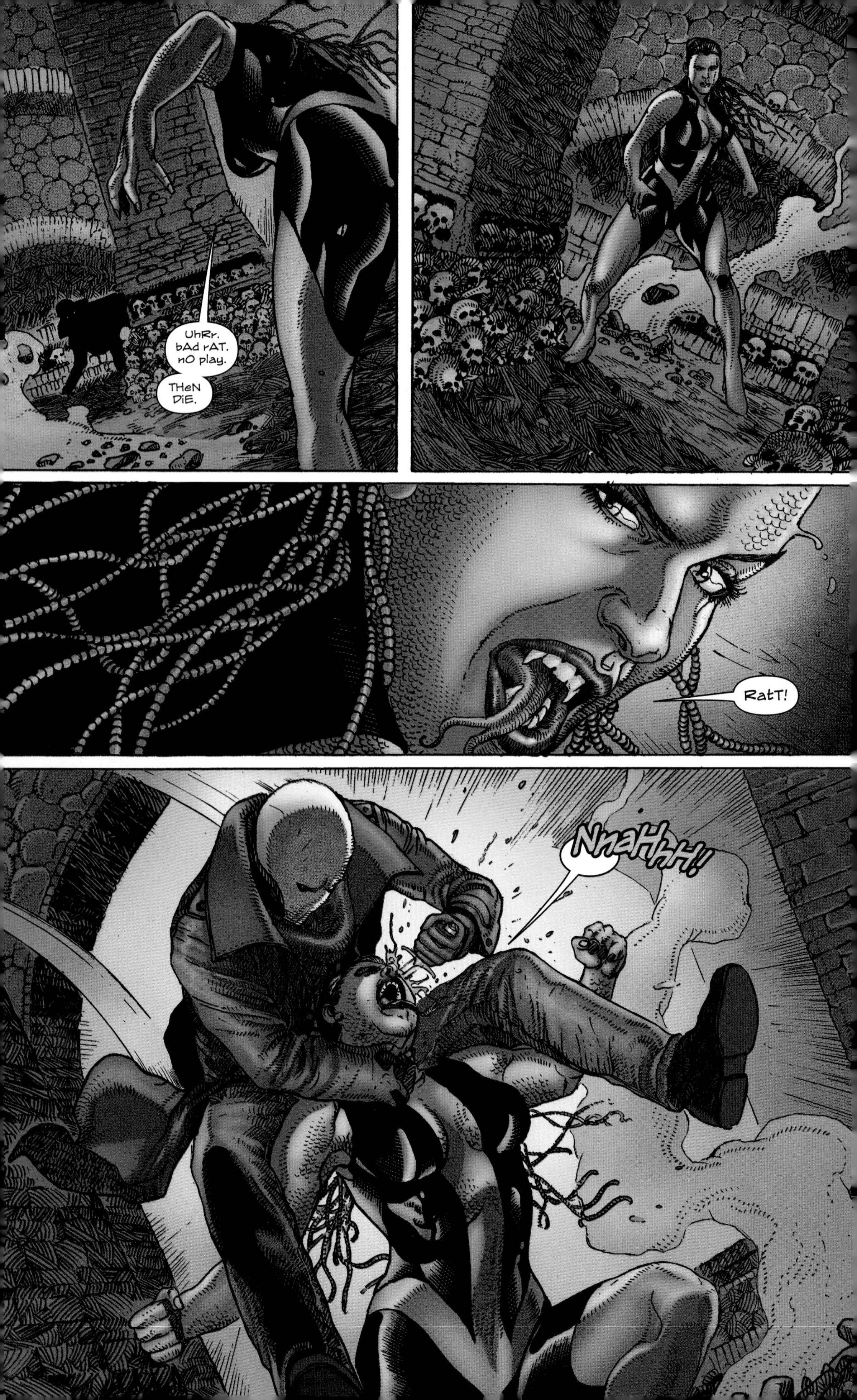
UhRr. bAd rAT. nO play.
THeN DiE.
RatT!
NnaHhH!

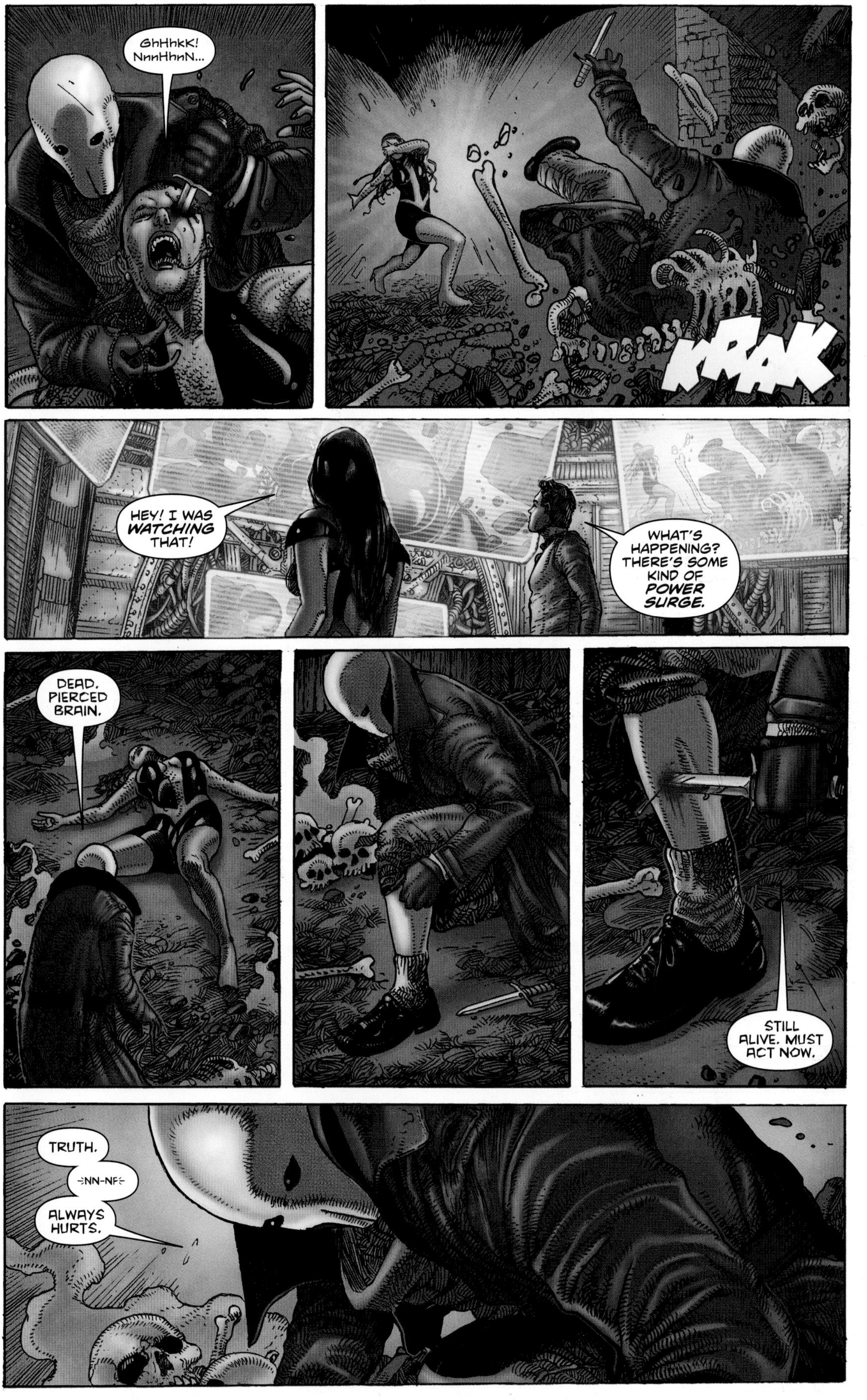
GhHhkK! NnnHhnN...
KRAK
HEY! I WAS WATCHING THAT!
WHAT'S HAPPENING? THERE'S SOME KIND OF POWER SURGE.
DEAD. PIERCED BRAIN.
STILL ALIVE. MUST ACT NOW.
TRUTH.
=NN-NF=
ALWAYS HURTS.

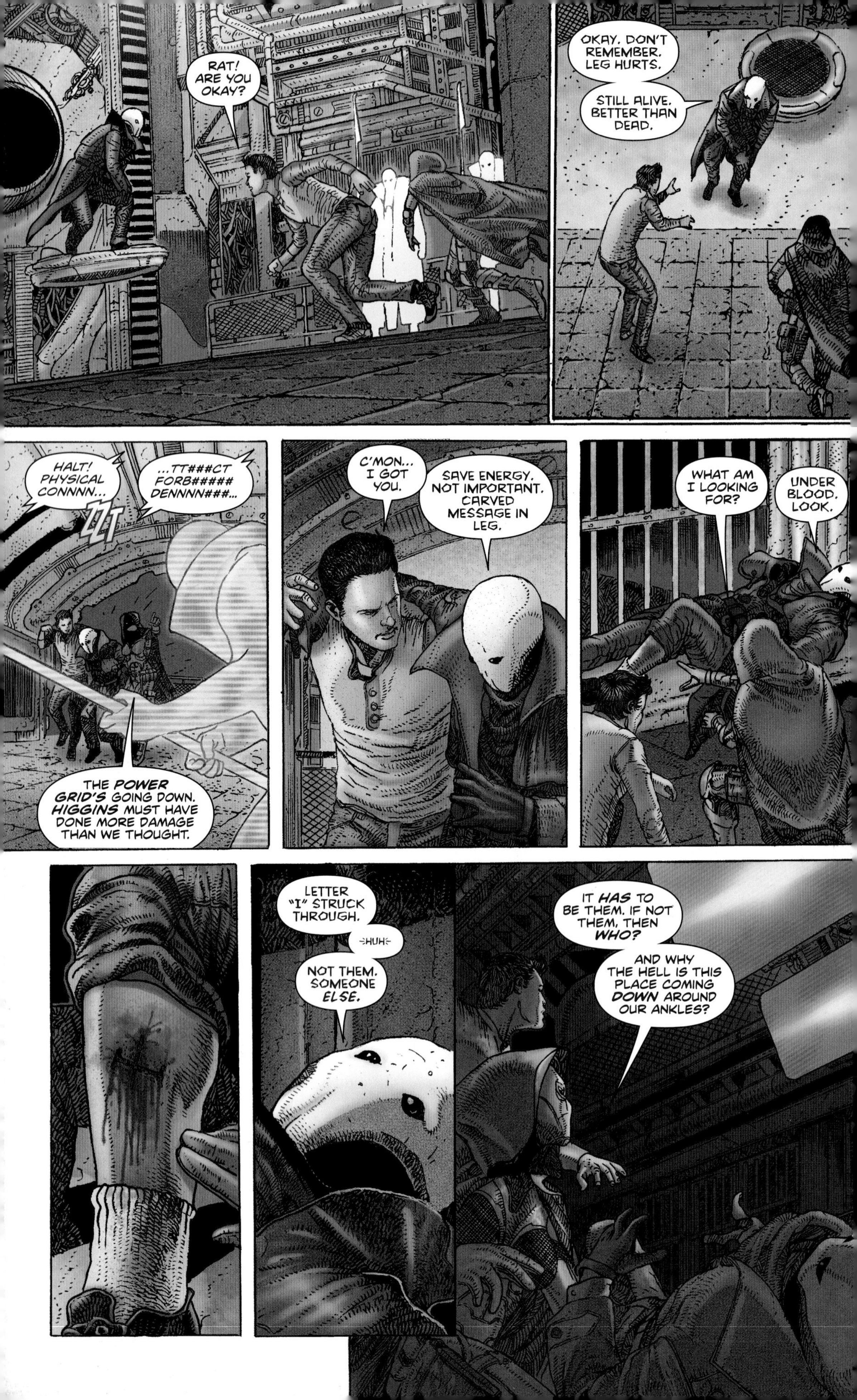
RAT! ARE YOU OKAY?
OKAY. DON'T REMEMBER. LEG HURTS.
STILL ALIVE. BETTER THAN DEAD.
HALT! PHYSICAL CONNNN...
...TT###CT FORB##### DENNNN###...
ZZT
THE POWER GRID'S GOING DOWN. HIGGINS MUST HAVE DONE MORE DAMAGE THAN WE THOUGHT.
C'MON... I GOT YOU.
SAVE ENERGY. NOT IMPORTANT. CARVED MESSAGE IN LEG.
WHAT AM I LOOKING FOR?
UNDER BLOOD. LOOK.
LETTER "I" STRUCK THROUGH.
HUH
NOT THEM. SOMEONE ELSE.
IT HAS TO BE THEM. IF NOT THEM, THEN WHO?
AND WHY THE HELL IS THIS PLACE COMING DOWN AROUND OUR ANKLES?

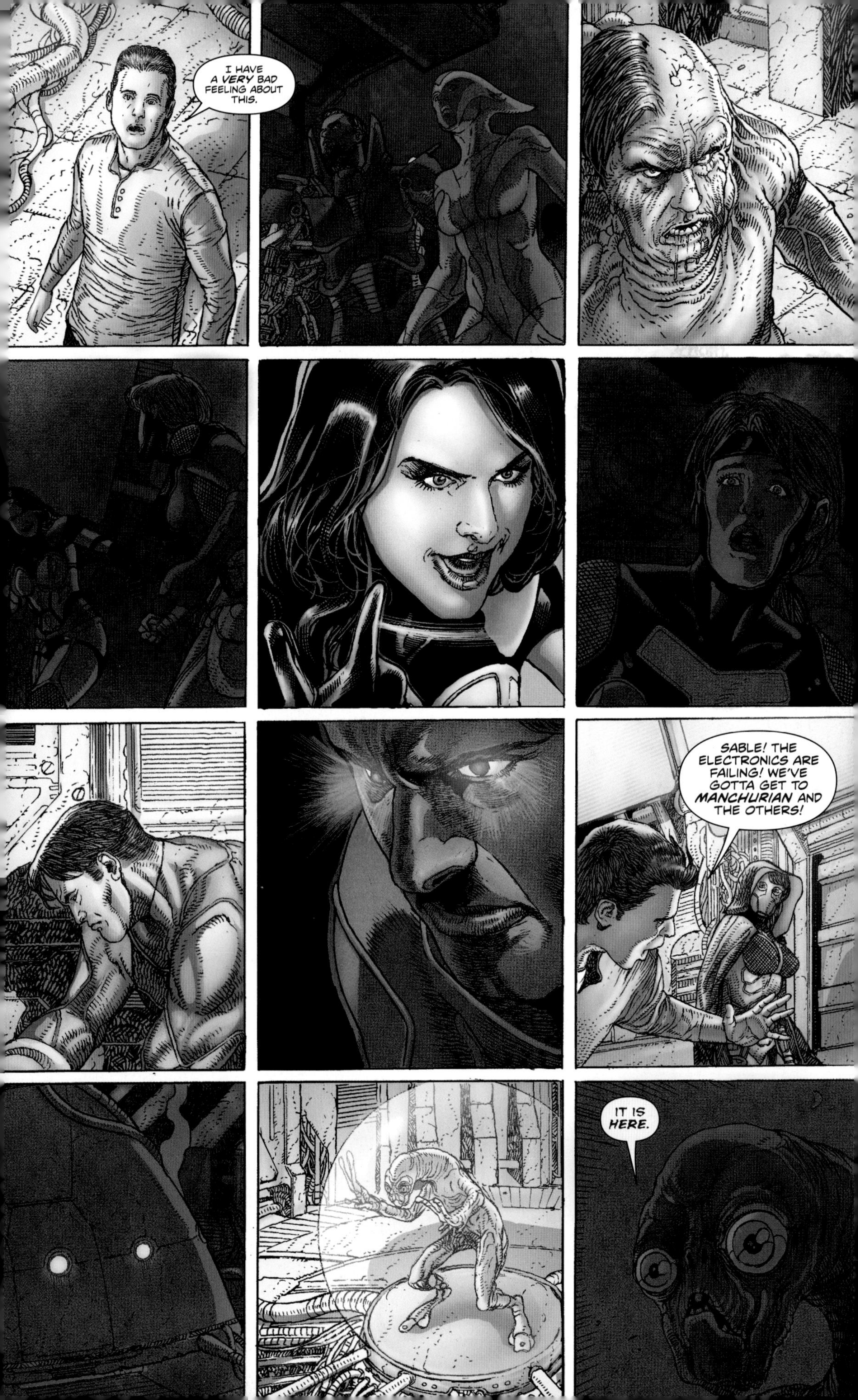
I HAVE A VERY BAD FEELING ABOUT THIS.
SABLE! THE ELECTRONICS ARE FAILING! WE'VE GOTTA GET TO MANCHURIAN AND THE OTHERS!
IT IS HERE.

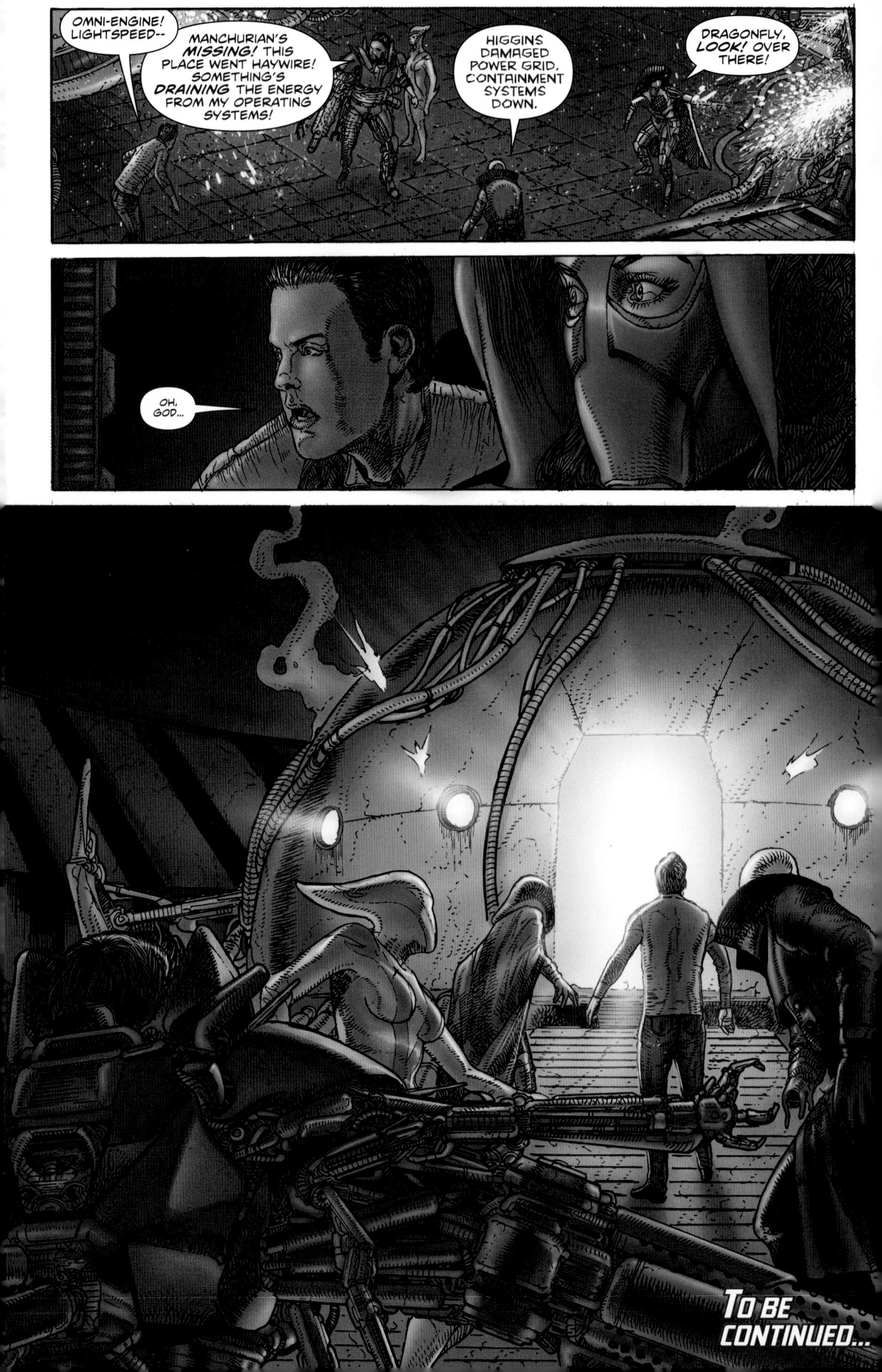
OMNI-ENGINE! LIGHTSPEED--
MANCHURIAN'S MISSING! THIS PLACE WENT HAYWIRE! SOMETHING'S DRAINING THE ENERGY FROM MY OPERATING SYSTEMS!
HIGGINS DAMAGED POWER GRID. CONTAINMENT SYSTEMS DOWN.
DRAGONFLY, LOOK! OVER THERE!
OH, GOD...
TO BE CONTINUED...

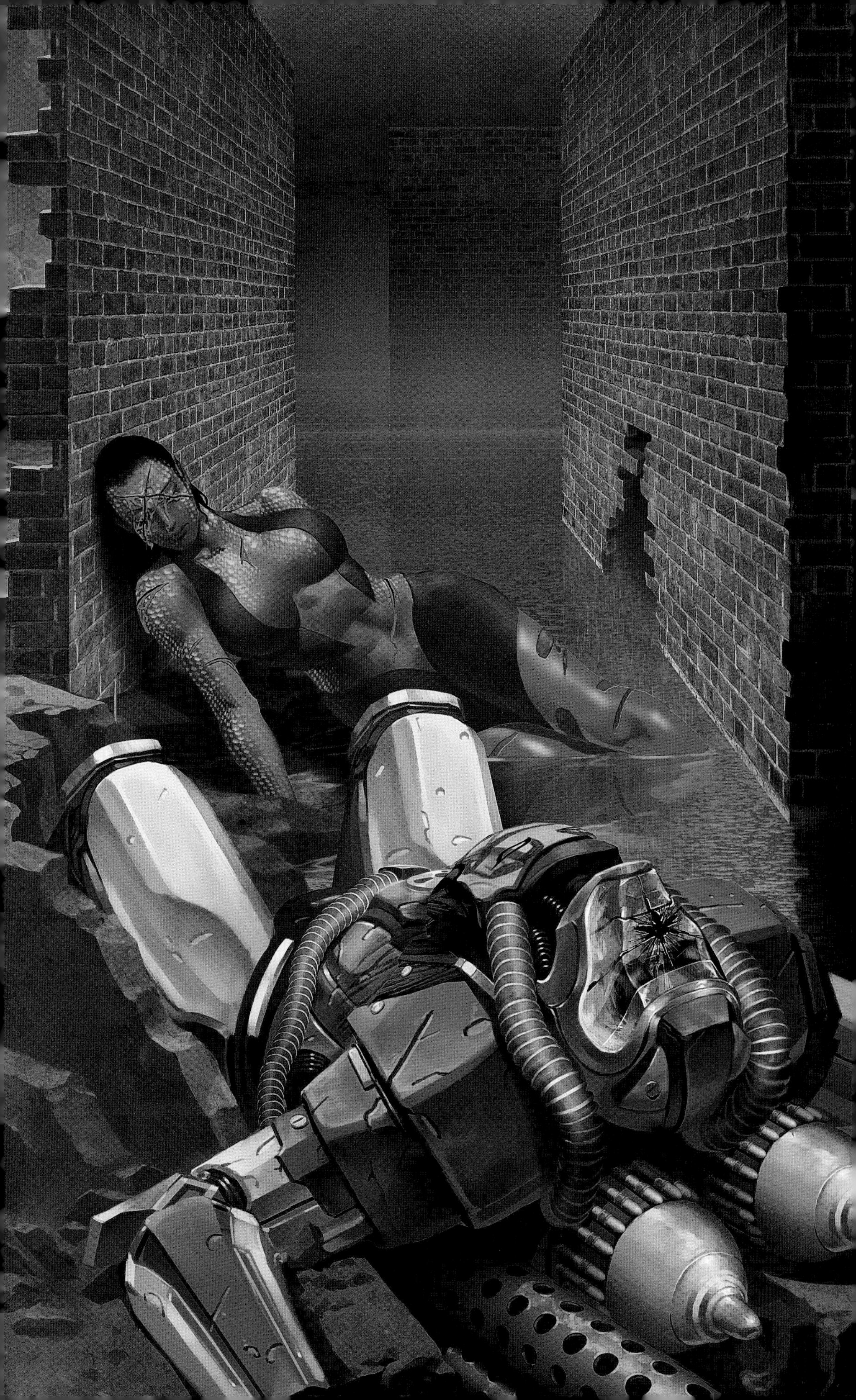

COVER GALLERY

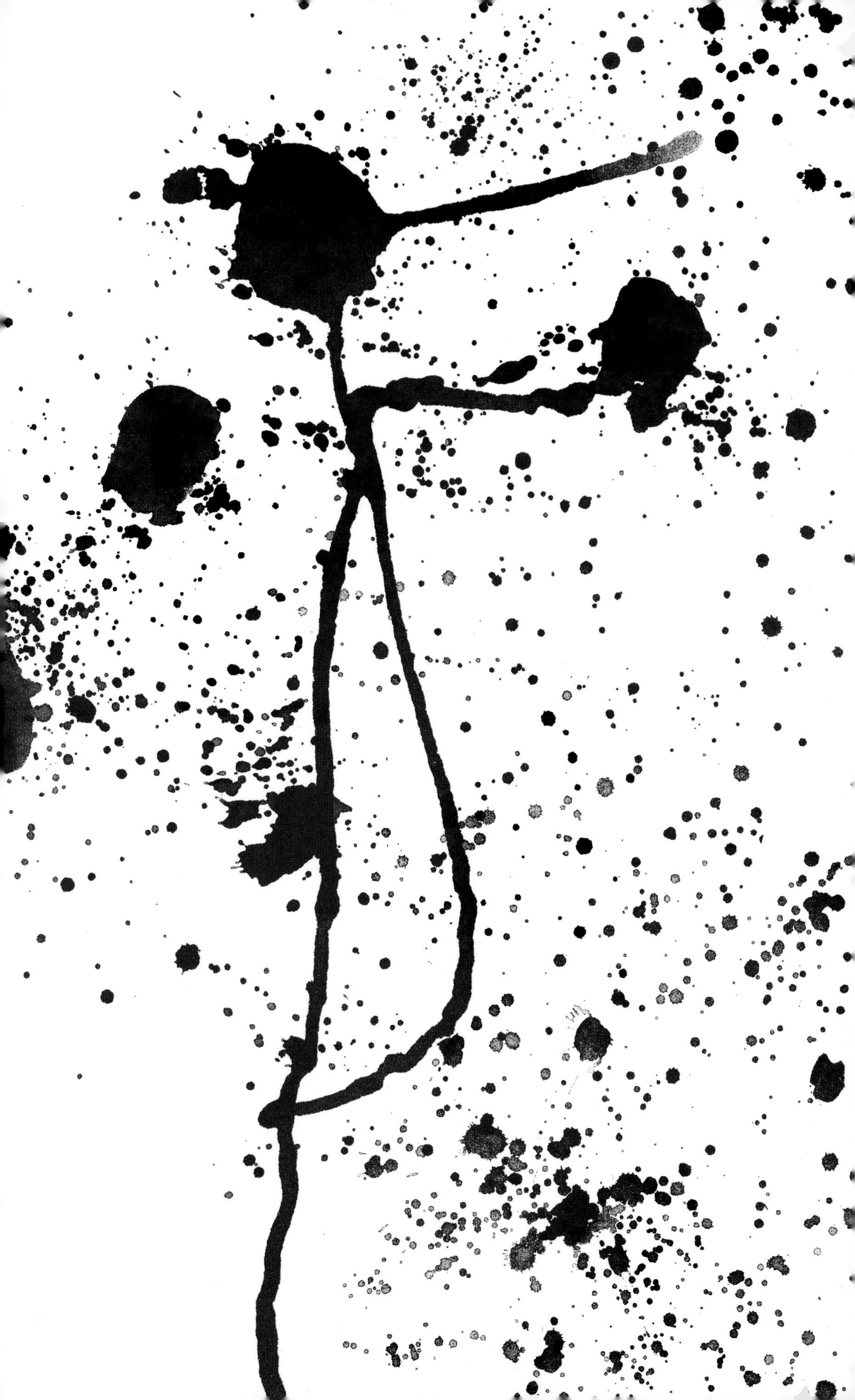

ISSUE ONE
WHILCE PORTACIO
WITH COLORS BY BLOND

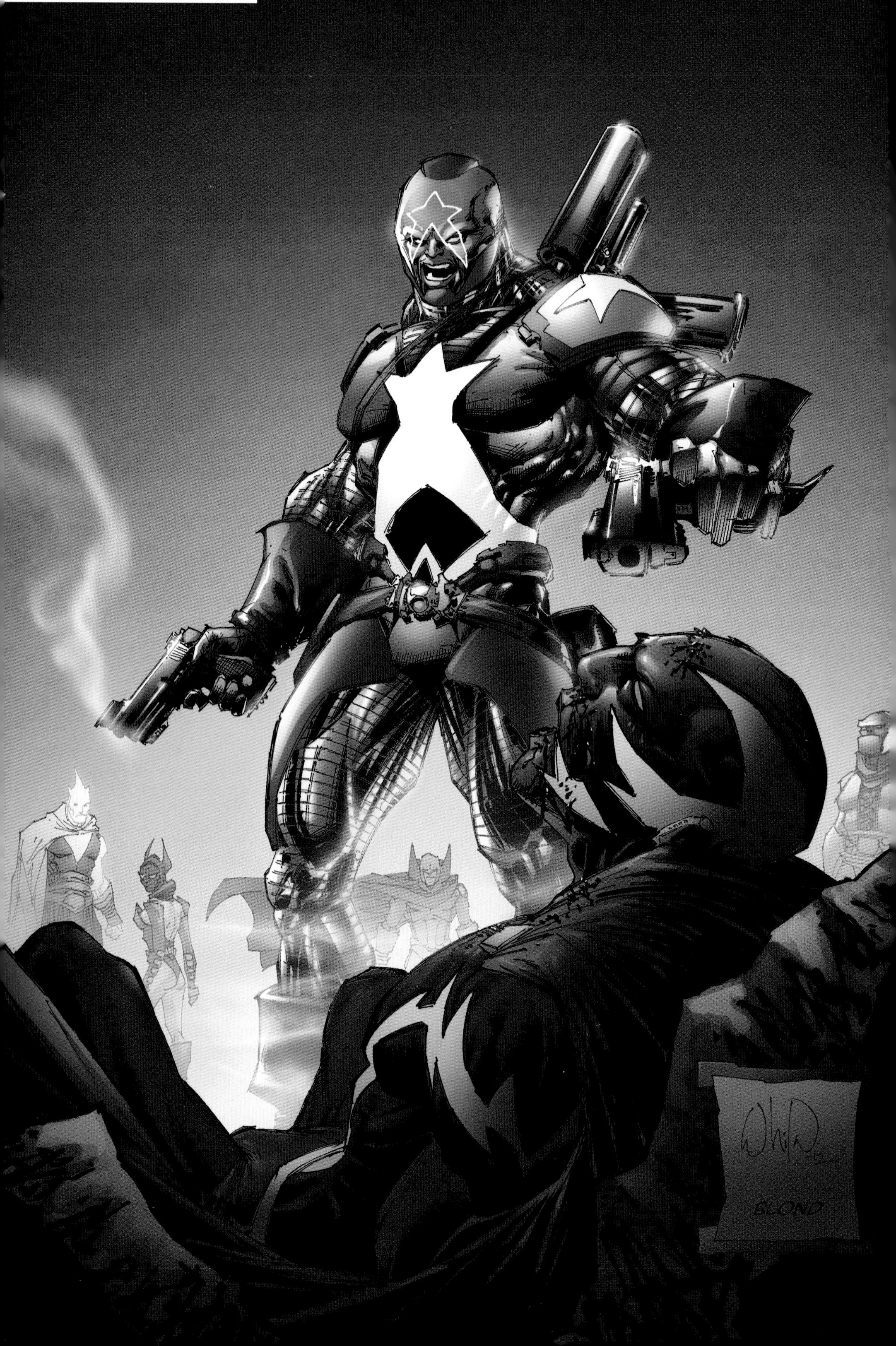

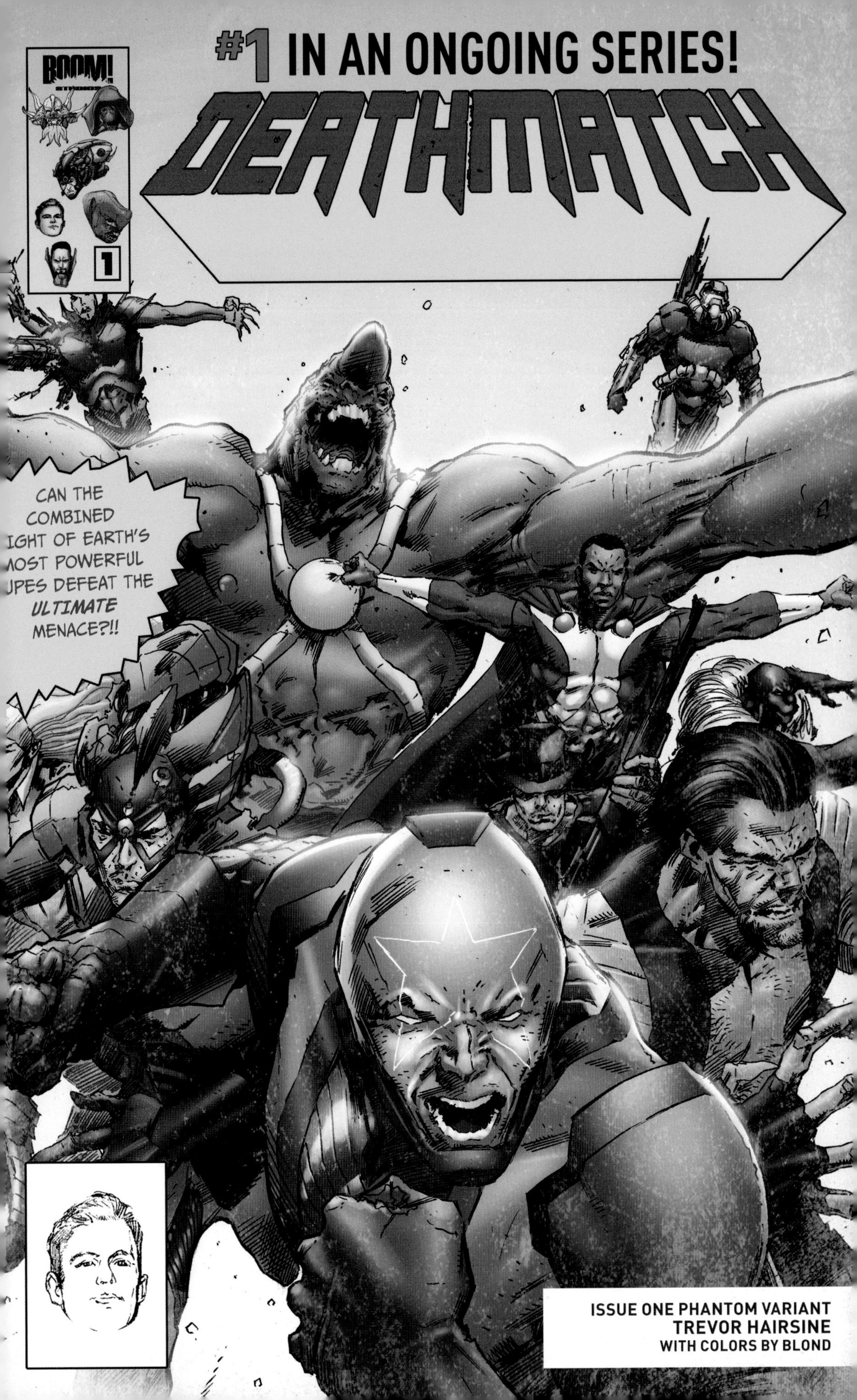
#1 IN AN ONGOING SERIES!
BOOM! STUDIOS
1
DEATHMATCH
CAN THE COMBINED IGHT OF EARTH'S OST POWERFUL PES DEFEAT THE ULTIMATE MENACE?!!
ISSUE ONE PHANTOM VARIANT
TREVOR HAIRSINE
WITH COLORS BY BLOND

ISSUE ONE
CARLOS MAGNO
WITH COLORS BY ARCHIE VAN BUREN

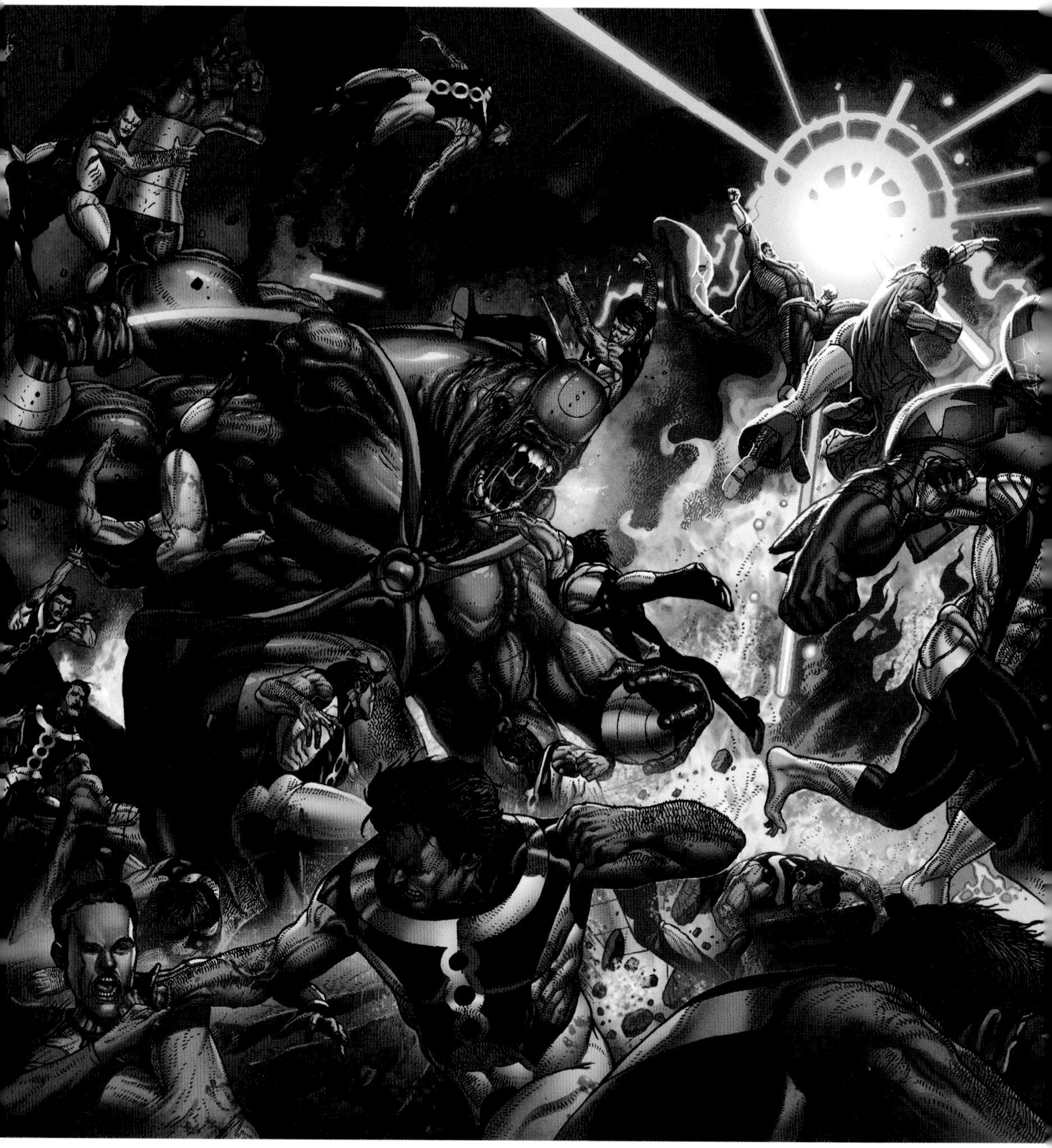

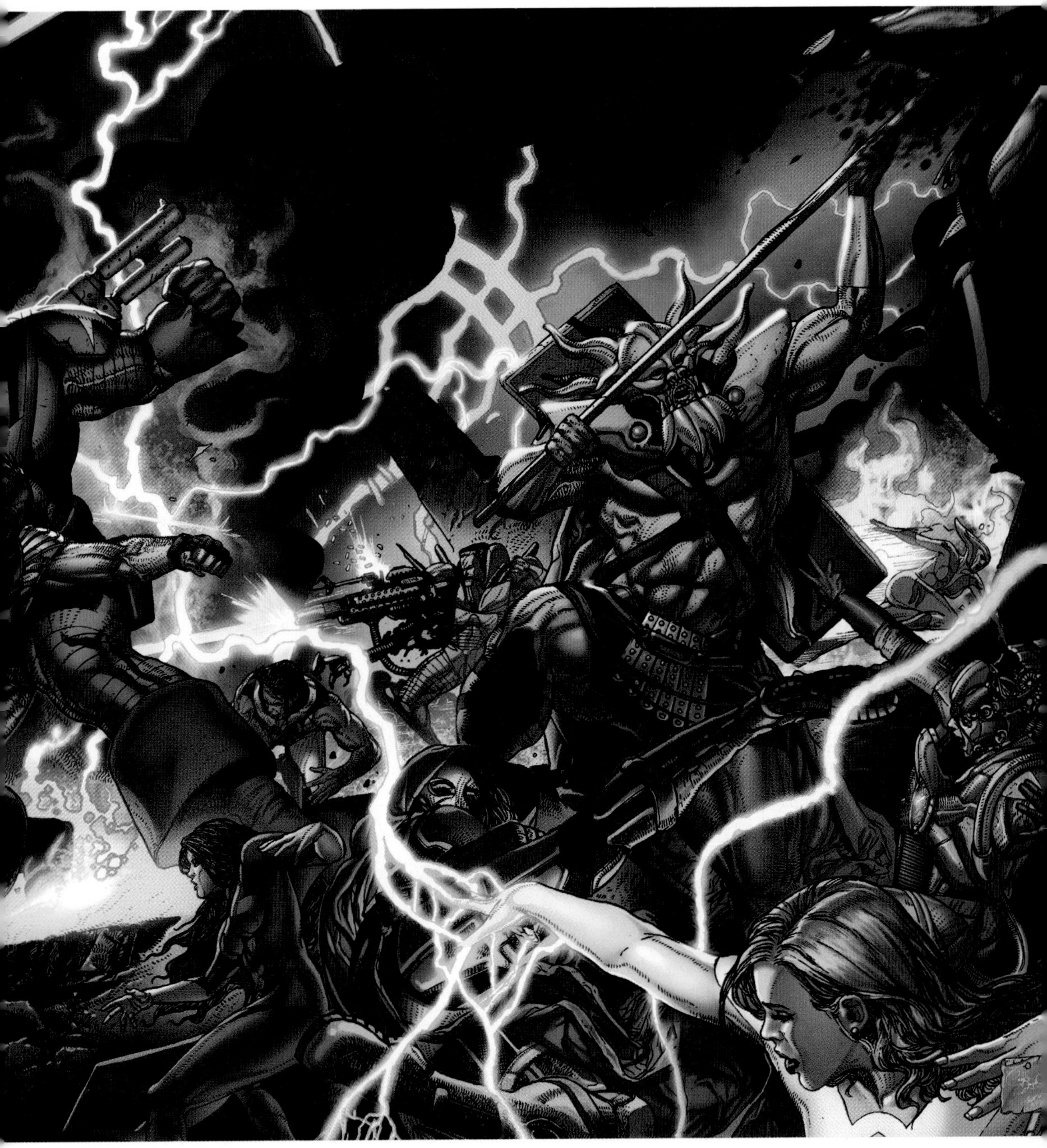

ISSUE ONE ECCC EXCLUSIVE
DAN PANOSIAN

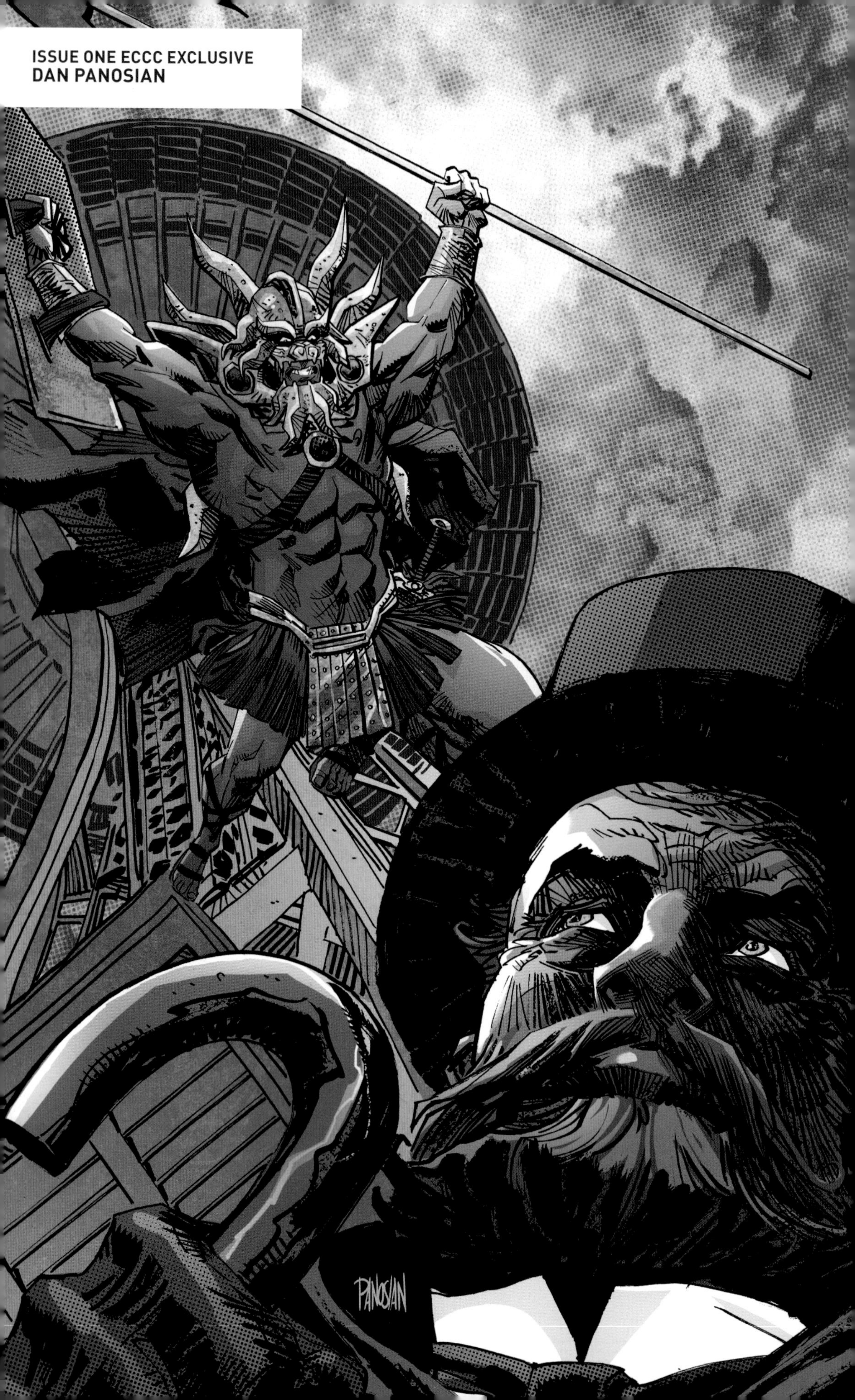
PANOSIAN

ISSUE ONE HASTINGS EXCLUSIVE
V KEN MARION
WITH COLORS BY BLOND

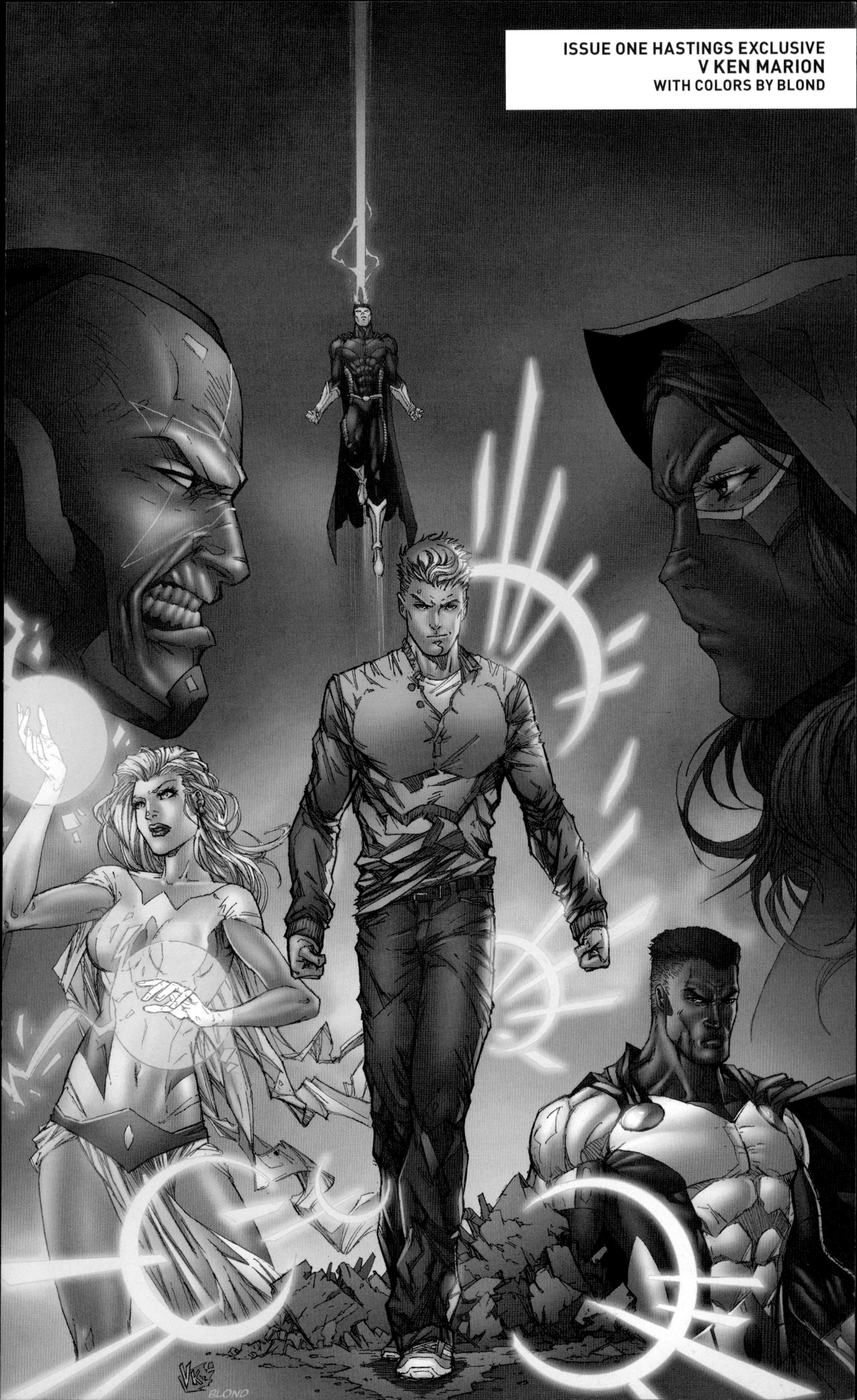

ISSUE ONE 2ND PRINT
TOM DERENICK
WITH COLORS BY BLOND

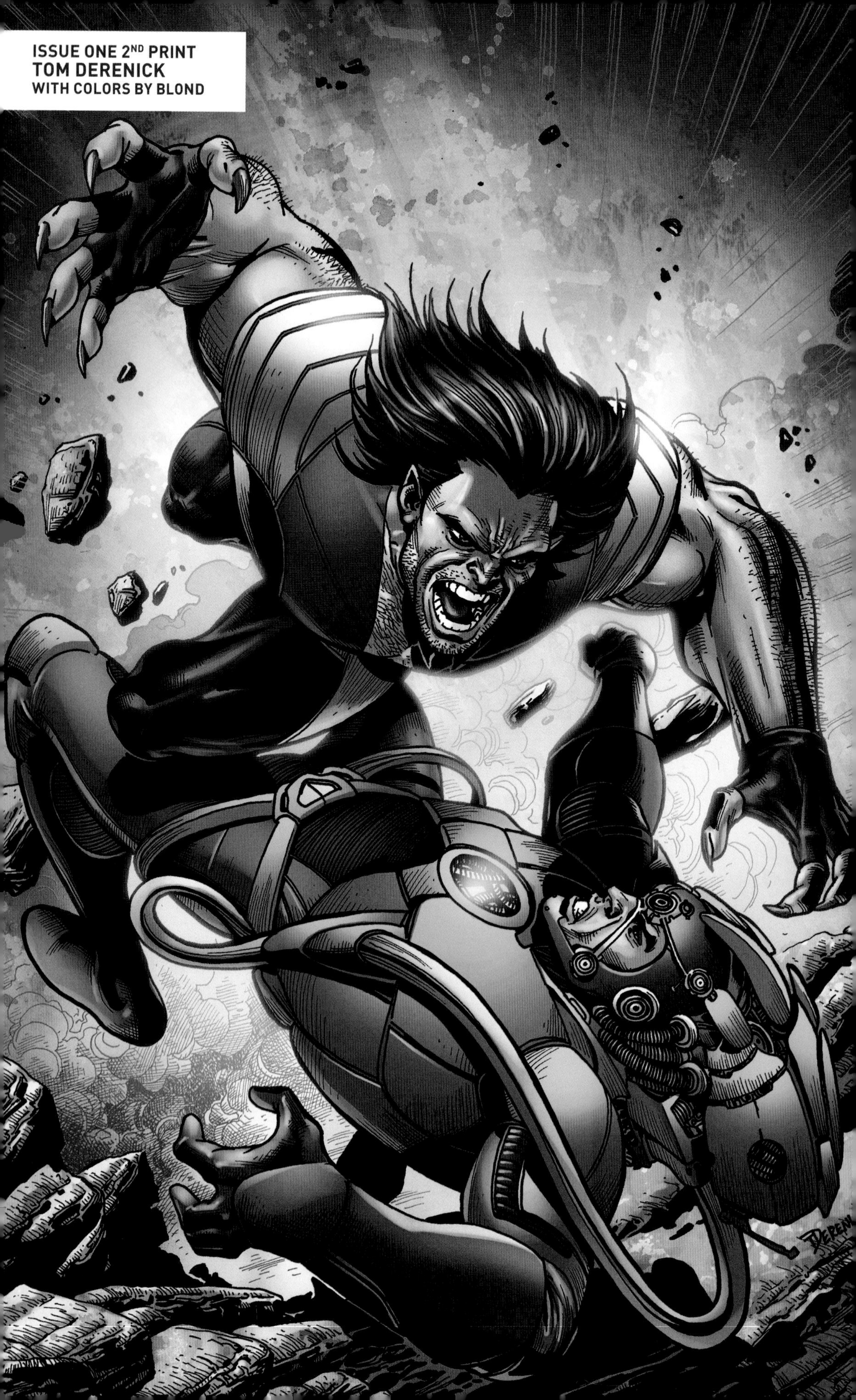

ISSUE TWO
WHILCE PORTACIO
WITH COLORS BY BLOND

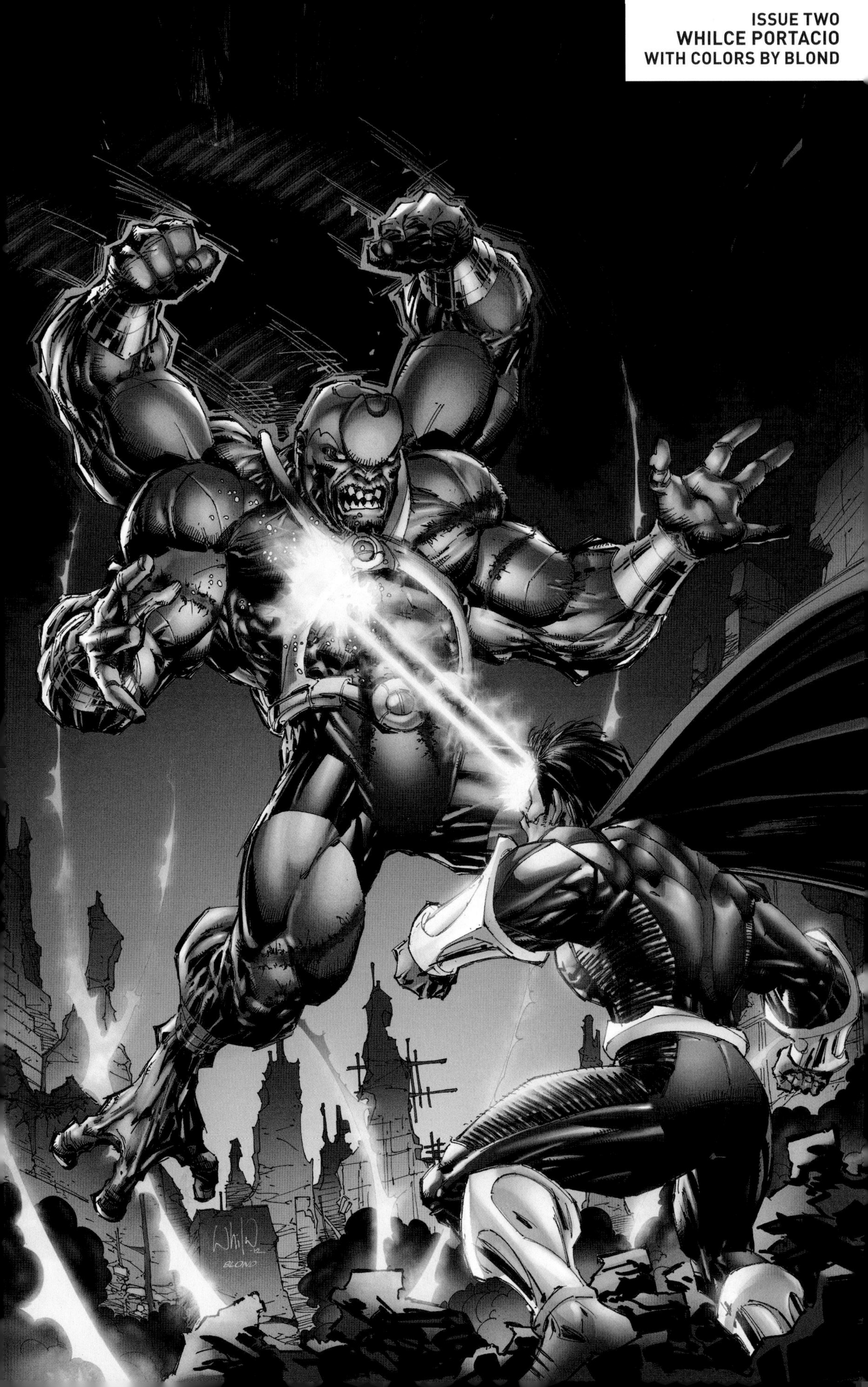

ISSUE TWO
TREVOR HAIRSINE
WITH COLORS BY ARCHIE VAN BUREN

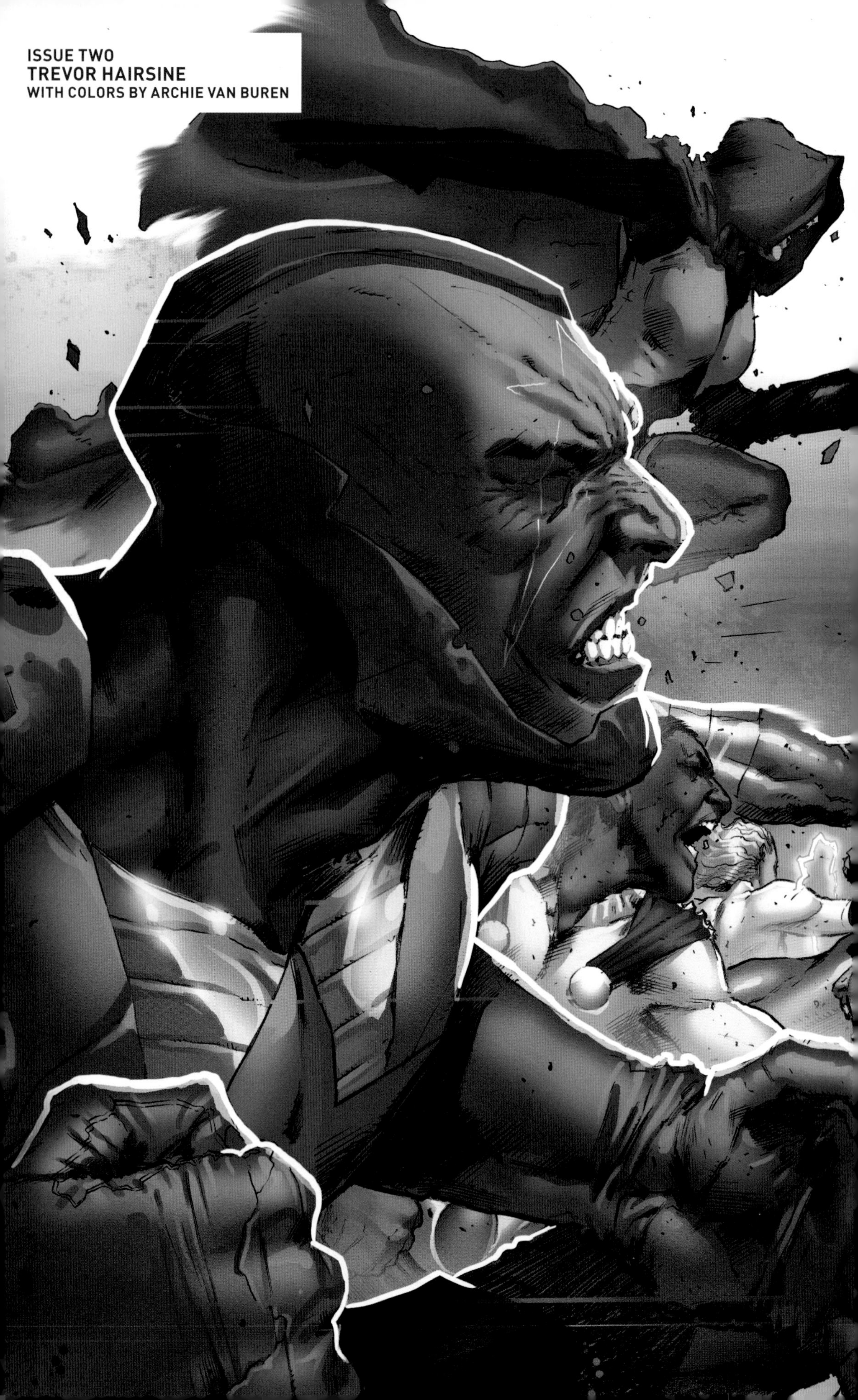

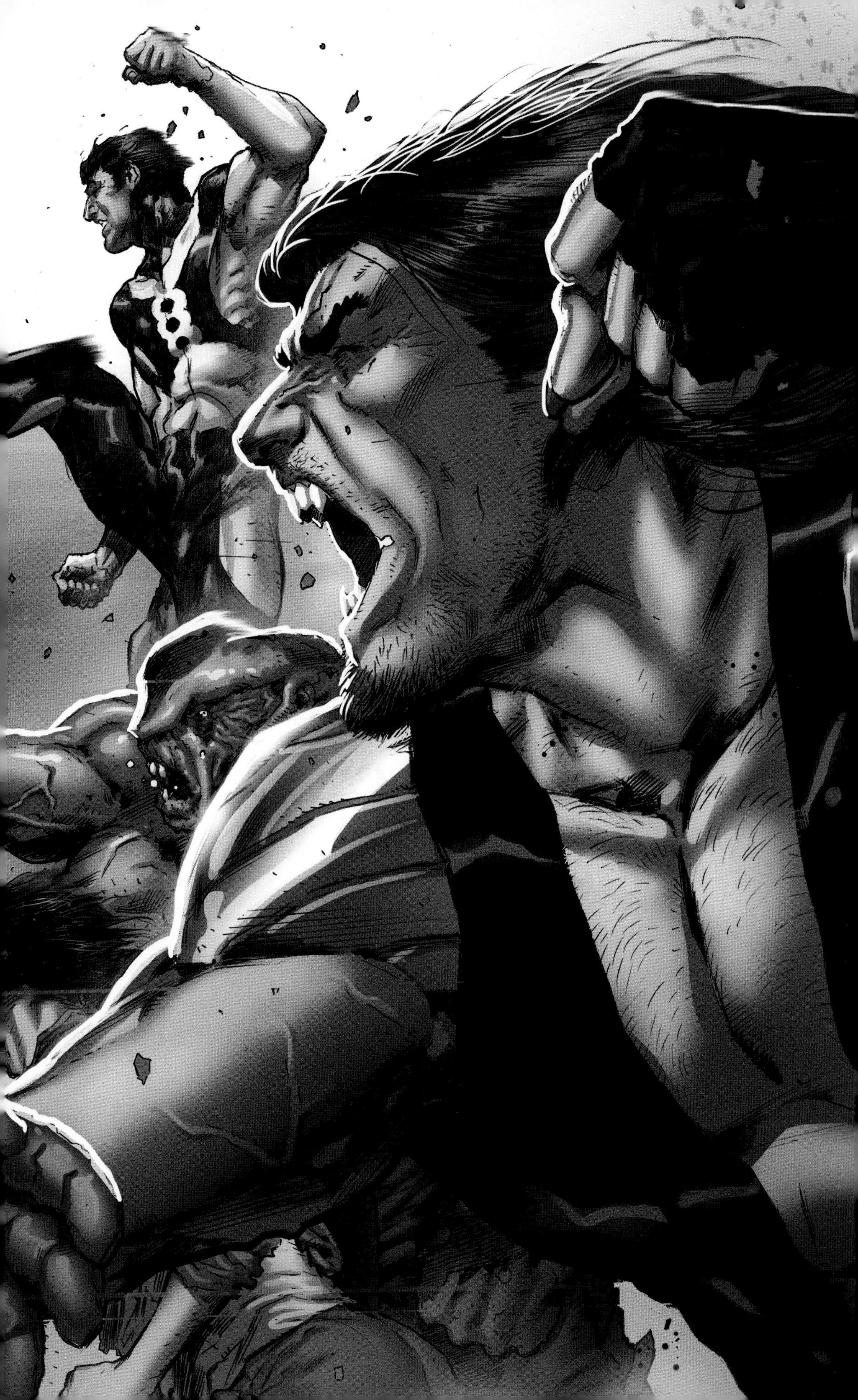

ISSUE TWO 2ND PRINT
TOM DERENICK
WITH COLORS BY BLOND

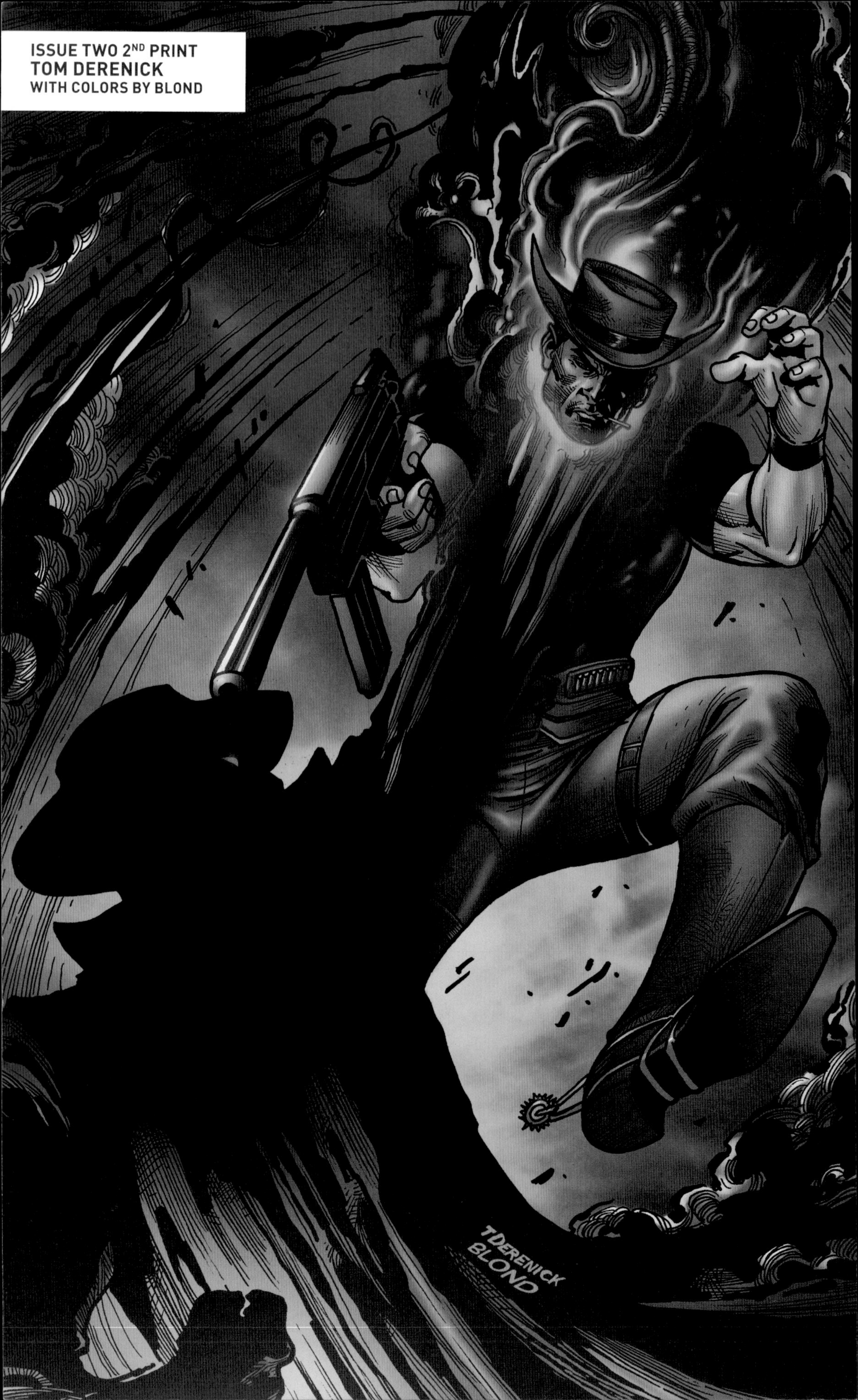
T DERENICK
BLOND

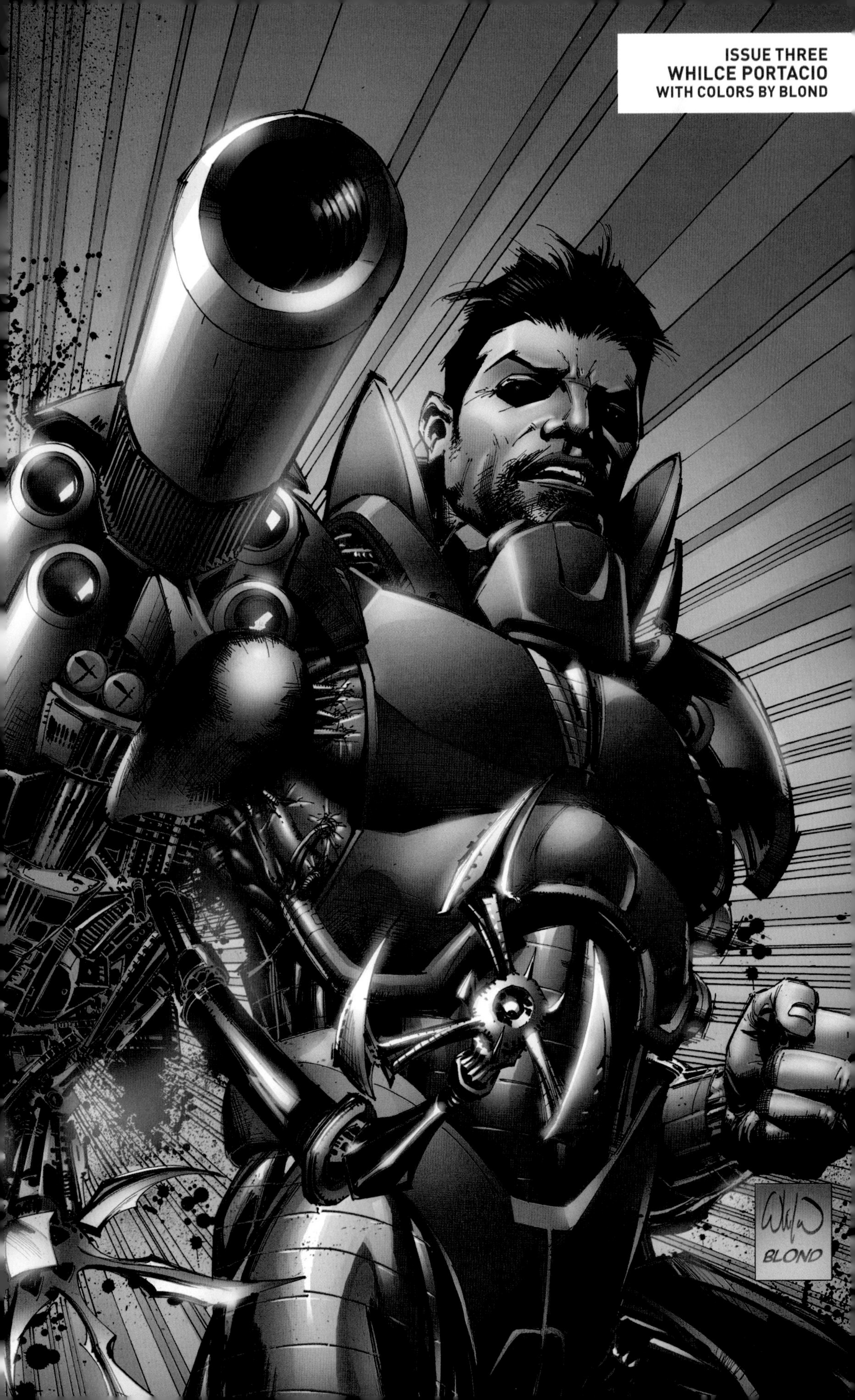
ISSUE THREE
WHILCE PORTACIO
WITH COLORS BY BLOND
BLOND

ISSUE THREE
CARLOS MAGNO
WITH COLORS BY ARCHIE VAN BUREN

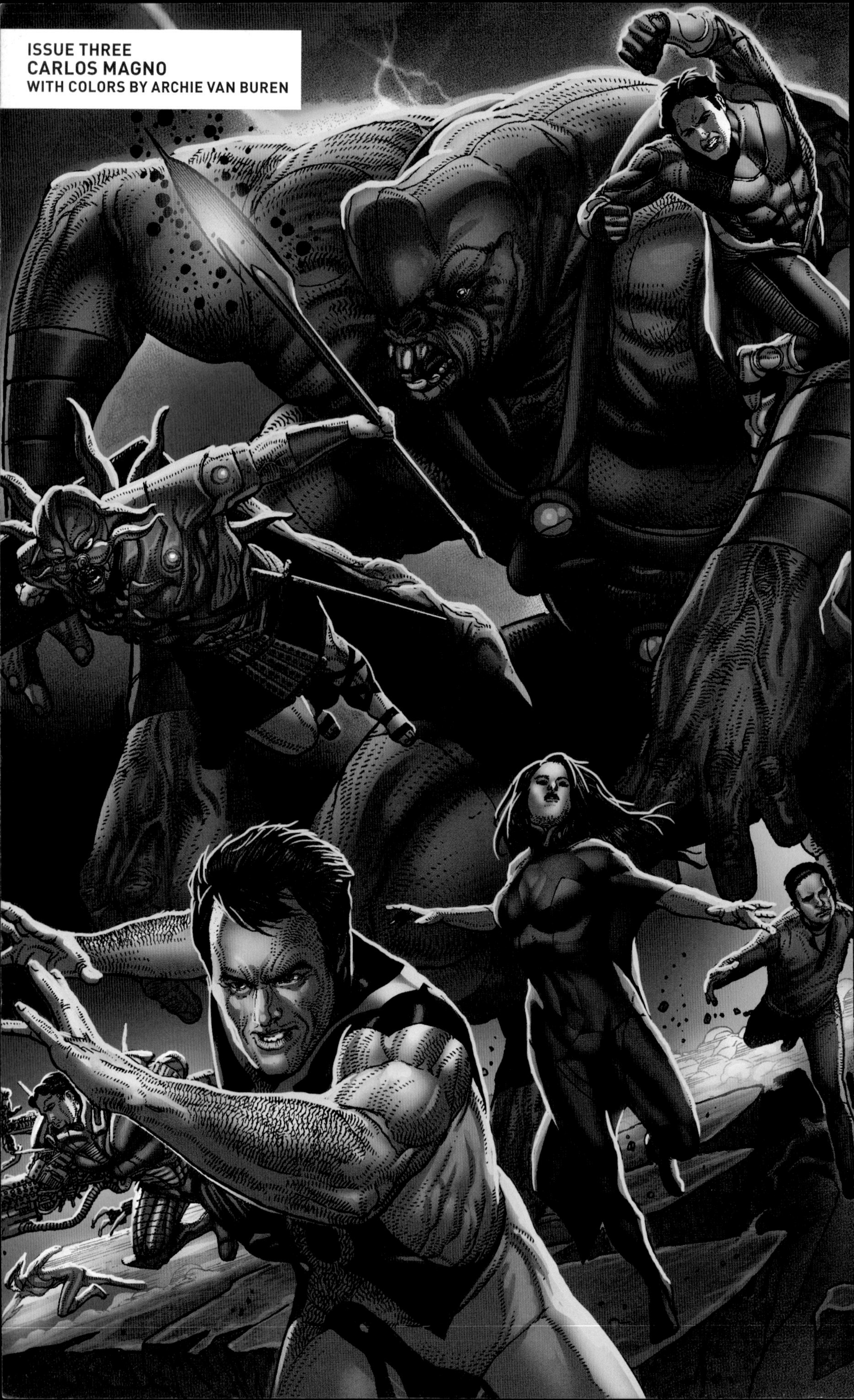

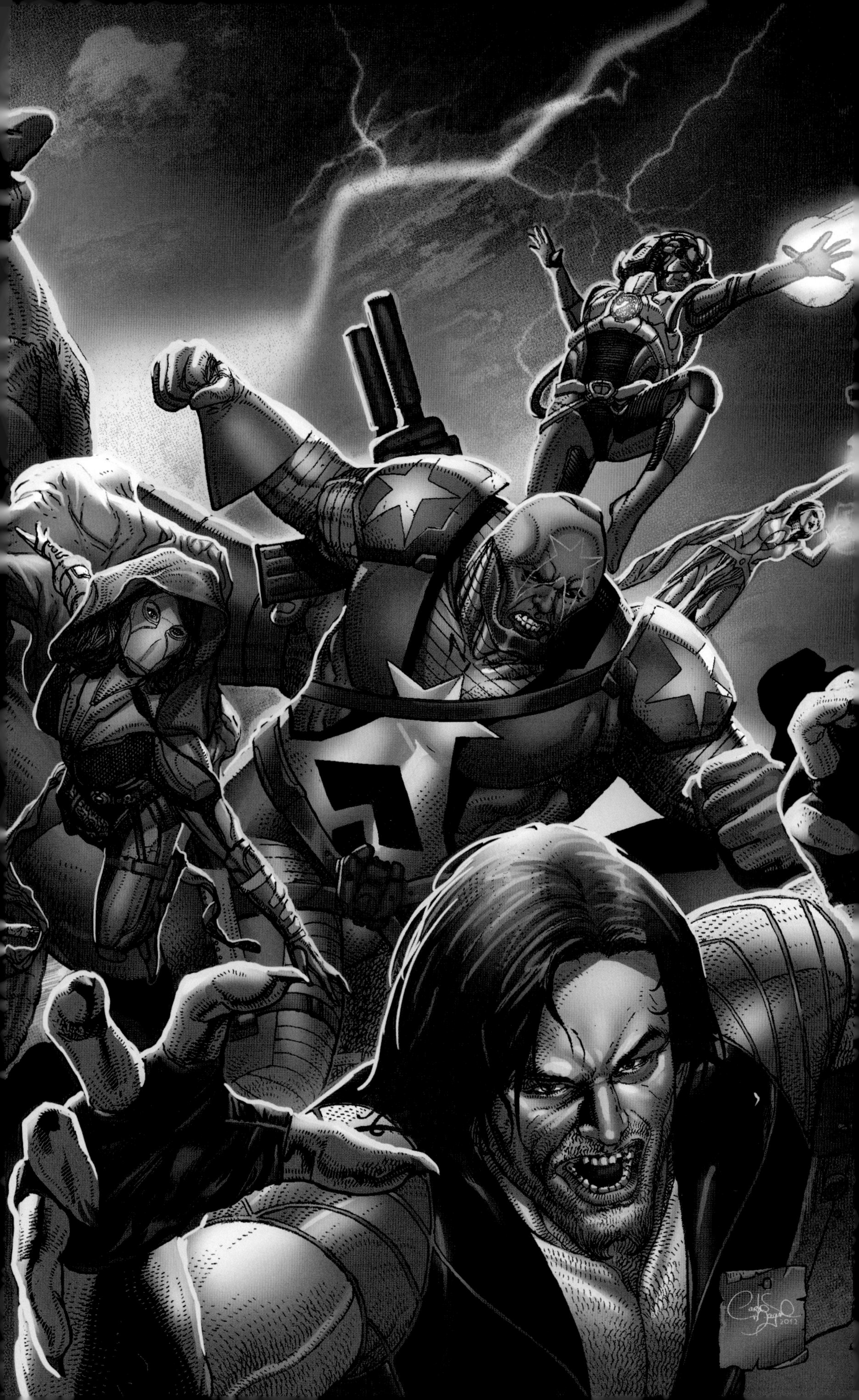

ISSUE THREE 2ND PRINT
TOM DERENICK
WITH COLORS BY BLOND

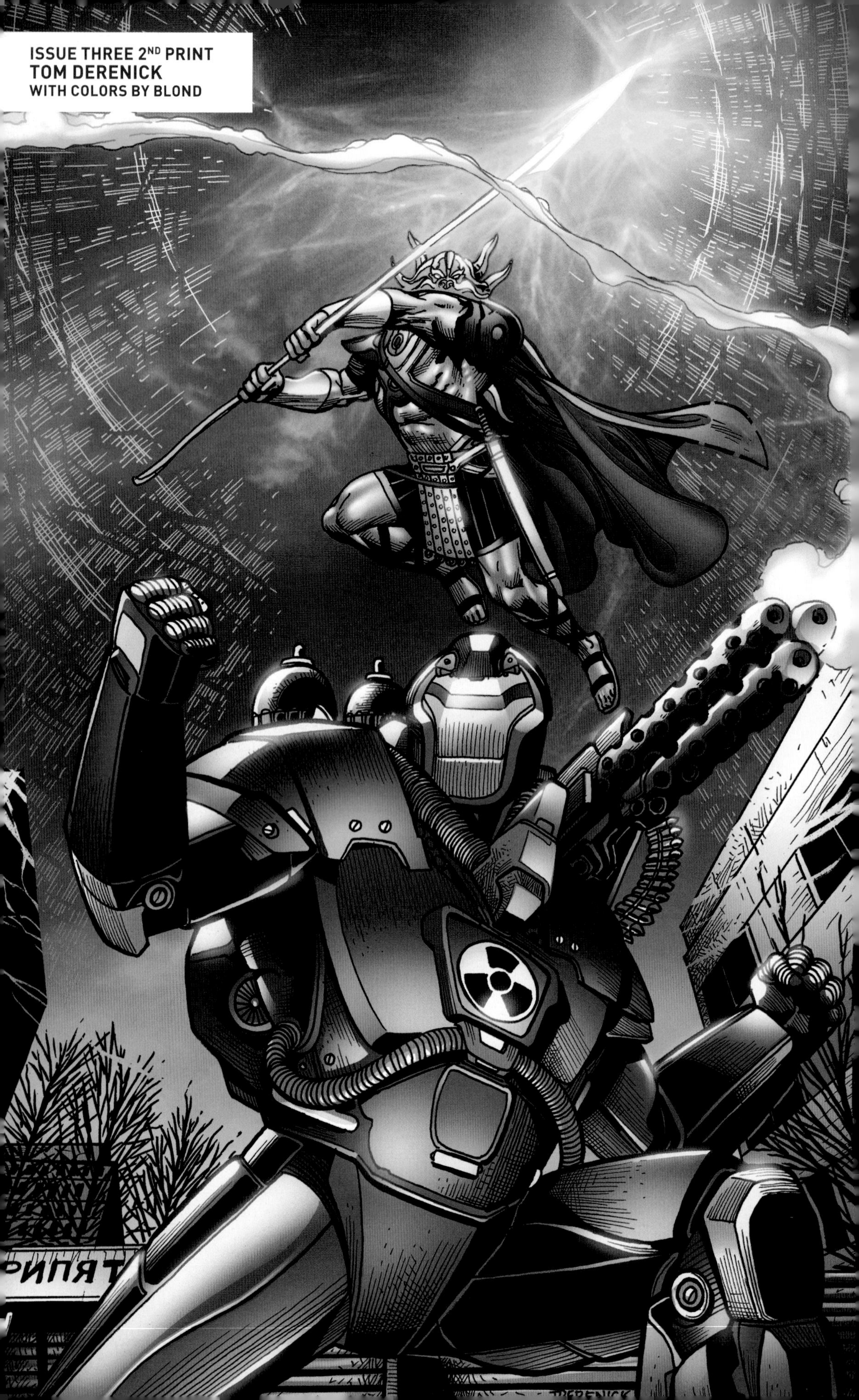

ISSUE FOUR
WHILCE PORTACIO
WITH COLORS BY BLOND

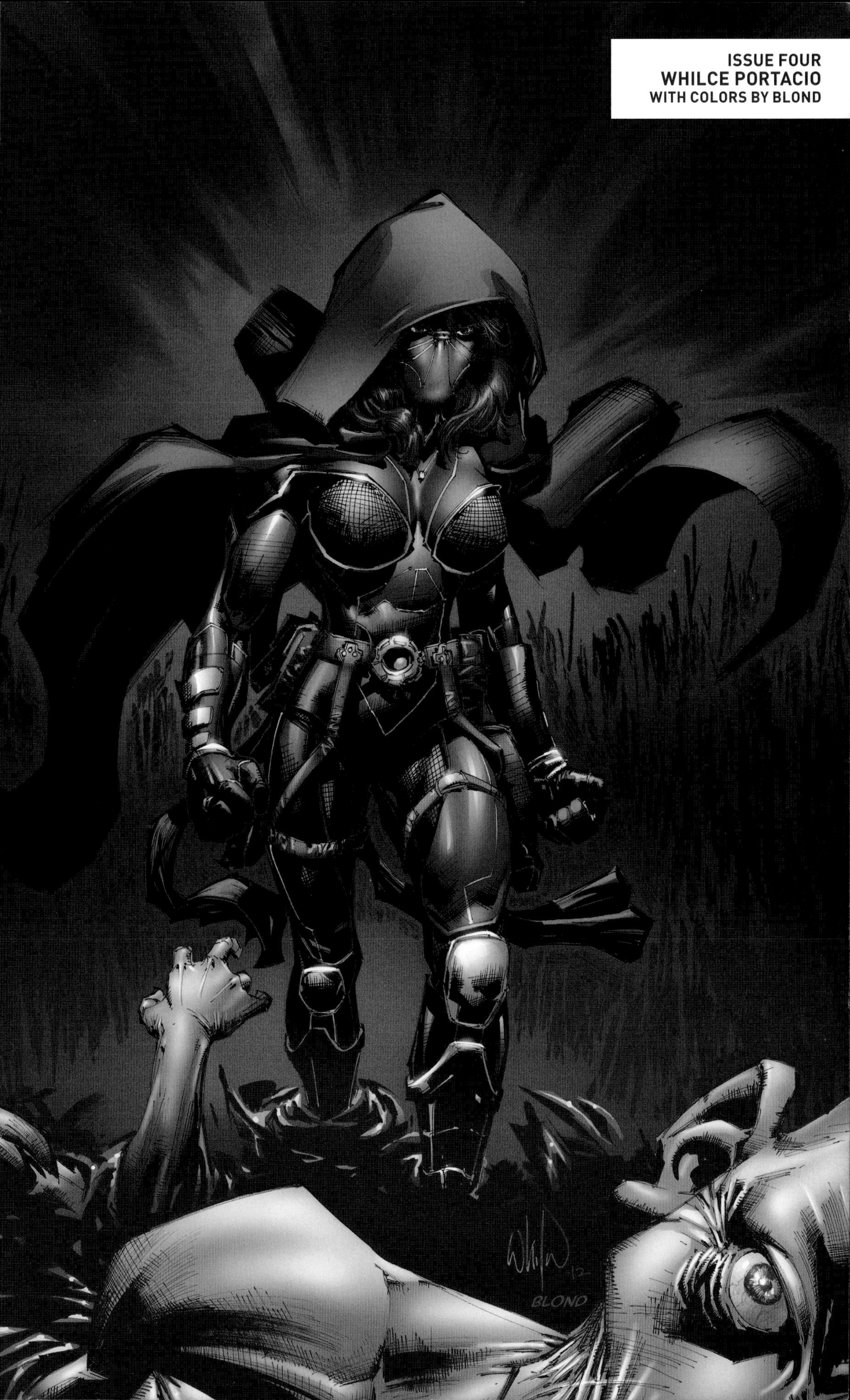

ISSUE FOUR
FRAZER IRVING

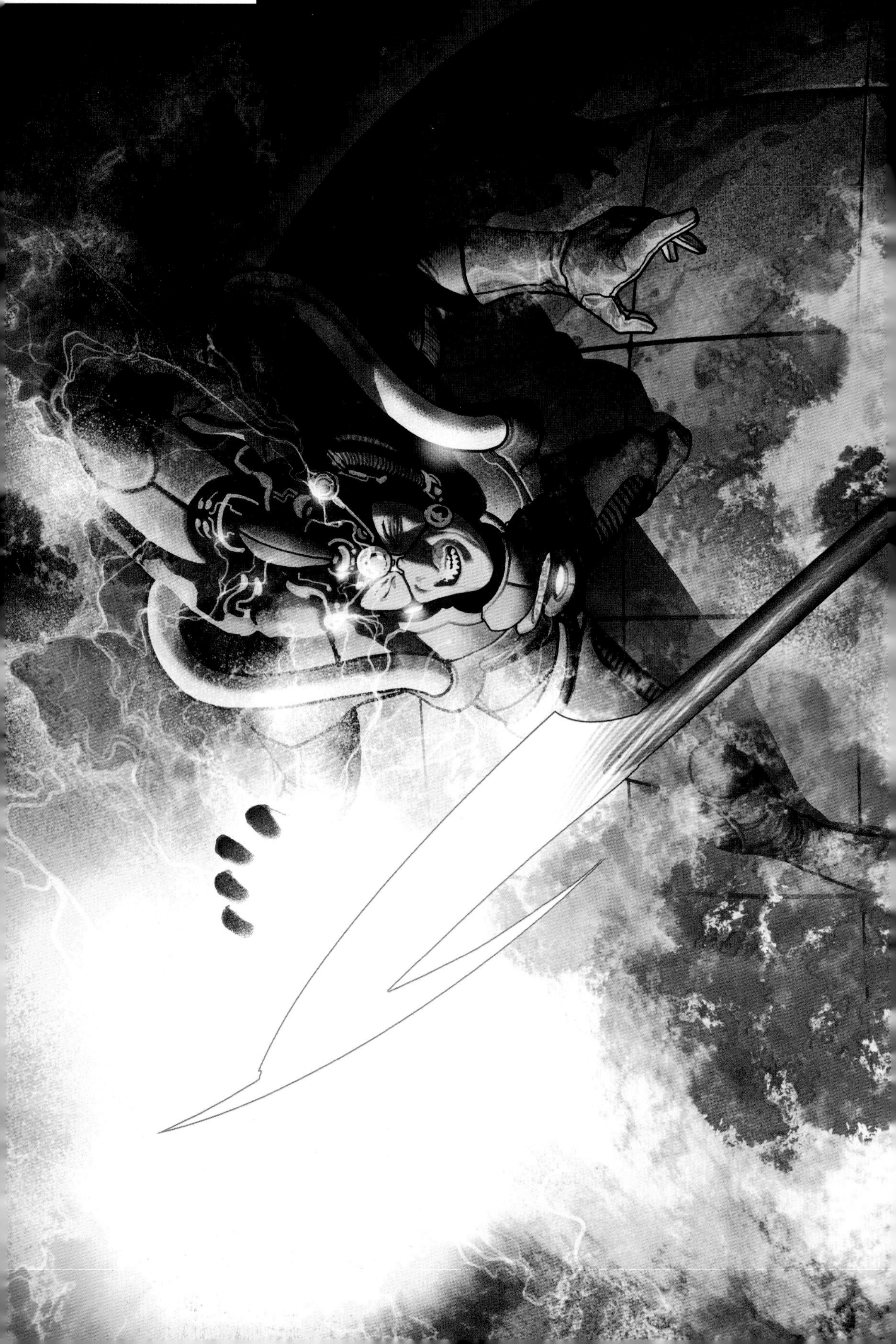

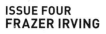

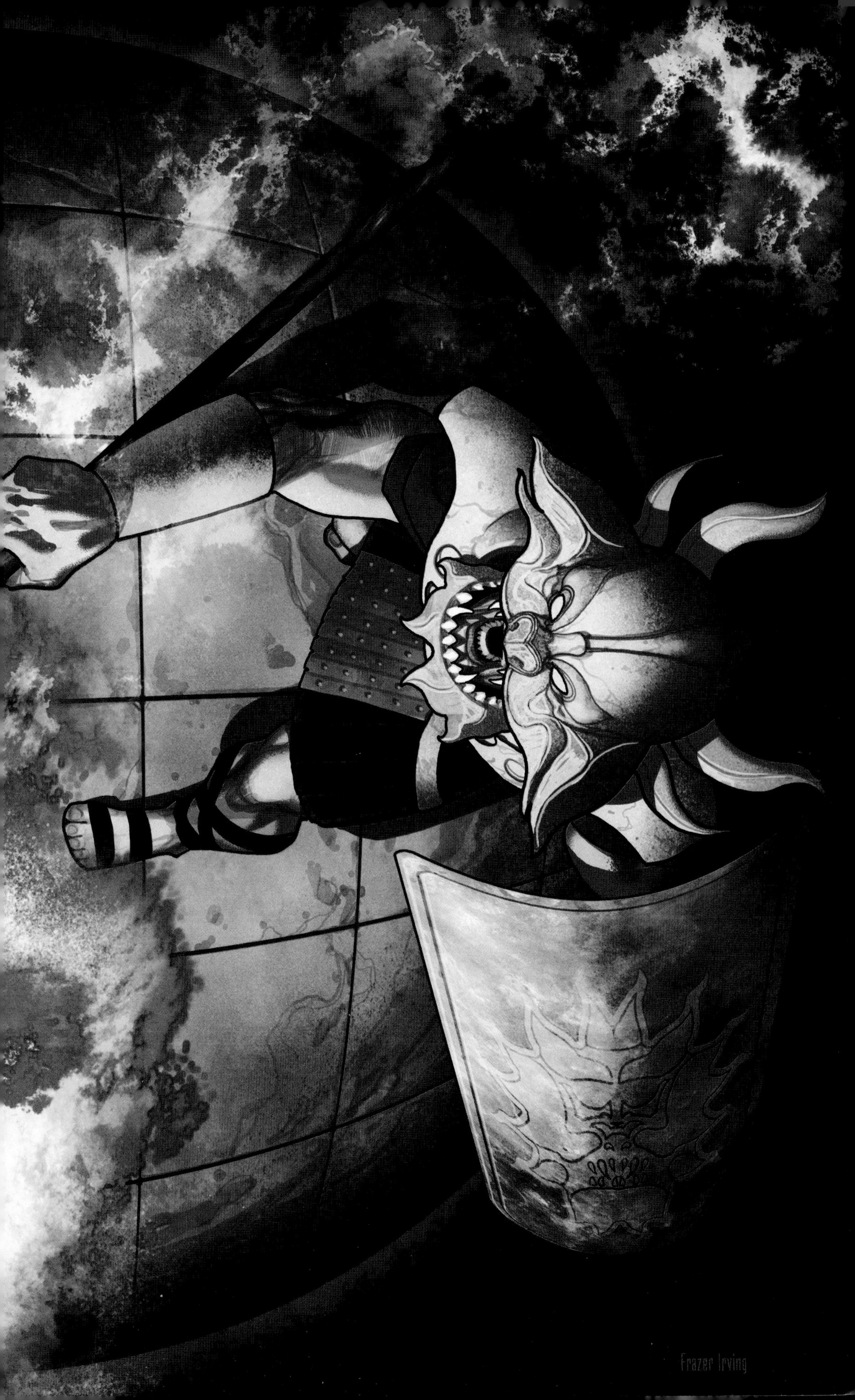
Frazer Irving

MORGUE VARIANT
CONNECTING COVERS
JUNG-GEUN YOON

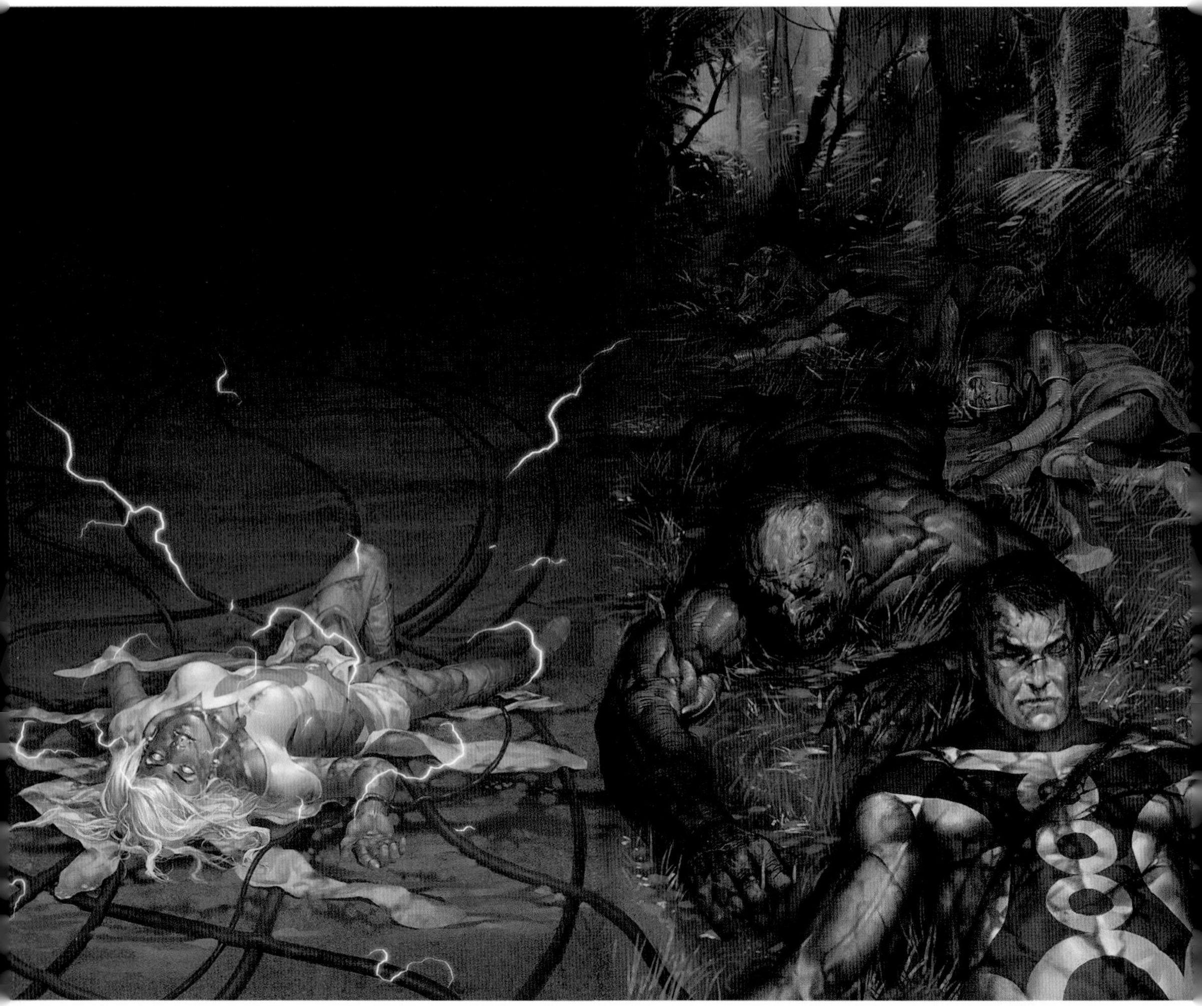

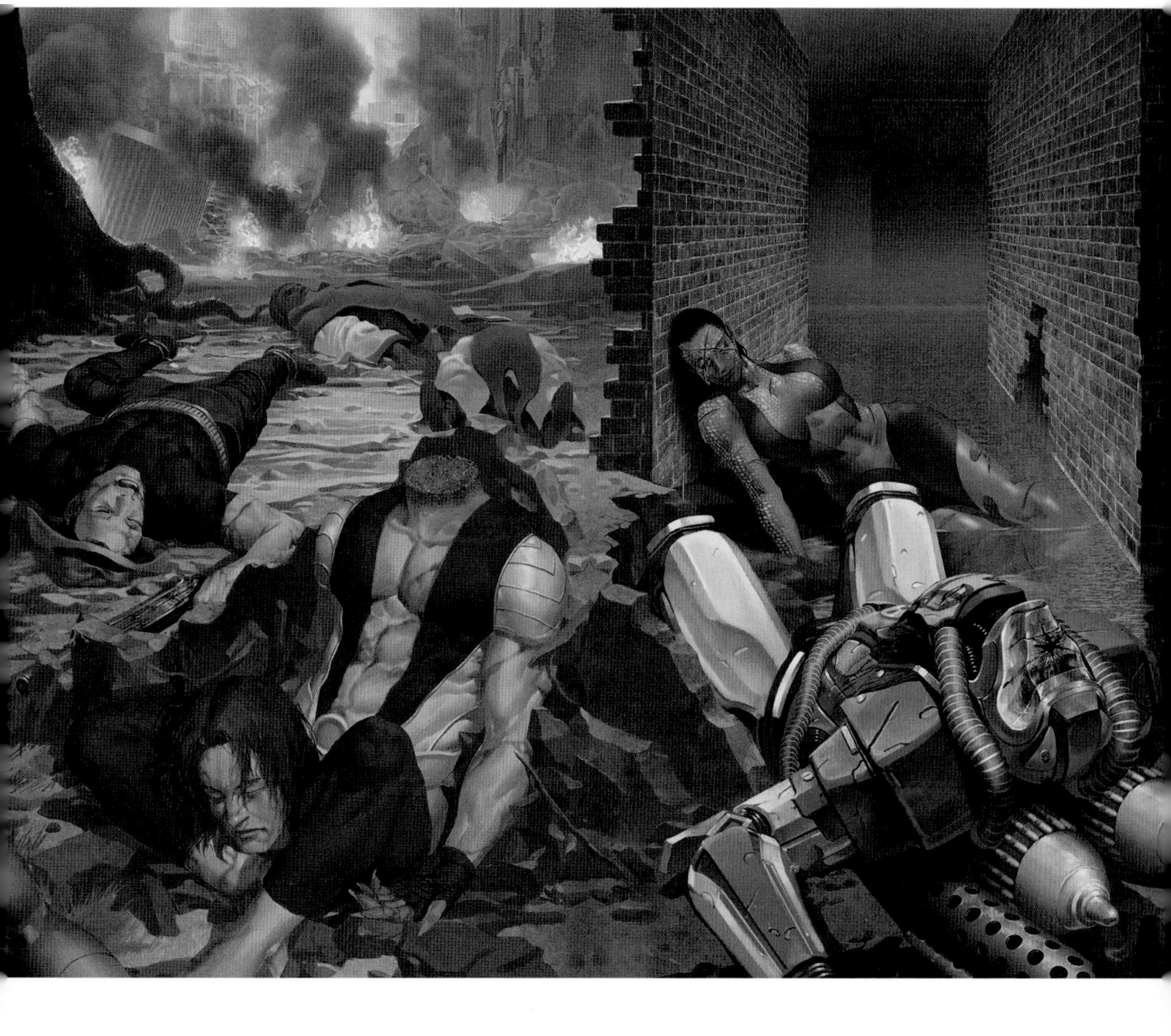

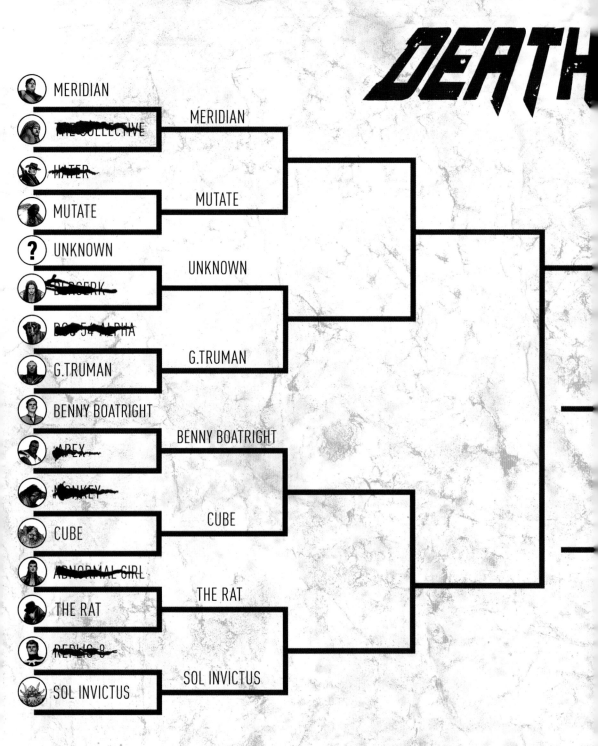

DEATH

Round 1

- MERIDIAN
- ~~THE COLLECTIVE~~
- ~~HATER~~
- MUTATE
- UNKNOWN
- ~~BERSERK~~
- ~~DOG 54-ALPHA~~
- G.TRUMAN
- BENNY BOATRIGHT
- ~~APEX~~
- ~~MONKEY~~
- CUBE
- ~~ABNORMAL GIRL~~
- THE RAT
- ~~REPLIC-8~~
- SOL INVICTUS

Round 2

- MERIDIAN
- MUTATE
- UNKNOWN
- G.TRUMAN
- BENNY BOATRIGHT
- CUBE
- THE RAT
- SOL INVICTUS

ABNORMAL GIRL
AMALGAM
APEX
BENNY BOATRIGHT
BERSERK
THE COLLECTIVE
CUBE
DOG 54-ALPHA

ELECTRONIKA
FALLOUT MAN
GEORGE TRUMAN
THE GLYPH
HATER
PROF. H. HIGGINS
LIGHTSPEED
MANCHURIAN

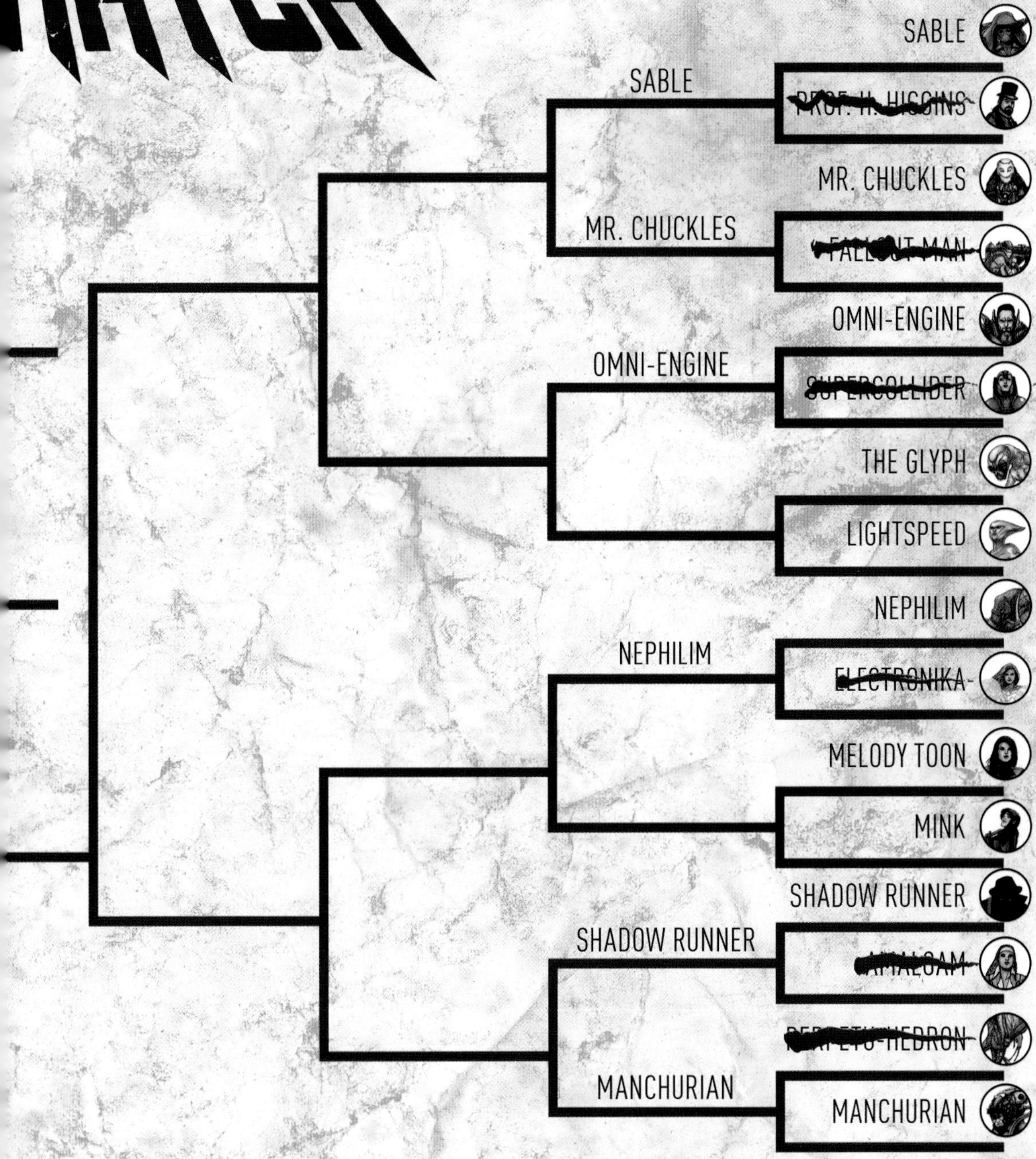
SABLE
~~PROF. H. HIGGINS~~
MR. CHUCKLES
~~FALLOUT MAN~~
OMNI-ENGINE
~~SUPERCOLLIDER~~
THE GLYPH
LIGHTSPEED
NEPHILIM
~~ELECTRONIKA~~
MELODY TOON
MINK
SHADOW RUNNER
~~AMALGAM~~
~~PERPETU-HEDRON~~
MANCHURIAN
SABLE
MR. CHUCKLES
OMNI-ENGINE
NEPHILIM
SHADOW RUNNER
MANCHURIAN

MELODY TOON
MERIDIAN
MINK
MR. CHUCKLES
MONKEY
MUTATE
NEPHILIM
OMNI-ENGINE

PERPETU-HEDRON
THE RAT
REPLIC-8
SABLE
SHADOW RUNNER
SOL INVICTUS
SUPERCOLLIDER
UNKNOWN

CHARACTER INDEX

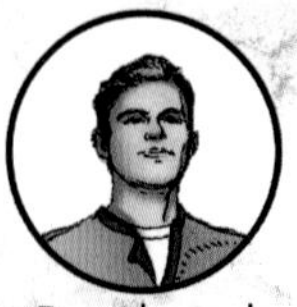

DRAGONFLY
a.k.a. Benny Boatright

Developed strange powers as a child after surviving the crash of a Br'kytt spacecraft that destroyed his family home and killed his parents.

Powers: dragon-flight, dragon barbs, proportionate strength of chitin

Killed Apex in 1st Round

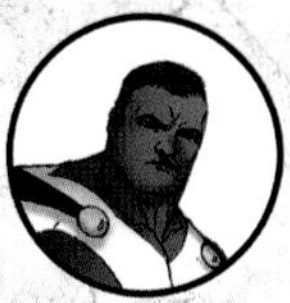

APEX
a.k.a. Michael Bedard

The last known survivor of a displaced race of super-beings that perished during a climactic event known as the Trek.

Powers: flight, heat vision, super-strength

Killed by Dragonfly in 1st Round

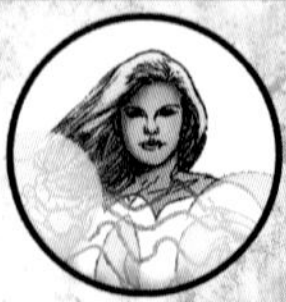

ELECTRONIKA
a.k.a. Teagan Harcrow

A former university professor endowed with powers after the U.S. Government stole her proprietary technology and an electronic anomaly erupted, killing her husband.

Powers: electricity manipulation, pulse spheres, static webs

Killed by Nephilim in 1st Round

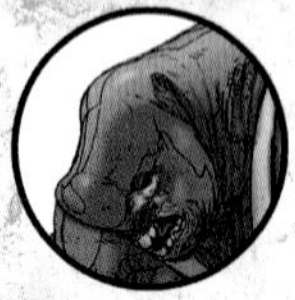

NEPHILIM
a.k.a. Abel Caan

The personification of ancient Hebrew lore, a construct born of ancient beliefs that manifested as a creature in what was once the city of Babylon.

Powers: super-strength, impervious to fear

Killed Electronika in 1st Round

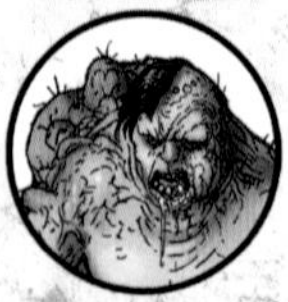

CUBE
a.k.a. Gordon Hume

A scientist obsessed with harnessing the venomous properties of the notorious box jellyfish injected himself with the substance, resulting in madness and a complex body alteration.

Powers: noxious tendrils, strength of virulent poisons, looks that kill

Killed Monkey in 1st Round

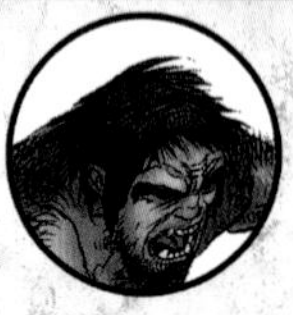

MONKEY
a.k.a. "Fred"

A primate test subject that was mistakenly injected with two separate formulas, which produced super-strength and human levels of intelligence within the beast.

Powers: proportionate strength of a Barbary ape, unbreakable teeth

Killed by Cube in 1st Round

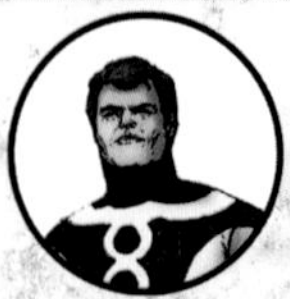

REPLIC-8
a.k.a. Simon Foster

A brilliant young scientist that discovered an interface between this and multiple other dimensions who unwittingly brought through eight other versions of himself.

Powers: control of eight identical avatars

Killed by Sol Invictus in 1st Round

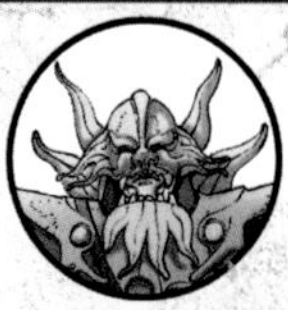

SOL INVICTUS

The only remaining heir to the sun, raised believing himself to be the son of a lowly Solar Warrior before defeating Nihilus Rex, reclaiming his throne, and subsequently being cast down to Earth.

Powers: solar rays, nuclear fission

Killed Replic-8 in 1st Round

MUTATE

Emerged from the disputed Kashmir region between India and Pakistan during provocative military maneuvers and quickly became a symbol of peace when his appearance catalyzed a cessation of hostilities.

Powers: super-strength, EMP roar

Killed Hater in 1st Round

HATER
a.k.a. Stuart Duncan

Subjected to biological experimentation after vanishing deep in enemy territory while serving with the 4th Psychological Operations Group Airborne, resulting in severe PTSD and enhanced senses.

Powers: the ultimate special ops agent

Killed by Mutate in 1st Round

THE COLLECTIVE
a.k.a. Kim Soon Park, Plethor Collective

A devolving alien species encountered a South Korean deep space probe and, seeking a host, spread to a young rocket technician named Kim Soon Park and the other members of Park's team.

Powers: symbiotic hive mind, consciousness infiltration

Killed by Meridian in 1st Round

MERIDIAN
a.k.a. Samuel Fox

A survivor of the tragic event know as The Trek, precocious Teen of Tomorrow Ssam-YI landed on Earth after his home dimension was devoured by a paradoxical implosion.

Powers: super-strength, super-speed, unlimited flight

Killed The Collective in 1st Round

SABLE

Origin is unknown, but her first recorded appearance involved an attack by her nemesis Mister Chuckles on a busload of tourists, which she stopped with her extraordinary intuition.

Powers: uncanny intuitive abilities, possible telepathic awareness, preternatural stamina

Killed Prof. H. Higgins in 1st Round

PROF. H. HIGGINS

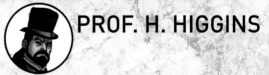

When the time stream began to flow backwards in Victorian England, Hieronymus Higgins secretly collected the data of the greatest minds of the era, subsequently murdering all but one.

Powers: control over the time stream, unique intellect

Killed by Sable in 1st Round

FALLOUT MAN
a.k.a. Nikolai Ivanov

The product of the Chernobyl reactor explosion near the Ukrainian city of Prypiat, which endowed him with incredible powers as he grew into his teenage years.

Powers: nuclear fission and fusion reactors, emits poisonous radiation

Killed by Mister Chuckles in 1st Round

MISTER CHUCKLES
a.k.a. Charlie Kain

A notorious street performer known for an unorthodox act which failed to entertain anyone, "Charlie Chuckles" discovered an aptitude for manipulation and crime, which he exploited to the fullest.

Powers: extremely intelligent and manipulative, clinically insane

Killed Fallout Man in 1st Round

DEATHMATCH™

VOLUME TWO
A THOUSAND CUTS

COMING SOON